PLAYWRITING
WOMEN

PLAYWRITING
WOMEN

7 Plays from the Women's Project

edited and with
an introduction by

Julia
Miles

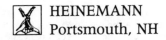

HEINEMANN
Portsmouth, NH

Heinemann
A Division of Reed Publishing (USA) Inc.
361 Hanover Street   Portsmouth, NH 03801-3912
Offices and agents throughout the world

Library of Congress Cataloging-in-Publication Data
Playwriting women: 7 plays from the Women's Project / with an
    introduction by Julia Miles ; edited by Julia Miles.
        p.   cm.
    Contents: Milk of Paradise / Sallie Bingham—O pioneers! / Darrah
    Cloud—Violent peace / Lavonne Mueller—Night sky / Susan
    Yankowitz—Approximating mother / Kathleen Tolan—Chain / Pearl
    Cleage—Late Bus to Mecca / Pearl Cleage.
    ISBN 0-435-08617-0
    1. American drama—Women authors.   2. American drama—20th
century.   3. Women—United States—Drama.   I. Miles, Julia.
II. Women's Project (New York, N.Y.)
PS628.W6P6   1992
812'.54080352042—dc20   92-24090
                                                               CIP

Designed by Adrianne Onderdonk Dudden
Printed in the United States of America on acid free paper
93   94   95   96   97   7   6   5   4   3   2   1

To my granddaughters—
Allie, Emma, Thea

Contents

Introduction

The question I asked in 1978, "Where are the women playwrights?" has been answered in 1992 with an astonishing outpouring of women's talent for the theater. There is now a nucleus of powerful women playwrights' voices and they write both women's-issue plays and public-issue plays. They write in order to explore human values and the desire for transcendence of self. They write with the hope—small and perhaps not always obtainable—that their audience will share an idea, a feeling, a dream they have struggled to make into a play. They have entered into the collaborative process of theater, often new and frightening, to enchant, hold, possess, and tell the audience their secrets. Theater's power stems from the coming together of a group of people—the audience—to share an experience that is alive and of the moment and at its best—universal. No wonder I admire playwrights; they have courage!

I'm very happy to introduce the seven plays in this, the Women's Project & Productions' fifth anthology. These plays are particularly American. They are about the American female's experience past and present, rural and urban and these experiences are often different from the male experience.

The plays also span many time periods from the pioneer experience to the Depression, to our military involvement in Central America in the 70–80s, to today's social and scientific worlds.

All the plays are about, among other things, hope and renewal. These playwrights, in their wisdom, know there is a yearning in our lives for both.

Sallie Bingham's *Milk of Paradise* was produced by the Women's Project in 1980 and had that special excitement of the first production of a new playwright. Set in the South in the 1930s, a young girl's coming of age and reconciliation to the danger and adventure of growing up is accomplished with the help of her Aunt Jane and servants both white and black. The playwright knows these people and writes of them in language both poetic and precise. The emotional landscape is true. The young girl, Missy, discovers that growing up is not "like dying" and finally begins her adulthood filled with hope; her Aunt Jane is perhaps renewing her own.

O Pioneers! commissioned and developed by the Women's Project and produced as a work-in-progress in 1988, was its first adaptation of a novel. It was a co-production with the Seattle Repertory Theatre in their "The Other Season" in Spring 1989 and was broadcast on PBS's *American Playhouse* in 1991. Willa Cather was a great lover of theater and in this novel she wrote to a friend, "I hit home pasture." Her authentic voice and talent came together in this great novel adapted for the stage by Darrah Cloud with music by Kim Sherman. Darrah Cloud's adaptation is a close but contemporary treatment of this classic. She retains both the spiritual dimension and intellectual rigor of the novel. This play embodies the American frontier experience and specifically tells of the necessary strength of one of its pioneers—Alexandra. She manages to grow up to protect her dream of the land and endure. Though she makes sacrifices and undergoes tragedy in her family, she is finally able to experience love and a renewal of hope when her life-long friend returns home to be with her.

When I actually stopped to count them, I was astonished to learn that *Violent Peace* by Lavonne Mueller is her seventh play that the Women's Project has produced. Lavonne's themes often are about families—made up, found, not by birth. I think we are her theater family. *Violent Peace* is a Pentagon term for a state of not all out war, but neither is it peace. The play describes many countries where we do and do not have a military presence as well as, symbolically, the relationship between the two characters. It deals with the reconciliation of the tortuous love affair between an army brat and the father figure who raised her. After a long night of confrontation Kim is ready to let go her love for Mark and start her new adult life.

Susan Yankowitz's *Night Sky* was inspired and directed by Joseph Chaikin. Joe has made a remarkable recovery from aphasia and asked his longtime friend, Susan Yankowitz, to write a play based on his experiences. In the play Anna, an astronomer, is in an accident and is shocked to awake to the sound of gibberish coming from her mouth. She is aphasic, unable to communicate. The cosmos and the mind are two of the remaining mysteries in the universe and Anna must confront them both. She struggles to regain her speech, express her love for her family, and come to terms with her life.

Approximating Mother by Kathleen Tolan is about a serious subject—children, an urgent concern for many young women and men today—told in a humorous style. It views the complexities of motherhood in the 90s from many angles and echoes the variety of emotion concerning motherhood with wit and honesty. Babies give hope and renewal to the women in this play: Fran gives new purpose to her life by adopting one, Jen is allowed to start her life over again by giving up hers, and Molly begins a new way of life by working full-time and hiring a part-time mother for her daughters.

The last two plays in this anthology, *Chain* and *Late Bus to Mecca* by Pearl Cleage, were commissioned by the Women's Project and the Southeast Playwright's Project. They had rehearsed readings in Atlanta and New York and gave off a different kind of special excitement—plays so powerfully and completely themselves as to be ready for the stage. They are in production as I am writing this. The playwright knows the young women in her plays and knows the effect our culture has on their lives.

Chain is a chilling portrait of a young, black, crack addict who is held prisoner in her home by her parents out of desperation and hope that she will be cured. The child is divided between love for her parents who saved her from a probable death among crack addicts and hatred for them for keeping her away from drugs. Cleage gives her the possibility of hope, but the odds are against her and sorrow fills the audience's heart.

Late Bus to Mecca is a different story. Two young women bond together waiting for the Atlanta bus due to the energy and will of one who aids the other—her new, silent friend. The audience is in awe of the spirit of Ava who has her plan and her standards in a hard and complex time. She is a realist and a survivor.

All of these works are remarkable both as plays and as records of the American female experience. They give women actors heroes to play and audiences women they recognize and with whom they can identify. Perhaps their most striking common feature is the talent and love with which they all were written. Where are the women playwrights? They are here and their voices are loud, clear, and strong.

Sallie Bingham

MILK OF PARADISE

Author's Introduction

The light that shines over and through this play is the same benign late-winter light that shone in the little study in a new suburb where I wrote it, in a brief, happy three-week period in the late 70s. I was newly returned to the state of my birth, in perhaps more ways than one, and had yet to understand the darkness and complexity attendant on that state.

Going home meant going back to memories buried for forty years; it also meant a new love-affair with the life of the imagination, without which a play about childhood could never be written. For nothing, of course, "happened" in my life as it happens in this play. Everything is transformed through the act of imagination that makes the past simple and bright as in fact it never was, or could be.

The first and only production of the play, by the Women's Project in a small basement theater in New York, was as brightly and palely lit, and as charming, as the script itself. "Impressions for Flute," by Ramson Wilson, set the tone. An atmosphere of acceptance, humor, and love seemed to unite, for a brief moment, cast, director, playwright, and producer. And while I may be sentimental in my memory of that first production of my first play, I do think there were in it the seeds of energy and hope that keep so many of us in the theater, against all reason.

Milk of Paradise was produced by the Women's Project & Productions under the directorship of Julia Miles at the American Place Theatre, New York City, from February 28–March 9, 1980. It was directed by Joan Vail Thorne with the following cast:

MISSY	Maia Danzinger
MILDRED	Birdie M. Hale
LOUISE	Sylvia Short
EULA	Verona Barnes
BILLY	Paul Carlin
CAPTAIN P.	Tom Brennan
FATHER (Mr. Robby)	David Bailey
MOTHER (Miss Alice)	Annie Murray
MISS KATY	Theresa Merritt
AUNT JANE	Patricia Roe

Set design by William Barclay
Costume design by Mimi Maxmen
Lighting design by Annie Wrightson

Stage manager   Mary R. Lockhart
Production assistants   Larry Neumann and Marianne Wolkstein

The play takes place in the nursery, kitchen, duckyard, and balcony of a large house in the upper South.

Act I: A Sunday in early June, 1937
    Scene i   early morning
    Scene ii   mid morning
    Scene iii   afternoon

Act II: The following day
    Scene i   early morning
    Scene ii   mid morning
    Scene iii   noon

TIME

Two days in June, 1937

PLACE

Kentucky

CAST

MISSY, a fourteen-year old girl
BILLY, her sixteen-year old brother
MISS ALICE, their mother
MR. ROBBY, their father
LOUISE, their nurse
CAPTAIN P., the gardener
MILDRED, the cook
MISS KATY, Mr. Robby's old nurse
EULA, a young maid
AUNT JANE, Mr. Robby's sister

ACT ONE

Scene: The nursery, kitchen, duckyard and balcony of a large house. The balcony is supported by columns; French doors lead off into the rest of the house. The nursery, below, contains a rocking chair and shelves for toys and books. The kitchen, center, is the largest area; it contains a stove, sink and an enormous deal table, surrounded by chairs and stools. The duckyard, left, holds a swing, window boxes, etc. There are no visible barriers between the areas.

At rise, in the kitchen, Mildred, a solid-looking black woman, about forty-five, is beginning preparations for Sunday breakfast. She fries eggs for the servants, sets up three breakfast trays and lays out cereal for the children. While she is working, she turns on the radio and listens to a revival program.

Missy, a pale skinny girl in a nightgown, comes into the nursery and sits in the rocking chair.

Billy, a tough sixteen-year old, wearing ragged clothes, enters the duckyard and sits in the swing.

Pale light deepens as the sun rises.

MISSY: This is the summer they said, Take a typing course. I'm almost fourteen, I know the Rhyme of the Ancient Mariner, the mourning dove calls, where the Jack-In-The Pulpit grows in the woods. I swung on those grapevines once, a long time ago. "It is an Ancient Mariner, and he stoppeth one of three." They said at school, Take a typing course, this summer. You go to a concrete building downtown, you sit in front of a typewriter with blurred keys. It's cooler here, ten miles out from town, there's a breeze from the river . . . (She looks at her nightgown.) Blood . . . This is the summer they are taking the typing course. This is the summer they are taking the bus downtown, going shopping, getting their hair done. "Gather ye rosebuds while ye may, old time is yet a-flying." (She looks at her nightgown again.) Blood . . . Blood on the stump where Captain P. guillotines the chickens. Blood where Billy shot the squirrel, it fell down from the tree like a sack, hit the road, burst. Blood when Louise was cutting Miss Katy's toenails, cut them down to the quick. No blood on me, never any blood on me, not even a mosquito bite. Louise says I'm too sweet. (*In the kitchen, Louise, a middle-aged white woman with a scarred face, enters and sits down. Mildred hands her a cup of coffee.*)

MILDRED: Billy and Missy going to church?

LOUISE: Missy is. I don't know about Billy.

MILDRED: They not going to fuss, this time. They heard what they daddy, Mr. Robby said.

LOUISE: (*Sitting down at the table, beginning to polish Missy's white shoes.*) Good children, Mildred.

MILDRED: All children is good, Miss Louise. You get after Billy and Missy, I tell them, Come to Mildred, you Mildred's babies. I was right here in this kitchen the day they was born.

LOUISE: You spoil them, Mildred. You don't spoil your own. Five kids loose in that house on Harrods Creek while you work here.

MILDRED: Lord, no, I don't spoil mine. Mine got to live! (*In the nursery, Missy looks at her nightgown.*)

MISSY: I must have cut myself, riding Billy's bike. I went flying down the hill, fast, fast. Louise, look! Oh, Louise, look! Fell, at the bottom . . . (*In the kitchen, a buzzer sounds.*)

MILDRED: They starting to ring for breakfast! Eula got to take these trays up . . . Eula! (*Eula enters, a pretty young black woman wearing a striped uniform.*) Girl, take these trays up. You want to lay in the bed all day?

EULA: I up, dressed, got my Sunday uniform on Miss Alice give me. How you like it?

LOUISE: Pretty!

EULA: I wish I had the day off, a ride into town. They fixing to go to church, down at the projects at Eighth and Kentucky. Everybody wearing hats, gloves . . .

MILDRED: Take them trays!

EULA: I put on my little white hat with the flower . . . (*She puts a napkin from the breakfast tray on her head.*) I start down the road to church, walking real slow, swinging my skirt . . .

MILDRED: (*Snatching the napkin off her head.*) You get! (*Eula exits, with tray.*)

LOUISE: Eula fixing to leave?

MILDRED: (*Sitting down at the table.*) She just talking. On this hill, they all the time talking about leaving. They got it too good, you ask me. Saps them. Young ones maybe has still got the juice.

LOUISE: Takes more than juice, Mildred. (*In the nursery, Missy begins to sing.*)

MISSY: "For I'll go no more a-roaming with you, fair maid." Daddy sings that. He told me to carry a stick in my hand for who-ever's in the bamboo forest by the creek. I walk in the stalks, I have the stick in my hand, the bamboo quivers . . . Bamboo slivers cut my legs, little lines of blood . . . (*In the kitchen, Eula enters.*)

EULA: They sitting up in the bed. Miss Alice got her white lace nightgown on. I'm going to get me a white lace nightgown one of these days, blue ribbons run right through the neck.

MILDRED: Quit that foolishness! (*Eula laughs, exits with an-other tray. A buzzer rings.*) That's Miss Jane! What she doing up so early? She ought to be sleeping late, after her trip. (*To Louise*) You got her pills?

LOUISE: Miss Alice brought me these pills soon as Miss Jane took them out of her purse. (*She takes two pill bottles out of her pocket, puts a pill on the tray.*) Don't want no trouble like the last time, Miss Jane sleeping two, three days in bed, heat pad on, burning her leg.

MILDRED: Miss Jane Mr. Robby's sister. She got to act right!

LOUISE: Who's going to take her tray up?

MILDRED: That Eula—she ever get back.

LOUISE: Well, I'm going in, I'll find her. (*Mildred and Louise exit.*) (*Lights up on Billy in the duckyard.*)

BILLY: Ellie . . . Come on, Ellie, it's morning. You got to get up and let me take you home. I know you don't feel like it but I got to take you home now. My parents would die if they saw you, mud on your dress, in the duckyard . . . Don't cry, Honey. Of course I love you. You know I love you. Would I ask for THAT if I didn't love you? (*Captain P. enters the duckyard and begins to rake.*) I'll walk you home now and tonight, if I can lay my hands on a car, I'll take you to the drive-in.

CAPTAIN P.: What are you talking about, boy?

BILLY: (*Startled.*) You got the lizzy fixed yet, Captain?

CAPTAIN P.: No. Pretty bad shape.

BILLY: Anybody else'd have it fixed by now! You just fool around, Captain. Ran into the gate, your last day-off, sat in the car like you didn't know what happened. Louise had to go down there and snake you out! Man, I thought that car was fixed by now.

CAPTAIN P.: You got plans for it?

BILLY: I'm fixing on going to the drive-in tonight.

CAPTAIN P.: Your mama don't want you going to no drive-in!

BILLY: They leaving, ain't they? How they going to know?

CAPTAIN P.: They leaving this afternoon. Not even going to be here for Missy's birthday tomorrow. You can't count on nothing . . . You fixing on going to the drive-in WITH somebody?

BILLY: Looks like I ain't going to the drive-in.

CAPTAIN P.: When you was going, was you going with somebody?

BILLY: Yes.

CAPTAIN P.: Somebody I know?

BILLY: No.

CAPTAIN P.: Somebody alive?

BILLY: Of course she's alive! You think I'm crazy?

CAPTAIN P.: Un huh!

BILLY: Pretty little blond, works down at Walgreen's drugstore. Her and me's going—

CAPTAIN P.: Going?

BILLY: When I get out of here.

CAPTAIN P.: You planning on leaving anytime soon?

BILLY: Soon as I can lay my hands on some cash.

CAPTAIN P.: Well, good luck! I been waiting seventeen years for the cash.

BILLY: You got your salary.

CAPTAIN P.: It just don't hardly seem to last. By the time I get me a few beers down at Harrods Creek, my groceries . . . When my wife died, I thought I'd commence to save, but that poor woman was cheap as air! I'm planning on a little trip, though—

BILLY: Where are you planning on going?

CAPTAIN P.: I'm going to cross the Big Four Bridge! Clear across to Indiana! I'm going to visit those four big cities: Cincinnati, Cleveland, St. Louis and Chicago. (*Talking, Captain P. and Billy exit.*) (*In the nursery, Missy begins to speak.*)

MISSY: I'm going to start to hope for something. Doesn't make too much difference what. Could be a dress to wear—wear to a dance! I hope hard enough, I'll get it, and a wind to lift me off my feet, carry me out of here on a gale of fiddle music. Then the wind'd drop me down, crash on the ground, break, tear, bleed . . . (*Calling.*) Louise! Louise!

LOUISE: (*Offstage.*) I'm coming.

MISSY: Far from home, bleeding, and nobody to say. It's all right, Honey, don't cry—kiss it and make it well . . . (*Louise enters.*)

LOUISE: What you want?

MISSY: I'm bleeding.

LOUISE: Bleeding! Where?

MISSY: (*Lifting up her nightgown.*) I must have hurt myself, riding Billy's bike.

LOUISE: You wearing your underpants to bed! How many times I told you, Take them off. You got to air out down there! (*She examines Missy's underpants.*) Honey—you didn't hurt yourself! You remember what your mother told you?

MISSY: No.

LOUISE: That book she gave you?

MISSY: No.

LOUISE: Why, you showed me that book, yourself! Remember the picture of the boy and the girl with all the labels so you'd know what everything—

MISSY: No!

LOUISE: Honey . . . (*Louise sits in the rocking chair, holds out her hands to Missy.*) This is going to happen to you every month till you're as old as I am! Here, take off those pants. I want to show them to your mother. (*Louise helps Missy slide off her underpants.*) You're turning into a young lady!

MISSY: I want to stay back, Louise. Young ladies don't go anywhere.

LOUISE: Why, they go out to lunch. They go out to dinner!

MISSY: I want the grapevines. I want the bamboo forest.

LOUISE: You got to leave all that. Now, you get dressed for church while I go see your mother. (*Louise exits. Missy sits in the rocker.*) (*On the balcony, Mr. Robby, a handsome middle-aged man, dressed for church, appears and begins to recite a poem. He does not see Missy.*)

MR. ROBBY:
"A damsel with a dulcimer
In a vision once I saw:
It was an Abyssinian maid,
And on her dulcimer she played,
Singing of Mount Abora . . .
Could I revive within me
Her symphony and song,
To such wild delight 'twould win me,
That with music loud and long,
I would build that dome in air,
That sunny dome! Those caves of ice!
And all who heard should see them there,
And all should cry, Beware! Beware!
His flashing eyes, his floating hair!
Weave a circle round him thrice,
And close your eyes with holy dread,
For he on honey-dew hath fed,
And drunk the milk of Paradise." (*Mr. Robby exits. Miss Alice, a beautiful woman wearing a negligee, enters and begins to speak to the audience. She does not see Missy.*)

MISS ALICE: No, I said, no. Not this Sunday, my darling. Excuse me, yet once more, from attendance. Communion service is so wearing! Everything said twice. I never can find enough sins to confess to fill up the space provided. The sun coming through the stained-glass windows boils like raspberry jelly. No, I said, no. Not this Sunday, my darling. Excuse me from attendance! (*Louise enters the area below the balcony.*)

LOUISE: Miss Alice!

MISS ALICE: Louise!

LOUISE: It's started!

MISS ALICE: What's started?

LOUISE: Missy—she's started to bleed!

MISS ALICE: I was fifteen when I started.

LOUISE: (*Taking underpants out of her apron pocket.*) I brought these to show you.

MISS ALICE: (*Turning away.*) You've talked to her, haven't you? You've given her the necessary supplies?

LOUISE: I can give her some of mine, but I thought you'd want to talk to her! (*Calling.*) Missy! (*Louise exits.*)

MISS ALICE: (*To the audience.*) The trouble is, it's so embarrassing . . . The Piazza San Marco, not an English-speaking drugstore in a thousand miles. Of course I couldn't explain my difficulty to the Italians. I was using the napkins from my breakfast tray. Of course I couldn't explain my difficulty to Robby. Men! They are so easily disillusioned . . .

LOUISE: (*Offstage, calling.*) Missy! Your mother wants to see you!

MISS ALICE: Wants! What woman can say she wants it! I tell Robby, it's not what I want, it's what you want, Darling. That makes for balance. That makes for twenty years of perfect poise!

LOUISE: (*Offstage, calling.*) Missy! Your mother wants to see you!

MISS ALICE: See you! It's hardly that. At the hospital, I said, Let me close my eyes awhile first. Twilight sleep! But no, they woke me up, thrusting the babies at me—little sausages in their white rolls. (*Louise enters, with Missy, dressed in a white petticoat.*)

LOUISE: Miss Alice . . . (*Louise exits. Pause. Missy climbs on a bench to get closer to the balcony.*)

MISSY: Mother . . . I want a corduroy skirt, for my birthday. Orange with three tiers. A new white petticoat, an off-the-shoulder gypsy blouse.

MISS ALICE: I'll tell Captain P. to drive you downtown. You can go to Stewarts.

MISSY: I want some little—some very little gold hoops to wear in my ears.

MISS ALICE: No. That's vulgar—that I won't allow.

MISSY: Some Tangee for my lips?

MISS ALICE: Your lips are perfectly fine the way they are. What will you wear on your legs?

MISSY: Stockings?

MISS ALICE: Not at fourteen! You'll wear your white socks, your patent-leather slippers. (*Missy jumps down off the bench, turns her back to her mother.*) Darling, you must realize your father and I have set a very high standard for you. Coming as you do from a family that has always made its contribution to the community . . . Three state senators, one governor, and a hopeful in the last presidential primary . . . (*Mr. Robby enters the balcony.*)

MR. ROBBY: (*To the audience.*) One surgeon with extraordinary hands . . . You can see them preserved in marble in the foyer of the medical college. One large-hearted businessman who gave the orphanage on Dixie Highway; you can see his bust in limestone over the portico.

MISS ALICE: And on my side, one state senator who single-handedly drove back the powerful reactionary force of the Klu Klux Klan; singlehandedly defended his negro tenants when the night-riders came.

MISSY: Just one pair of stockings. I promise I won't let them get a run.

MR. ROBBY: And on my side, one judge known in and out of the state for his fairminded decisions . . . (*Dance music begins, off-*

stage. Mr. Robby picks a daisy from the vase on the balcony and presents it to Miss Alice, who puts it in his buttonhole.)

MISS ALICE: In seven days, Paris . . . Eula is packing my elbow-length white gloves, my hat with artificial lily-of-the-valley. Do you think the artificial lily-of-the-valley is too much, Darling? Do you think I should tell Eula to take it off?

MR. ROBBY: Sweetheart, on you, the lily-of-the-valley . . . (*He kisses her.*) It's a pity Missy didn't get your eyes.

MISS ALICE: She got your nose—your mouth, too. And it looks like she's going to get your height. She's grown out of all her summer dresses. I have to go in, make a list of what she needs so Captain P. can drive her down to Stewarts. (*Miss Alice exits.*)

MR. ROBBY: (*Noticing Missy for the first time.*) Get your collection money, Missy. You know I expect you to give at least a fourth of your allowance to the church . . . Why, Missy, you're not dressed. Better hasten along. Gather ye rosebuds while ye may!

MISSY: Old time is yet a-flying!

MR. ROBBY: And this same flower that blooms today—

MISSY: Tomorrow will be dying! (*Mr. Robby turns towards exit.*) Is that true, Daddy? Is it like dying?

MR. ROBBY: What, Honey?

MISSY: Growing up.

MR. ROBBY: Why, Missy, of course it's not. You're going to find whole kingdoms opening up for you. You're going to find the lotus fruits just dropping in your mouth! "For he on honey-dew hath fed, and drunk the milk of Paradise!" A pretty girl, Honey, a pretty girl will have the whole world at her feet.

MISSY: What if I'm not?

MR. ROBBY: Not what?

MISSY: Not pretty.

MR. ROBBY: Why then you'll cultivate a talent. Sing, write, paint. But Honey, it looks to me as though you won't have to fall back on that solution.

MISSY: How will I know?

MR. ROBBY: Look in the mirror!

MISSY: I don't know what to look for.

MR. ROBBY: Look for blue eyes. Look for fair hair! Look for little pink ears that fill up with poetry.(*Mr. Robby exits. Missy runs into the nursery to look at herself in the mirror.*)

LOUISE: (*Offstage.*) Where are you, Missy? (*Louise enters the nursery.*) I brought you what you need. (*Louise takes a kotex and belt out of her apron pocket.*)

MISSY: All that?

LOUISE: The whole contraption! Here, take off those pants. (*She helps Missy take off her underpants.*)

MISSY: I was scared, at first.

LOUISE: Everybody's scared at first. Here, slip into this belt. (*She helps Missy into the kotex and belt.*)

MISSY: Were you scared?

LOUISE: Yes, I was, but I got over it.

MISSY: I'm not comfortable, Louise. All these things—they sort of grate.

LOUISE: Lots of things in this life grate, Honey. Come on, now—let me get you dressed for church. (*Louise and Missy exit.*) (*Miss Katy, a massive black woman in late middle-age, enters the duck-yard and begins to plump a pillow.*)

MISS KATY: (*To the audience.*) . . . Mr. Robby called that monkey Parpeetus. Brought him back in a great big box from New Orleans. Had him dressed up just like a doll. Little red hat, little red jacket, blue kneebritches with a place cut out for his tail. Brought that monkey back and turned him loose in the house. I say, Mr. Robby, we can't have no monkey loose in this house. Mr. Robby just laugh, say, They's plenty of monkeys loose in this house already, one more not going to make a bit of difference! (*Miss Katy exits into the kitchen, sits down at the table by a laundry basket full of sheets. She drinks a cup of coffee.*) (*Aunt Jane, a handsome middle-aged woman wearing a tailored robe, comes out onto the balcony.*)

AUNT JANE: Whew, I'd forgotten how hot it is down here . . . (*She goes to the balustrade, speaks to the audience.*) Frightful trip, coming down from New York on the sleeper. The engine gave out somewhere in the mountains, I lifted up the shade, we're standing in one of those godforsaken little towns. I thought, Oh God, I'm going back . . . (*She fans herself with a handkerchief.*) Amelia couldn't come to see me off so Bruce insisted on doing the honors. I hadn't seen him since that terrible dinner party, but there he was at Grand Central, box of chocolates, violet nosegay—even the look on his face matched . . . I don't need you, Honey. I don't need your talk, I don't need your arm, getting in and out of taxis, I don't even need your cock—(*In the kitchen, Miss Katy gets up abruptly.*)

MISS KATY: Got to count my sheets! (*She carries the laundry basket into the area under the balcony.*) Miss Alice say we use these linen sheets only on they bed, take them off and wash them twice a week, iron them out good while they's still damp. That Eula don't have no sense. She ball them sheets up in this basket, try to iron the wrinkles out—

AUNT JANE: Katy! I need my coffee!

MISS KATY: How you, Jane? (*She sits down on a stool, begins to fold sheets.*)

AUNT JANE: Where's my breakfast, Katy? You told me last night you'd fix me a two-minute egg, nice little slice of white toast, just a smidgeon of butter . . .

MISS KATY: That Mildred won't let me near her stove.

AUNT JANE: You don't bring me my breakfast, I'll fill up on something else. Start with that good Kentucky bourbon. Then I'll raid your little basket of hot rolls. Lick the butter balls off the silver butter plates! I'll blow up like a great big hot-air balloon, Katy. Only my feet'll be little—little dainty feet in high-heeled slippers.

MISS KATY: You ought to get yourself married, Miss Jane. Then you could stick to your diet.

AUNT JANE: They all love my girlish figure, my little flat rearend. They know they can get their fingers around me—no lumps, no detours. Every man who's ever loved me—

MISS KATY: What you talking about?

AUNT JANE: Nobody, really . . . Robby and I used to roll down the hill, below this house. Side over side, hands and heels hitting; your neck clicks, you think your head's going to roll off. Lie at the bottom and laugh, pick leaves and sticks off each other . . .

MISS KATY: I'll bring you your coffee. (*She starts towards exit.*)

AUNT JANE: Katy, Katy, don't leave me. You're the only one comes when I call. At night when I can't sleep, I hear you rocking back and forth across the nursery floor. Maybe you know what happened when we quit rolling down the hill.

MISS KATY: I'll get you your pills, maybe a large glass of fresh orange juice. (*Miss Katy exits.*)

AUNT JANE: Well, I got to get a loan, see my lawyer. Maybe take a trip to Hatteras, roll the way we rolled in the breakers . . . (*Missy enters the area under the balcony. She is dressed for church.*) The summer before Missy was born.

MISSY: Me?

AUNT JANE: (*Ignoring her*) Poor Alice, big as a house . . . I said to Robby, Let's take a week off from this heat, this waiting, those dresses of Alice's with the puritan collars. Let's go to Hatteras like we used to when Papa was alive, let's go to Hatteras and roll in the waves.

MISSY: (*Climbing on bench*) Aunt Jane! I want to go to Hatteras, too.

AUNT JANE: Why, Missy! It's not all it's cracked up to be. I was there once, you know. It didn't change my life.

MISSY: I want to get off this hill.

AUNT JANE: Why, there's plenty to do, right here . . . I never see you helping your poor mother. I've seen her coming in the house, arms so full of magnolia boughs she couldn't even open the front door—and where were you?

MISSY: Out. In the back woods—wandering. Daddy calls it roaming.

AUNT JANE: That's a pretty occupation!

MISSY: Aunt Jane, at church they say, Blessed are the meek, for they shall inherit the kingdom of heaven. Did you ever expect to inherit the kingdom of heaven?

AUNT JANE: I never thought much about it. I just wanted to be loved, Missy, just plain old loved. Funny thing is, I've got it now, after ten years of looking for it, scraping for it. Found it sitting by its mother's fire, little piece of fine embroidery in its hands. Put that thing down, I said. We're going out and find us the driest martini ... Well, looks like Katy's forgotten me again—she is getting old! I'm going in and ring hell out of that buzzer by my bed. (*Aunt Jane exits. Missy stares after her as Louise enters the area below the balcony. She is carrying a hairbrush and a ribbon.*)

LOUISE: There you are, Missy! I'm going to fix your hair—your Daddy's waiting for you. (*She begins to brush Missy's hair, and to tie on a ribbon.*) Your mama's going to have to get you a brassiere, one of these days. Then before long it'll be your first long dress. Your mama'll want to do it right, she'll take you down to Stewarts, dress you clean from the skin out, dress you in pure white taffeta, little puff sleeves, seed pearls down the front. By and by you'll make your debut, next thing you know, you'll be standing on that balcony, throwing your bouquet ... Honey?

MISSY: I'm going down the hill, catch the bus into town.

LOUISE: Bus don't run on Sundays. All the help that's got the day off leaves Saturday night. (*She gives Missy a tiny purse.*) Your daddy's waiting.

MISSY: Mother's going to buy me a corduroy skirt, Louise. Three tiers, orange. I'll put that skirt on, catch the bus into town, go to the Paradise Inn on Third Street—

LOUISE: Who ever heard!

MISSY: And dance to the juke box playing "Moon Over Miami!"

LOUISE: All by yourself, Missy?

MISSY: Maybe there's another one of me out there.

LOUISE: You're going to church, young lady! (*Missy exits. Captain P. enters, whistling. Louise picks up a basket of mending and sits down on a stool.*)

LOUISE: Morning, Captain. (*She begins to darn a sock.*)

CAPTAIN P.: Morning. (*He begins to fill window boxes with soil.*)

LOUISE: Those kids—always talking about leaving!

CAPTAIN P.: They get those notions once in a while. Always packing, saying this time they mean it.

LOUISE: Missy had that little old canvas bag, you remember? Had ducks on it. Her Daddy give her that when she was five years old—five years old and a month. He brought it back from England. She was all the time putting her little things in it.

CAPTAIN P.: Remember that time Billy made it all the way down to the bus stop? Miss Alice sent me to get him. He was standing there looking at the river, said, "Captain P., I saw the E.T. Slider go by. She was pushing twelve barges!" Then got right on in the car . . . Couldn't have been more than eight years old—

LOUISE: Seven and a half, that summer.

CAPTAIN P.: (*Taking seed packets out of pocket*) What you think, these little yellow marigolds? Missy always did love them.

LOUISE: Morning glories are her favorite flower.

CAPTAIN P.: (*Showing another seed packet*) Got some of them, too. (*He begins to plant the seeds in the window box.*) You think one of these days they going to leave, for good?

LOUISE: They got to grow up, first.

CAPTAIN P.: Billy's a big boy.

LOUISE: Big, and don't know a thing.

CAPTAIN P.: (*Sitting down in the swing*) Said he had a girl down here, yesterday.

LOUISE: Girl!

CAPTAIN P.: Yeah! She works at Walgreen's. He's fixing to take her to the drive-in—

LOUISE: Drive-in! What kind of girl—

CAPTAIN P.: I don't know. Don't know nothing about it. Just do what I have to do—plant my seeds.

LOUISE: You can't fool me, Captain. You know a whole lot more than you let on! You've been here as long as I have.

CAPTAIN P.: Seventeen years. I was here the day you come! (*Pause; he looks at Louise.*) My, you were pretty—you were sweet!

LOUISE: Don't start that, now. You were a married man.

CAPTAIN P.: When I saw those shoes . . . Those little black nursie shoes . . . Felt like they was stepping on my heart!

LOUISE: (*Stretching out her feet.*) They got big in seventeen years, didn't they?

CAPTAIN P.: Well, I don't know about that!

LOUISE: I come here looking just about the way I do now. You were seventeen years younger, that's all. Had these same scars on my face . . . (*Tentatively, she touches her face.*) Had them since I was five years old. Mama was afraid the kids'd fall in the fire. She hollered at me from the front room, Louise, put that firescreen up! I was too little to reach the handles, I climbed up on a big old stool . . . (*She looks down at the sock she is darning.*) It don't hardly pay to darn these cotton socks, Billy runs through them so fast. Sometimes I think his heels must just burn . . . They're growing up, Captain—both of them. Won't be any job for me here, a few more years . . . (*She begins to fold up her mending.*) Sometimes I wonder . . . Seventeen years ago . . . If I hadn't of had these scars . . . If you hadn't of been married to Laurie—

CAPTAIN P.: Her with that goiter like a gobbler's under her chin! (*He makes a turkey gobble.*)

LOUISE: Red as these old scars . . . (She stands up.) We got to go out next Sunday, if we can get the time, trim the ivy on her grave. (*Louise exits. Captain exits.*)

BLACKOUT

Lights up on balcony. Miss Alice, still in her negligee, and Mr. Robby are standing close together.

MR. ROBBY: (*Examining Miss Alice's neck.*) Just the little crepe lines you've always had, Darling. Venus' necklace.

MISS ALICE: (*Exhilarated.*) You're wrong, Robby. It's started. I can feel it. I don't even need to look in the mirror to know I'm starting to change. Oh, I know what to do about it—you don't need to console me. I know what to do about my own skin—my own bones, my flesh. Flesh . . . What an ugly word!

MR. ROBBY: (*Concentrating on the details of her body.*) Your legs are just the same. Your hips haven't spread. That waist's only an inch bigger than it was twenty years ago—after two children!

MISS ALICE: I never could do all those things, after the children came. I didn't have the energy. Not that you ever asked—you wouldn't ask, being your own darling considerate self—

MR. ROBBY: Lovely, slender ankles, legs like a young filly—

MISS ALICE: It's just a spasm—that's what they call it—I've read those books! But you know I never had that spasm. You were missing something!

MR. ROBBY: Hips with that lovely gentle slope—

MISS ALICE: It mattered! Don't try to tell me it didn't matter!

MR. ROBBY: (*Holding out his arms.*) Why, Alice—I love you! I love our life together, the things we do—even just driving you into town, watching the way you light up when we go into Stewarts.

MISS ALICE: Shopping for one of our trips.

MR. ROBBY: You're always ready for our trips—our lovely times together! Rome, Venice, Cap D'Antibes . . . We're not tied to this hill, Honey, we can go anywhere. You know what that means? It means we're free . . . (*He kisses her.*) Now, Darling, you go in and see about the packing. I'm going to study my maps. (*Miss Alice exits. Mr. Robby sits down, begins to look at maps.*) (*In the kitchen, Eula and Mildred enter. Mildred is carrying a bowl of cut-up fruit.*)

MILDRED: Get me them glass bowls, girl—the ones with the pleats. I got to get this fruitcup ready for they dinner. (*Eula searches in the cabinet.*) No! The top shelf—I can't stand here all day! (*Eula brings the bowls to the kitchen table. Mildred begins to fill them.*)

EULA: I'm leaving this place tomorrow, soon as I'm paid. I'm going down to the distillery—they pay fifty cents an hour!

MILDRED: How you going to live? You got to pay rent, buy clothes and food out of that fifty cents.

EULA: Mildred, I wants to get married! I wants me a little baby! Ain't no way out here I'm ever going to meet somebody to get married.

MILDRED: You got your day-off, girl. I met my Beuse on my day-off. I was up to that boat place at Harrods Creek and he was shoving off—oars just tipping the water! "Anybody interested in coming after some catfish?" I stepped right in.

EULA: He died on you, left you five kids.

MILDRED: I just stepped right in! He wiped off the seat with a piece of newspaper and I set myself down. Didn't know nothing about fishing. Still don't know nothing about fishing! Lord, Lord . . . Girl, take these fruit-cups and ring that dinner bell. My roast'll be dry as a stick. (*Eula and Mildred exit.*) (*On the balcony, Aunt Jane enters and stands watching Mr. Robby study his maps.*)

MR. ROBBY: It'll take us a little over an hour to drive from Le Harve to Deauville. In Deauville we'll be staying at the Pension Fougat. Lovely clean rooms, a view of the rose garden. Much more character than the Grand Hotel—

AUNT JANE: Where we stayed the summer you were winning races.

MR. ROBBY: Twenty years ago! I wanted to see, just once, before I got married—

AUNT JANE: That was coming up, in the fall.

MR. ROBBY:—Whether I could bet on every race, every day of the meet, and come up with a certain percentage of success.

AUNT JANE: You bought me this string of pearls.

MR. ROBBY: Yes, but I never told you the percentages. You were much too young to understand percentages!

AUNT JANE: I saw your money at the jewelers. Your billfold was crammed!

MR. ROBBY: I only won twenty-two percent of the time. That necklace took about all of it.

AUNT JANE: Robby! I never knew that! I thought you only spent a part of your winnings on me.

MR. ROBBY: The diamonds for Alice were paid for out of Papa's estate.

AUNT JANE: All these years, I never knew . . . (*She puts her arms around Mr. Robby.*) Remember the way the roses smelled, in the garden behind the Grand?

MR. ROBBY: (*Putting her off.*) There was no rose garden.

AUNT JANE: No rose garden?

MR. ROBBY: No. That was at the Pension. The Pension Fougat . . . You'll be all right while we're gone?

AUNT JANE: I intend to enjoy myself! I intend to eat! I'll melt down some vanilla ice cream and drink it out of a crystal goblet. I'll get fat, Robby, fat and respectable. I'll read the Bobbsey Twins to Missy—

MR. ROBBY: Missy is far too old for that.

AUNT JANE: Well, I'll read the Hardy Twins to Billy.

MR. ROBBY: I don't expect you to entertain the children, Jane. Leave that to Louise and the other servants. I simply expect you to maintain a certain tone . . . Promise you'll avoid the old problems. No whiskey bottles under the bed for Katy to poke out—

AUNT JANE: And display with unholy glee.

MR. ROBBY: No guests to disrupt the children.

AUNT JANE: Not even a woman friend?

MR. ROBBY: Why, certainly–if she'll make a contribution.

AUNT JANE: She'll tell Missy stories. She has the most wonderful collection. They travel with her in her fitted leather travelling case. Brush in its own little sling, make-up bottles anchored, giant stories, goblin stories, each in its pocket.

MR. ROBBY: I don't want you to be lonely while we're gone. I want you to be happy, Jane.

AUNT JANE: (*Seizing his hand.*) Take me back, Robby!

MR. ROBBY: (*Disengaging his hand.*) We can't go back, Jane.

AUNT JANE: Take me back to the Grand Hotel. Take me back to the rose garden. I don't care about the pearls. I only want to go back to the Grand, hear your voice on the gravel below our window, ordering our breakfast: "Deux croissants, s'il vous plaît."

MR. ROBBY: We can't go back, Jane. We've talked about it many times. All I can do is offer you a home, now you've run through all your money . . . I'll see you get back for another trip, before long. Maybe your friend with the stories would like to consider a little excursion to France, after we return . . . Jane, Dear, compose yourself. (*Mr. Robby exits. Miss Jane snatches off her pearls. Then she picks up the telephone.*)

AUNT JANE: (*Into telephone.*) Operator? Would you place this call to New York, please? New York City . . . Yes, I'll wait . . . Hello, Amelia? Darling, are you awake? You don't sound awake . . . Yes, I know it's early. Chicken crow at daybreak, down here on the farm . . . No, I didn't call just to call, I've got something to say. Amelia—Darling—do you think you could pack up that little leather travelling case and get yourself down to Grand Central— now? . . . I know you have your plans. I'm not trying to ride roughshod—It's just it's so utterly bleak down here . . . No, I've got to stay, it's my place, you see, still is. But there's nothing for me to do . . . (*Billy enters the duckyard and stands looking up at Aunt Jane on the balcony.*)

BILLY: I ain't been up there since I was six—that's what Captain P. says. I had the double pneumonia and they carried me up there to say goodbye.

AUNT JANE: (*Into telephone.*) Yes. Robby did say something about a trip, I think it means Europe . . . No, no details now. Goodbye, Amelia. (*She hangs up the telephone. Unaware of Billy, she puts the pearls on the table.*)

BILLY: Aunt Jane?

AUNT JANE: Billy! I haven't seen you since I got here . . . What's that terrible shirt you've got on—and your hair . . . Where've you been?

BILLY: Around.

AUNT JANE: Why, Honey, you've grown so tall. Taller than your dear father, it looks like. Where'd you get all those good tall genes? (*Billy climbs on the bench.*) Can I do something for you, Billy?

BILLY: Aunt Jane, I got to get out of here.

AUNT JANE: The eternal cry of youth!

BILLY: Trouble is, I'm a little short on cash.

AUNT JANE: Now, Billy, surely you can't expect me . . . Your parents are leaving you in my care! "I could not love you half so much loved I not honor more . . ." (*Billy jumps off bench.*) Your sister lives on poetry.

BILLY: I used to get down under the sofa and put my fingers in my ears when he read that stuff.

AUNT JANE: If poor Robby could hear you!

BILLY: Poor Robby ain't going to hear me! What'd he ever give me I could either use or sell? He don't know nothing about me . . . You used to give me peppermint sticks.

AUNT JANE: I did?

BILLY: You brought me a package of peppermint sticks, the ones that are hollow in the middle. Then you took a lemon and gouged a hole in the end and showed me how to suck the juice through the peppermint stick!

AUNT JANE: I did that?

BILLY: You sure did!

AUNT JANE: Billy, I'd love to help you, but my position here is so precarious. Your dear mother would have me out of here in a minute if she could find an excuse.

BILLY: What happened to your money?

AUNT JANE: Well, it seems I spent it. Never did quite understand how! I used to get these enormous checks in the mail—these really enormous checks! Seemed like I'd never be able to spend all that money. Then it'd turn out some of that money was supposed to be saved for taxes, so when tax time came, I'd have to borrow . . . After a while the checks stopped coming. Eaten up ahead of time, somehow.

BILLY: Don't you have anything just sort of laying around?

AUNT JANE: Now, young man: I disapprove, I strongly disapprove of your plan! (*Aunt Jane touches the pearls on the table.*)

BILLY: If I do get away, will you wait awhile before you send them word?

AUNT JANE: Certainly not! What an idea! Besides, there's absolutely no chance. I mean, we're buried out here. You'll have to wait—just like me—for the Captain to drive you where you want to go . . . (*Aunt Jane turns towards exit. She glances down at Billy, who is sitting on the bench with his head in his hands.*) Did you know I ran away from boarding school? Slid down three knotted sheets, got all the way to the train station! They wouldn't have caught me if it hadn't been the full moon . . . I guess I could wait a little while.

BILLY: Thank you!

AUNT JANE: I'm glad to see you haven't entirely lost your manners. You're welcome. (*Aunt Jane exits. Billy begins at once to look for a foothold in the nearest column. After some difficulty, he manages to swarm up to the balcony. He climbs over the balustrade and grabs the pearls.*)

EULA: (*Offstage.*) They fixing to leave!

CAPTAIN P.: (*Offstage.*) Tell them the car's ready . . . (*Billy climbs down off the balcony and hides in the duckyard. Miss Alice and Mr. Robby come onto the balcony, dressed for travelling. Missy comes into the nursery and sits down in the rocking chair.*)

MISS ALICE: All ready, Darling! Twelve matched pieces of pigskin, each one tagged with our name and address . . . (*Turning to the audience, she waves.*) Goodbye! Goodbye!

MR. ROBBY: (*Waving to the audience.*) Goodbye!

MISS ALICE: Sometimes, when we're all ready to leave, I see their faces looking up at us like from the bottom of a well.

MR. ROBBY: Train won't wait, Darling. (*He takes Miss Alice towards the exit. Suddenly she turns back, wrenches open her purse, and empties a rain of pennies over the balustrade. Billy runs out from his hiding place and begins to collect the pennies.*)

CURTAIN

ACT TWO

The following morning. The nursery alone is lighted. Missy is sitting in the rocking chair, holding a large doll.

MISSY: (*To the audience.*) They go for the button, first, at the top, under the collar. Then they go down to the second button, and the third, and all the time, you're telling them, No! You can feel their fingers through the material, you can feel their nails slide on the little pearl buttons. They're not quick about it. Then you start to say, No, again, real loud, and you argue. Sometimes they answer you back and then you get them off the track with an argument about the way people ought to behave, about respect. Other times, they don't even bother to answer you, they just go right on. You can't argue all by yourself—that's no distraction . . . Then they get down to the waist and they start to undo your skirt. If you've got on your school uniform, they have to hitch their fingers inside the waistband to get a purchase on that big button. Of course if it's hot weather, after-school time, and you've got your shorts on, that makes it easier . . . Soon as they get that button undone, they stick their fingers in and feel your skin. They say, Ooh—you hear them draw their breath. They're feeling your skin. It's cool, it's smooth, they say it feels like silk. You don't need to go on arguing, then, you just need to lie still and listen to them saying, Ooh, ooh . . . (*Missy takes off the doll's skirt.*) Why, you don't have any underwear on, Darling! How can you go out in public with nothing over your little weewee? (*She turns the doll over and spanks it.*) Spank you, Darling, for your own good . . . It hurts me more than it hurts you! (*Billy enters the nursery.*)

BILLY: You still fooling with dolls?

MISSY: I was just practicing.

BILLY: What you want to fool with this thing for? (*He takes the doll, presses his lips against the face.*) Um—she tastes good. Almost as good as my own little girlfriend.

MISSY: Oh, Billy, I'm so glad! You seem mad at me, most of the time.

BILLY: (*Hugging doll.*) Not when I'm with my baby.

MISSY: Sometimes I take her to bed and just hug her.

BILLY: (*Throwing doll back.*) Here, you take her.

MISSY: (*Laying doll aside.*) Billy, I've started to bleed.

BILLY: What you talking about?

MISSY: I've started to get my curse.

BILLY: You shouldn't be talking to me about that.

MISSY: I thought you'd be pleased. I'll have my hair cut, my dresses let down. Maybe I'll start going to parties. Does it show, Billy?

BILLY: Does what show?

MISSY: The curse.

BILLY: You know it doesn't. You look like the same silly old . . . (*He throws his arms around her.*) The same silly old sister! (*They embrace. Missy kisses him. Billy spins her away.*) What are you doing, necking with me?

MISSY: That's not necking. I know the difference.

BILLY: How you know?

MISSY: Mother gave me a book.

BILLY: About necking?

MISSY: That, and some other things.

BILLY: (*Inspecting her.*) You getting big. Any breasts yet?

MISSY: No.

BILLY: They starting to grow?

MISSY: Not really.

BILLY: Let me see . . . I'm not going to touch you! What you think, I want to touch my sister's titties? You think I'm like those guys you park with, trying to get their fingers in your pants—

MISSY: I don't do that, Billy! I'm never going to do that!

BILLY: I bet!

MISSY: I'm never even going to wear lipstick!

BILLY: That a promise?

MISSY: Yes!

BILLY: Cross your heart and hope to die?

MISSY: Yes.

BILLY: On the Bible?

MISSY: Yes.

BILLY: On our parents' graves?

MISSY: Oh no, Billy, not when they're crossing the ocean!

BILLY: Well, I guess you promised on enough stuff. I'll let you off that last one.

MISSY: Thank you . . . You're not fixing to go away, are you, Billy? Not before the end of summer?

BILLY: I don't get out of here before cold weather, I'll be stuck till spring!

MISSY: Billy—would you wait for me?

BILLY: How long?

MISSY: Till I'm old enough to go with you anywhere—to Captain P.'s saloon at Harrods Creek! Even to the Paradise Inn on Third Street . . . I passed by there once: big plate-glass window. They were all dancing, inside, in front of a great big mirror. One lady in a red dress was dancing WITH the mirror, had her hands pressed up against the hands in the reflection.

BILLY: That what you want? Borrow trouble?

MISSY: I never have had a red dress in my life.

BILLY: Well, girls don't wear red. (*He picks up a piggy bank from the toy shelf.*)

MISSY: You ever get that strong feeling, Billy? Like you want to open yourself up and take in the whole world?

BILLY: Not to talk about . . . How much you got in this thing?

MISSY: I don't know. Louise and I are saving for a trip to Bardstown, see My Old Kentucky Home.

BILLY: How you get it open?

MISSY: It doesn't open. Louise says when the time comes, I can break it.

BILLY: Well, the time has come! (*He holds the piggy bank over his head and drops it on the floor where it shatters.*)

MISSY: Oh, Billy—you broke it! I've been saving my money . . . Louise's extra dimes . . . (*She tries to get the money from him. They scuffle.*)

BILLY: I got to get out of here, Missy! Don't you want me to live?

MISSY: Of course I want you to live, Billy!

BILLY: Then stop trying to get in my way! (*He scoops up the rest of the money, stands up.*)

MISSY: It's not going to be enough, anyway!

BILLY: You'd be surprised! (*Billy runs out into the duckyard. Missy chases him. They grapple; Billy throws her to the ground. Aunt Jane runs out onto the balcony.*)

AUNT JANE: Billy! (*Billy exits.*) Missy! Oh, Missy! Are you hurt? Turn around, Honey—let me see your face! Why, you're crying . . . Shouldn't be down there, all by yourself, crying . . . Missy, why don't you come up here, let me . . . Let me comb the tangles out of your hair . . .

MISSY: Louise takes care of my hair.

AUNT JANE: . . . I remember when you were a little bit of a thing, couldn't have been more than five years old, all dressed up for some little girl's birthday. Louise was putting on her coat to go with you, and you told her, "Now, Louise, you won't be going to parties with me the rest of my life . . ."

MISSY: I said that to Louise?

AUNT JANE: Oh, in the sweetest way. You knew what was coming. (*She takes a lipstick out of her purse.*) I bought this in New York. It's a new shade, called Persian Melon. Want to try it?

MISSY: I promised Billy I wouldn't wear lipstick.

AUNT JANE: Never?

MISSY: That's what I said.

AUNT JANE: Billy's going to leave here, isn't he?

MISSY: Yes! I wanted him to wait . . .

AUNT JANE: For you?

MISSY: He won't. I'll never get off this hill by myself. (*She begins to cry again.*)

AUNT JANE: Honey, don't cry. Here . . . Blow your nose. (*Aunt Jane drops her handkerchief off the balcony; Missy picks it up and blows her nose.*) Now, why don't you come up here?

MISSY: I haven't been up there since I was three. I threw up on Mother's dress.

AUNT JANE: Well, you won't throw up on me, and if you do, I wash! Come along. I've got a lot to tell you . . .

MISSY: What?

AUNT JANE: I lived in this house when I was your age.

MISSY: I thought they sent you away to school.

AUNT JANE: They tried, but I came home. They couldn't hold me! Robby and I used to roll down the hill to the river. He ever tell you about that?

MISSY: No.

AUNT JANE: We were close. But I was the one who left, in the end. Your father stayed.

MISSY: Men don't ever stay.

AUNT JANE: Robby did. He met your mother and forgot about everything else. But I caught the itch, somewhere in these woods, the itch for the big world. I knew it was somewhere, spread out like a big bright-colored rug, maybe just the other side of the Ohio River.

MISSY: Where the cornfields are?

AUNT JANE: Corn all leans west. You ever notice that?

MISSY: What?

AUNT JANE: Leans towards the open spaces.

MISSY: I was trying to tell Billy about the open spaces.

AUNT JANE: You want them, don't you, Missy? You want to feel that breeze! Cornfields—next best thing to the ocean!

MISSY: I want to see myself in a room with mirrors, see myself dancing to the juke box playing "Moon Over Miami."

AUNT JANE: You got to learn how to dance, first.

MISSY: You going to teach me?

AUNT JANE: Maybe.

MISSY: Aunt Jane, you ever find another one of you out there, other than in mirrors?

AUNT JANE: You'd be surprised how learning to dance brings on the partners. (*Missy and Aunt Jane dance. Missy exits.*)

LOUISE: (*Offstage.*) Miss Jane . . .

AUNT JANE: Yes? (*Louise enters.*) What is it, Louise?

LOUISE: I hate to worry you.

AUNT JANE: Looks like I'm here to worry.

LOUISE: It's Missy. She needs somebody to help her, tell her things. I can't tell her what she needs to know. I never have been across that bridge!

AUNT JANE: And I have?

LOUISE: Ever since that time you slept in the bed forty-eight hours straight, heat pad on, burning your leg—

AUNT JANE: I was drunk.

LOUISE: But you got up, put that red dress on, went to the dance with Mr. Robby. Ever since that time, I knew if you wanted something, you were going to get it.

AUNT JANE: Thanks!

LOUISE: You're welcome.

AUNT JANE: What exactly do you want me to do, Louise?

LOUISE: Missy's stuck here, stranded . . . Makes me think of that fish we saw last December, frozen in the creek under a foot of cloudy ice. Missy wanted me to get a shovel, knock that ice apart but I told her, There are a lot of things I can do, and there are a lot of things I can't do and one of the things I can't do is free swimming things that are stuck tight . . .

AUNT JANE: You think I have the shovel?

LOUISE: And the muscles, too!

MILDRED: (*Offstage.*) Miss Louise! (*Mildred enters.*) Captain's looking for you!

LOUISE: Well, he can look. (*Louise exits.*)

MILDRED: Miss Jane . . . You done already finished with the ordering?

AUNT JANE: (*Picking up a list.*) Afraid I haven't even started.

MILDRED: (*Producing her own list.*) You better get started. They don't deliver after noon.

AUNT JANE: What is that number?

MILDRED: I wrote it down on the list.

AUNT JANE: Oh, yes, here it is. (*She picks up the telephone.*) Hello? Taylor 271, please . . . Is this Harper's Market? Good. This is Miss Jane Anderson, out on River Road—you know the place?

Of course you know the place! (*To Mildred.*) They better! (*Into receiver.*) We'd like to order . . . Yes. Let me see, now. Sixteen lamb chops . . . No, I don't believe we want rib chops. I don't believe that's what . . . (*To Mildred.*) Do we want rib chops?

MILDRED: Loin. More meat.

AUNT JANE: Sixteen loin chops. They have more meat. (*Reading from list.*) One pound pork?

MILDRED: Pork fat, for the beans.

AUNT JANE: Oh, I see . . . Bacon, five pounds. That seems like a lot.

MILDRED: We uses a lot.

AUNT JANE: Three pounds brussels sprouts . . . Rice, five pounds. Butter, four pounds, unsalted. Ten pounds flour. Well, that seems to be it. Oh—do you carry beer? Good . . . Let me have . . . Oh, say a dozen bottles. (*To Mildred.*) That's in case we have company. (*Hangs up.*) That's quite a list you gave me.

MILDRED: We got to feed eight people, and what they eat has got to be right. I makes everything from scratch . . . A dozen eggs for Missy's birthday cake—(*Missy enters.*)

MISSY: You going to make me a cake?

MILDRED: Why, Honey, you know I am. A dozen eggs and a pound of sweet butter.

MISSY: You going to ice it?

MILDRED: Ice it, and write your name on it, too, I knew how.

AUNT JANE: I'm good at icing. I can make letters.

MILDRED: Well, I never was much of a hand with one of them icing tubes.

AUNT JANE: Then you just leave it to me!

MILDRED: I believe I will. (*Mildred exits.*)

AUNT JANE: (*To Missy.*) How come you came back?

MISSY: I thought you invited me.

AUNT JANE: I'm glad.

MISSY: You going to tell me some poems?

AUNT JANE: No, indeed. I'm going to tell you about when I used to live in this house.

MISSY: Good!

AUNT JANE: The time I'm remembering is after I was thrown out of that boarding school. I came home aching and complaining—ashamed, and too proud to admit it—and Papa asked me what in the world I wanted to make me feel better. I told him I wanted a trip to Europe. Abroad. I'd seen New York and Boston by that time but the grey Atlantic was still stretching between me and the rest of the world. Papa wanted to buy me a diamond necklace, wanted to buy me a debut—great big party on the lawn here, yellow-and-white striped tent, three kinds of oysters flown here from the coast. I told him I'd rather be one of the oysters. He let me go, finally. He always let me go, finally. Paris, London, Rome—

MISSY: All by yourself?

AUNT JANE: I had a friend, from school. We were three years older than you are now. Two girls alone on the old Queen Mary but the way we dressed and acted—nobody treated us like children. It was the Captain's table every night. I remember I had a certain summer suit. I bought it at a little place in Paris that offered Toutes Pour Les Jeunes Filles . . .

MISSY: Jeunes Filles?

AUNT JANE: Young girls . . . I'd outfit you from the skin out, depending on your darling father, of course, to pay the bills . . . I'm going to take you to Paris. We'll visit the flower market, the bird market, we'll feed our breakfast croissants to those great big carp in the Tuilleries pond.

MISSY: I don't think Mother will—

AUNT JANE: Here, let me see your hand. I want to see if there's a travel line in it. There it is! Winds clear around your thumb. Why, that line'll take us to China.

MISSY: That's my lifeline, Aunt Jane. Louise told me.

AUNT JANE: Well, a long life, and a lot of travelling: isn't that the same thing?

Now, just imagine this: if we run into a storm in the middle of the Atlantic—end of summer, storms start brewing then—you'll hear a lot of groaning and complaining, you'll see the dining saloon empty out. You and me won't be doing any groaning. We'll get our coats and go up to the bow. Stand there and watch her plough through those big seas. Watch the bow rise up as high as this house, fall down into a trough, burrow into a solid wave. But always coming up, streaming water, streaking foam . . .

MISSY: What are they going to say?

AUNT JANE: Who? Our friends downstairs?

MISSY: And my parents.

AUNT JANE: Robby promised me this trip. You're going to learn when you want something hard enough, the obstacles just melt away.

MISSY: You always get what you want?

AUNT JANE: Well, I work for it. I pay the price. I'll tell you something else: the price has been high. Maybe too high. I want to see you get it cheap.

BLACKOUT

Lights up in the kitchen. Louise, Mildred and Miss Katy are sitting at the table. Miss Katy has her foot in Louise's lap.

LOUISE: I'll take care of these toenails, Miss Katy, but you got to do something about these bunions. They going to bust out of your shoes.

MISS KATY: Take a razor and slash the sides.

LOUISE: Slash the sides of your shoes?

MILDRED: She ought to go be operated.

MISS KATY: I ain't going under no knife. You done forgot what they did to Beuse, Mildred? Wasn't a thing in the world wrong with him till he went to that white doctor. Said he got to cut that carbuncle off the side of his neck. Went under the knife in the morning and was dead by two o'clock.

MILDRED: Cancer. Said they wasn't a thing they could do about it. Beuse always was poor-looking. His daddy was the same way. (*Eula enters with tray.*) Kids eat they lunch?

EULA: That Billy just picked. Just picked! He seen them good stewed prunes you fixed for dessert, he just about had a fit. Miss Jane going to have to do something about that Billy cause he's getting too wild!

MISS KATY: Miss Jane not going to do nothing about nobody. Miss Jane down here for a good rest.

LOUISE: Miss Katy, this big toenail's as thick as a piece of horn . . . There! There it goes . . . Miss Jane going to do something about Missy, keep her out of trouble.

MISS KATY: (*Putting shoe back on.*) Now one thing: Miss Jane know about trouble. Grew up with trouble—her mother dying so young. Old Colonel sent her off to school and she come back just as wild! That school took her sweetness. Come back, seventeen years old, great big bottle of whiskey in her suitcase, saying one thing in the world she wanted was to cross the ocean. Never would have nothing to do with them men used to come calling.

MILDRED: Lord, no!

MISS KATY: Miss Jane ain't studying no men! (*Missy enters.*)

MISSY: Louise, Aunt Jane wanted me to use her lipstick. I told her I promised Billy I never would wear lipstick.

LOUISE: Why, Honey, you'd look pretty in the right shade. You're growing up, going to start doing different things—

MILDRED: Cut off all that long wild hair!

EULA: Look out and find you a boyfriend.

MISSY: I don't want a boyfriend. I don't like boys, I don't even like Billy, most of the time.

LOUISE: Don't talk that way, Honey.

MILDRED: She can say what she wants to in this kitchen.

MISS KATY: She can say what she wants to in this house!

LOUISE: You all going to egg her on?

EULA: What's on your mind, Missy?

MISSY: Aunt Jane's talking about taking a trip.

MISS KATY: She going again?

LOUISE: What trip?

MISSY: With me. To Europe. Abroad . . . I never have been across the ocean. Might get seasick, throw up everywhere.

LOUISE: That what you worrying about?

MISSY: Aunt Jane's the only grownup ever asked me to go somewhere.

LOUISE: Why I'd take you anywhere in the world, Missy, anywhere I had the power to take you. But just think how we'd look: me with this face scares most people—they don't ask what it is, just look the other way. How'd you look, alongside of me in the diner on a train? They'd treat you funny—little girl going someplace with her nurse. You don't want to be treated that way no more. You don't deserve it!

MISSY: (*Putting her arms around Louise.*) I don't want to leave you, Louise. I want to sit on the back porch in the dark, with you, and listen to the big owl out in the woods calling, who cooks for you!

LOUISE: Who cooks for you!

MISSY: I want to walk down the back road, with you, pick up walnuts, mockoranges, a bluejay feather. I want to pick the honeysuckle flower, taste the drop of honey on the end . . .

MISS KATY: You want to ride you a wild pony.

MISSY: I never had a wild pony.

LOUISE: She wants more than that!

MISSY: What?

LOUISE: Out there. The rest of it.

MISSY: For he on honey-dew hath fed, and drunk the milk of Paradise . . . (*Missy exits.*)

MILDRED: (*To Louise.*) Ain't you scared to talk that way?

EULA: Talk about egging her on!

LOUISE: Of course I'm scared.

MISS KATY: They going to have to catch that Missy soon. Catch her and get her started before it's too late.

EULA: Too late for what?

MILDRED: Here, Eula, start drying. (*She hands Eula a dishtowel.*)

LOUISE: Miss Katy just talking.

MISS KATY: Just talking, nothing. I seen the same thing with Jane. Missy the spitting image! . . . Thirty years ago, now. Old

Colonel didn't know how to handle Jane after she come back from that school. Gave her a little grey pony, let her go out on it every day, stay out till dark. Nobody knowed what she did on that little grey devil. Nobody knowed where she went. Come back all red in the face—I'd be waiting for her, her bath drawn. "Where you been, Jane, till this hour of the night?" She'd look at me all excited. "I been by myself, Katy, I been by myself!" That's all she ever would say. Missy's going the same way.

LOUISE: Now you listen to me, Miss Katy. Things is different for Missy. She never did ride no wild pony!

MISS KATY: Huh! (*Louise exits.*)

CAPTAIN P: (*Offstage.*) You got any coffee, Mildred? (*Captain P. enters.*)

MILDRED: Saved you some, like I always do. (*She pours him a cup.*)

CAPTAIN P.: (*Outside the kitchen door.*) Reckon I'll take it out here.

MILDRED: You want some of that good heavy cream?

CAPTAIN P.: Just a spoonful.

MILDRED: Eula, get the Captain some of that cream. (*Mildred hands the coffee cup out the door to the Captain. Eula brings the cream.*)

EULA: Cream's so thick a spoon'll stand up in it!

CAPTAIN P.: Good! (*He spoons cream into his coffee, surreptitiously adds whiskey from a bottle in his pocket.*)

MISS KATY: (*Calling.*) You seen the boy?

CAPTAIN P.: No, I ain't seen the boy. Boy's no business of mine!

MISS KATY: Some not too far off might have a different opinion! Didn't Miss Alice tell you to keep an eye on Billy while they gone?

CAPTAIN P.: Didn't say nothing to me.

MISS KATY: She don't want that boy tomcatting around!

MILDRED: He's sixteen years old—what do you expect?

EULA: Plenty old enough!

MISS KATY: Watch yourself! You been in the whiskey, or what?

EULA: I seen the way he looks up at me when I'm passing the food. I can always tell what they got on they minds!

MISS KATY: Eula!

MILDRED: Hush, now!

CAPTAIN P.: Talk like that's bound to lead to trouble.

MISS KATY: You remember that Fritz we had here?

EULA: Yes . . .

MISS KATY: Had that little redheaded girl—that Jenny?

MILDRED: Oh, Lord!

CAPTAIN P.: She was pretty!

MISS KATY: Too pretty! Miss Alice had her eye on her. Day she come sashaying in here, high-heeled shoes, looking for Billy—claiming she wanted to play jacks!—Miss Alice give Fritz his notice.

EULA: Poor little Jenny. Wonder what happened to her?

MILDRED: What about her daddy? Out of work after five years on this hill.

MISS KATY: Miss Alice didn't have no choice!

CAPTAIN P.: (*Outside door.*) Sure was a pretty little girl. Couldn't have been more than fourteen when they left here . . . You all seen Miss Louise?

EULA: She was looking for you!

MILDRED: She's somewheres in the house.

CAPTAIN P.: Well, tell her, when she's through with what she's doing—

MISS KATY: Now, hold on a minute, Captain. You want to see Miss Louise, you just march yourself in and set down and wait. Ain't none of us paid to carry your messages.

CAPTAIN P.: I believe I'll wait out here! (*They all laugh.*) What you howling about now?

EULA: You afraid maybe it's catching?

CAPTAIN P.: What you talking about?

MILDRED: Seventeen years, you ain't been in this kitchen once! The plates and cups I done handed out the window! Cold weather, freezing to death, hot weather burning up in the sun . . .

Well, I had enough of this foolishness. I'm going in, see if my groceries come. (*Mildred exits.*)

CAPTAIN P.: Miss Alice told me from the first. Stay on the outside! Said I was paid to do outside work, not hang around in that kitchen.

EULA: Well, they gone now. This is bachelor hall! (*Eula drags Captain P. into the kitchen.*)

MISS KATY: You foolish girl! Don't you know things don't change?

BLACKOUT

Lights up in the duckyard. Louise is sitting working on crepe-paper flowers. As she works, she hums to herself. Captain P. enters.

LOUISE: I'm making these crepe-paper flowers for Missy's birthday . . . (*Captain P. comes closer but does not sit down.*) You going someplace?

CAPTAIN P.: Going up to Harrods Creek, cash my paycheck.

LOUISE: Don't you come back here drunk tonight—I'm warning you!

CAPTAIN P.: Why, what are you going to do about it?

LOUISE: Just because Mr. Robby and Miss Alice is gone, don't think you can get away with murder!

CAPTAIN P.: You going to stop me?

LOUISE: I'm going to tan your hide!

CAPTAIN P.: You just try it!

LOUISE: Well, I will! (*She bats him playfully with a roll of crepe-paper.*) I just believe I will, you come back here drunk tonight!

CAPTAIN P.: Only one way to make sure that doesn't happen.

LOUISE: Stay at home!

CAPTAIN P.: I stay at home six days a week! Only sure way is—you come with me.

LOUISE: (*Startled.*) Me!

CAPTAIN P.: Yes. You, Miss Louise.

LOUISE: Now you know I can't leave this hill.

CAPTAIN P.: Why not?

LOUISE: I got responsibilities!

CAPTAIN P.: Name one.

LOUISE: Well, I got to finish these crepe-paper flowers for Missy's birthday. I got to shine her patent-leather shoes . . . I got to see whether Billy's shoes need cleaning . . . I got to . . . (*She looks up at Captain P..They both begin to laugh.*) I got a lot . . . A whole lot to do!

CAPTAIN P.: Just drop everything and come! (*Louise hesitates. Then she begins to cut another flower.*)

LOUISE: I got to finish these flowers, for Missy.

CAPTAIN P.: Will you come with me some time? Will you, Louise?

LOUISE: Well, now I don't know, Peter . . . Whew, it is getting hot out here. I'm going to take these inside, finish them where it's cooler. (*Louise rises, picks up flowers. Captain P. catches hold of her apron strap.*)

CAPTAIN P.: Well, I tell you one thing. I'm going to be counting on it. (*Louise smiles and exits. Captain P. notices some shreds of paper on the ground and leans down to pick them up. Billy enters.*)

BILLY: You going to Harrods Creek, cash your paycheck?

CAPTAIN P.: I might drop in there later.

BILLY: Thought the lizzy was broke.

CAPTAIN P.: Got fixed in a hurry.

BILLY: Fixed to carry you where you want to go! I'm coming with you, Captain.

CAPTAIN P.: To Harrods Creek? You too young to go in that saloon.

BILLY: I'm sixteen. They let you in if you're sixteen.

CAPTAIN P.: You look about fourteen and a half.

BILLY: I got proof!

CAPTAIN P.: What kind of proof?

BILLY: The best!

CAPTAIN P.: I don't know what you're talking about, boy.

BILLY: You wouldn't know, at your age!

CAPTAIN P.: What you talking about?

BILLY: That girl. She keeps after me.

CAPTAIN P.: You bite off more than you can chew?

BILLY: I can't get her voice out of my ears. "Come on and do something for me, Honey. Come on and show me how much you love me." I can't show her all the time. I got other things to do! (*Pause. Captain P. looks at Billy with new respect.*)

CAPTAIN P.: You going to keep quiet if I ride you up there?

BILLY: You know me.

CAPTAIN P.: Louise'd skin me.

BILLY: You scared of old Louise? She's not going to say nothing. She's looking for you to marry her!

CAPTAIN P.: I already been married once in my life–twenty-seven years with a woman with a goiter. Big and red as a turkey gobbler's wattles! (*He begins to gobble.*)

BILLY: You going to take me, or not? (*Captain P. hesitates.*)

CAPTAIN P.: Come on! (*Captain P. and Billy exit.*) (*Mildred and Eula, followed by Missy, enter the kitchen. Mildred is carrying the cake and ingredients to make icing.*)

MILDRED: (*To Eula*) Miss Alice leave you your paycheck?

EULA: Yes. I'll have to wait to cash it till I get in town. Can't hardly do nothing with one day-off a week—

MILDRED: Sift that flour. (*Mildred hands Eula a sifter, begins to mix eggs in a bowl.*)

EULA: I got my eye on them projects on Eighth and Kentucky. Each of them apartments got a living room, bedroom, kitchenette and bathroom with a pink tub, a pink washbasin and a pink toilet!

MISSY: What'd you do, living in town?

EULA: I'd enjoy the view! The rainiest day, that pink just sits in there and GLOWS! Sunny day, I'd put me a chair out on the porch and watch the world go by. Then I'd get me a job down at the distillery, watch them whiskey bottles marching by, slap on the labels—(*She slaps the sifter. Flour spills.*)

MISSY: If I was you, I'd try it.

MILDRED: Hush, Honey, you don't know what you're saying. Ain't you finished sifting that flour yet?

MISSY: Well, at least you can think about it.

EULA: I think about it, Missy. I think about it most all the time. (*Whispering.*) You heard about boyfriends?

MISSY: That why you want to move into town?

EULA: What I going to do out here? You want me to shrivel up? Nothing out here but a bunch of women worrying about cleaning and cooking. Nothing but Billy and the Captain to kind of lend a little contrast!

MILDRED: You done said enough, Eula. Hand me that sifter. (*Eula hands Mildred the sifter.*)

EULA: Well, I know one thing. I got to get out of here.

MILDRED: Well, then, get! I heard enough of your complaining.

EULA: (*Dismayed.*) I don't have no way to get into town.

MILDRED: Captain's going up to Harrods Creek. You can catch the bus from there.

EULA: What about my things?

MILDRED: We'll send them on to you once you get located.

EULA: I don't give no notice, Miss Alice ain't going to give me a reference.

MILDRED: What you want with a reference? You through with this line of work, ain't you?

MISSY: Maybe she just wants to think about it.

MILDRED: Well, I tell you one thing, I heard just about all I want to hear about getting out. Get now, Eula, or quit talking. Just do your job and quit talking!

EULA: I can't just go, Mildred. I got no place to live!

MILDRED: You never will, long as you sit out here!

MISSY: Maybe you could go to a hotel.

MILDRED: Hotel! Well, I'm putting this icing on to boil, and I'm setting this timer. (*She does so.*) You better make up your mind, Eula, before this timer rings.

MISSY: You just going to sit there and wait for it to ring?

EULA: Missy, I got a whole lot on my mind!

MILDRED: (*Sweetly.*) Missy, Baby, come on and help Mildred find the icing tube . . . Miss Jane says she's going to decorate your cake. What you want on it, Baby? (*Missy reluctantly finds the tube in the cupboard, returns with it to the table.*) You want your name on it? You want "Happy Birthday"? . . . You know how long I been in this house?

MISSY: Since before I was born.

MILDRED: Seventeen years I been in this house. Seventeen years, morning, noon and night.

MISSY: Oh, Mildred, what would I do if you weren't here to make my birthday cake?

MILDRED: Honey, you'd find somebody else to make your birthday cake. (*Enter Louise, with a large basket of paper flowers.*)

LOUISE: Look here, Missy. (*She spreads out the flowers on the table.*) I made you a whole bunch! Here's a red one—two red ones—and a purple with a yellow middle. How you like that yellow middle? Looks like a cat's eye!

MISSY: Pretty, Louise! (*Enter Aunt Jane, wearing an apron, followed by Miss Katy.*)

AUNT JANE: Here I am, you all! All prepared to do the icing!

MILDRED: It's just about ready . . . (*Timer rings; Mildred brings icing from stove.*) (*To Eula.*) You made up your mind?

MISS KATY: She going someplace?

EULA: No. I'm staying right here.

MILDRED: Showing some sense, for once.

MISS KATY: Starting to see how lucky she is! (*Aunt Jane begins to ice cake.*)

MISSY: Don't you want that all-pink bathroom?

EULA: Trouble is, Missy, I don't have any family to fall back on. My family's all in Hopkinsville. I don't want to go back there, live next to the colored graveyard.

MISSY: You'd have us to fall back on.

MISS KATY: Once gone is gone.

MILDRED: Out of sight, out of mind!

EULA: Mildred's right, Missy. Rent would eat up everything I made. I guess the trouble is I'm better off staying right here.

MISS KATY: Now you're talking!

AUNT JANE: Where's the icing tube? (*Missy hands it to her.*) Think I'll put on the star-shaped point . . .

MISSY: Where'd you learn about icing?

AUNT JANE: You don't know about the home-grown side of me.

MISS KATY: It was when you was getting ready to be born, Missy. Your Aunt Jane was staying here in the house, waiting for you to come, and you wouldn't come, and you wouldn't come, and your poor mama was fit to be tied! Laying in the bed, washrag over her eyes, every shade in the room drawn. Well, your Aunt Jane decided to try a little distraction.

MISSY: What'd she do?

MISS KATY: (*To Aunt Jane.*) You want me to tell it?

AUNT JANE: Go right ahead!

MISS KATY: Well, your Aunt Jane come in this kitchen, run all of us out, cooked up the biggest cake you ever did see. Used every egg in the house and every bit of butter. Had flour everywhere! Sink full of pots and pans! Cooked this great big cake and spent the entire afternoon icing it—sweated right through her pretty blouse. Sure enough, you was born that night.

MISSY: (*To Aunt Jane.*) What you going to write on my cake?

AUNT JANE: You'll see . . . (*Writing.*) J . . . (*Telephone rings.*)

LOUISE: Now, Missy, don't you look . . . (*She answers the telephone.*) Hello? Captain! I didn't expect to hear from you! What you doing, calling me on the phone? . . . He is! Billy's with you? Well, you bring him straight home! . . . No, you can't take that child to Indiana! (*She slams down the reciever.*) Captain's gone clear out of his head! Says he's fixing to take Billy across the bridge!

MISSY: Across the bridge!

AUNT JANE: (*Icing.*) . . . A . . .

LOUISE: Captain's got more sense. He'll be back around midnight, Billy wore out, asleep in the back seat. I'll be waiting for him!

AUNT JANE: (*Icing.*) ... N ...

EULA: Maybe they'll get across the bridge.

MILDRED: Bridge, nothing. What they going to do for gas money?

LOUISE: Captain probably cashed his paycheck!

AUNT JANE: There! It's finished! (*Aunt Jane stands up, takes off her apron. All crowd around the cake.*)

MISSY: What does it say?

AUNT JANE: You read it.

MISSY: J-A-N ... Jane! That what you wrote on my mother's cake?

AUNT JANE: Yes. She was wild! Thought I meant the cake was for ME. I told her, This cake is for your baby—that was going to be born that night. And I said to Robby, "Name her for me. Write it on her birth certificate. I won't care what you call her."

LOUISE: I called her Missy. She was such a little bit of a thing.

MISSY: (*To Aunt Jane.*) Were you claiming me?

AUNT JANE: Not then.

MISSY: Are you claiming me now?

AUNT JANE: Come here, Missy. (*They move away from the others.*) I want you to have something of mine, for your birthday. (*Aunt Jane takes off her scarf, ties it around Missy's neck.*)

MISSY: Thank you! (*She throws her arms around Aunt Jane.*) What are we going to do now?

AUNT JANE: Today's Monday ... You and I are the only two people in this house that's got nothing to do on Monday. Maybe the only two people in the entire world! It'd be nice if we could amuse each other ... Maybe we could hire a car, drive to Bardstown.

LOUISE: See My Old Kentucky Home.

MISSY: You know how to drive?

AUNT JANE: I could make a stab at it! You want to go?

MISSY: What time we going to get back?

AUNT JANE: Louise, what do you think?

LOUISE: Well, you leave now, you'll be back in plenty of time for supper.

MISSY: I thought we were going . . . further . . .

AUNT JANE: We have to practice first. For the big trip.

MISSY: All right. Let's go!

BLACKOUT

After a pause, the voices of Billy and Captain P. are heard over the sound of a car engine.

BILLY: You going to cross the Big Four Bridge?

CAPTAIN P.: Going right up on it now!

BILLY: We going to visit those four big cities?

CAPTAIN P.: Cincinnati, Cleveland, St. Louis and Chicago!

Lights up on the balcony. Dance music in the background. Mr. Robby and Miss Alice are standing by the balustrade, wearing evening clothes. A Spot picks up Missy and Aunt Jane, in the area below the balcony.

MR. ROBBY: A little rough, earlier, but now, look—it's smooth as a plate. I'm so proud of you, Darling. Our last crossing, you were so uncomfortable.

MISS ALICE: Made your life a misery! Couldn't keep a thing on my stomach . . . You know, I believe you've forgotten. Today was Missy's birthday.

MR. ROBBY: I didn't forget. Just didn't want to cloud the day.

MISS ALICE: Cloud the day! You think we were wrong to leave her alone?

MR. ROBBY: She won't be alone.

MISS ALICE: Well, no . . . You know, I can't imagine what they all do when we're not there.

MR. ROBBY: You mean the children?

MISS ALICE: The children. And the others.

MR. ROBBY: Why, they keep things going. We have to let them spread their wings, Darling. They can manage without us—but you and I—we can't live without this. (*He begins to dance with Miss Alice as the music grows louder and then abruptly ends.*)

MISSY: (*To the audience.*) We'll take the train from the river station, eat our dinner off a white tablecloth, watch the Ohio sliding by. In the morning, they'll be hollering, Grand Central Station! We'll get off, take a taxi to the boat. We'll get on! I'll unpack all my dresses, wear the prettiest one that night. Sit at the Captain's table, go up afterwards to the saloon and dance . . . Mother! Father! Look at me! I'm learning . . . (*She gives her hand to Aunt Jane.*) I'm learning how to dance! (*Aunt Jane and Missy dance a few steps.*)

CURTAIN

Darrah Cloud

O PIONEERS!

Author's Introduction

When I first read *O Pioneers!*, I thought it was the most accurate portrayal of how a woman thinks—at least a white, American woman—that I had ever read. I had long been obsessed with questions of how to create a female hero and yet not betray what is intrinsically female about her. It's easy to give a woman male traits and easy for American audiences to appreciate masculine women. But how to elevate such feminine accomplishments as intuition and nurturing to the high status of such classically male acts of heroism as the conquering of villians by physical prowess, or the driving of a race car, deeds which set our hearts beating faster and make us want to be "just like them?"

I was then struck by the immense responsibility I was taking on in attempting to adapt *O Pioneers!* to the stage. Willa Cather's book contains little dialogue and even the land is cast as a character. Cather fans are downright violent about defending her work; I could never presume to alter her intent or her plot. How would I marry Cather's voices to my own and still remain loyal to hers? Beyond those problems was one other: in a culture that devalues many feminine attributes, how do you make them as relevant and important as male ones? How could I make *O Pioneers!* as visceral and necessary to men as to women, to old as to young, to Black and Hispanic and Asian and Native American as to White European? How could I go on believing that a woman's simple experiences could mean that much to anyone, even women?

The answers, of course, were in the novel. If an individual's life could stand for a kind of empty but fertile landscape, then Alexandra's character would be like that of the land. Everyone has a life that is an open and green thing that one must take responsibility for creating. Everyone of us is a pioneer. On every page of the novel there was a basic human truth or foible, beauty or weakness, that I recognized in myself and others. Alexandra's greatest fault is her egotistical inability to see beyond her own repressed sexuality to the passionate desires of those around her. But her greatest strength is her utter courage in confronting her own weakness, pushing through her rage and sorrow over her brother's death to face his murderer at the end, asking him to forgive her for being blind and judgmental; and then forgiving him. She does this not to achieve anything but a deeper state of being in the world.

Now that is a truly universal, heroic act. That is the person I tried to create. If the culture insists on devaluing this kind of personal human struggle, then I will insist on giving it value in my work. Writing *O Pioneers!* taught me that.

Willa Cather's *O Pioneers!* was coproduced by the Seattle Repertory Theatre and the Women's Project & Productions under the directorship of Daniel Sullivan and Julia Miles as part of the Other Season at the Seattle Repertory Theatre in April 1989. It was directed by Kevin Kuhlke with the following cast:

ALEXANDRA	Mary McDonnell
CARL LINSTRUM	Randle Mell
ANGELIQUE/ILSA	Marsha June Robinson
AMEDEE/MAN IN DREAM	Scott Rabinowitz
MARCEL/FINN	Kevin McDermott
JOE TOVESKY/NELSE	Michael C. Hacker
YOUNG MARIE	Dorothy Longbrake
ANNIE LEE/OLD MRS. LEE	M. Elizabeth Kennedy
LOU	Peter Lohnes
FRANK SHABATA	Christopher Noth
SIGNA	Angela Fie
MILLIE	Shona Curly
OSCAR	Kevin C. Loomis
IVAR	Clayton Corzatte
FATHER	C.R. Gardner
YOUNG EMIL	Jeffrey Zimmerman
MOTHER	Kathryn Mesney
EMIL	Dougald Park
MARIE	Jennifer Rohn

Music by Kim D. Sherman
Lyrics by Darrah Cloud

Singers:

Soprano	Mary Jo DuGaw
Alto	Shirley Harned
Tenor	Jeffrey Francis
Baritone	Brian Higham

Musicians:

Conductor	Brian Russell
Piano/Synthesizer	Todd Moeller
Violin	Dorothea Cook
Cello	Meg Brennand
Clarinet	Jennifer Nelson
French Horn	Cindy Jefferson

Set design by John Wulp
Costume design by Mary Ellen Walter
Lighting design by Jeff Robbins

Managing director   Benjamin Moore
Music director   Brian Russell
Assistant music director   Todd Moeller
Stage manager   Jodi Molever
Sound designer   Steven M. Klein

TIME AND SETTING

Act I   Hanover, Nebraska, 1890s.

Act II   Sixteen years later, late spring.

Act III   That winter.

CHARACTERS AND VOICE BREAKDOWN

Alexandra Bergson: a strong Swedish woman
Emil Bergson, her brother: young, morose, intense
Lou Bergson, her brother: sly, full of himself
Oscar Bergson, her brother: slow, ox-like
Carl Linstrum: German, sensitive, artistic
Ivar: a mystical old Norwegian
Marie Tovesky: Bohemian—a spitfire
Frank Shabata: Bohemian—out of place, angry with the world
Annie Lee: brassy, modern/Soprano

Angelique/Ilsa, French and Swedish girls/Soprano
Mrs. Bergson/Mrs. Lee, Old Swedes/Mezzo Soprano
Signa, Swedish maid/Alto
Amedee, French young man/Tenor
Mr. Bergson, Swedish man/Tenor
Marcel, French/Lyric baritone
Guard/Dream Man, Bass
Milly, Teenage girl/Soprano
Little Emil, Five years old/Soprano
Little Marie, Ten years old/Soprano
Immigrants, Played by all singers

SET

Nothing but land and sky. Nebraska, late 1880s-early 1900s.

SCENE ONE

Music Cue 1—Land Music

A bare stage, nothing but land and sky. Alexandra stands alone in silhouette, wearing a man's coat and hat. We're unsure of whether this person is a man or a woman, at first. Lights come up as Poor Immigrants begin arriving at the Hanover rail station, bundles at their sides, some in traditional dress. All sorts of countries are represented. To the foreground of the crowd comes the Bergson Family: Alexandra, in her late teens, her mother, father, brother, Lou, and Oscar, in their teens, and Emil, who is five years old. They too are very poor.

Music Cue 2

FIRST IMMIGRANT:

MARCH 1873

LEFT MY HOME AND WALKED TWO DAYS.

BOARDED SHIP AND CROSSED THE SEA.

TAKING ONLY WHAT I COULD CARRY.

SECOND IMMIGRANT:

AUGUST 1874

LEFT THE CITY, TOOK THE TRAIN.

WHEN THE TRACK RAN OUT I WALKED

TO THE SHORES OF THE PRAIRIE.

THIRD IMMIGRANT:

APRIL 1875

THOUGHT COMING HERE WOULD MAKE US FREE.

GOT SO FREE WE NEARLY STARVED.

LOST MY YOUNGEST BABE AND LOST MY MIND.

FOURTH IMMIGRANT:

FOURTH OF JULY

MADE IT HERE, AND ALL ALIVE.

SEND US WHAT YOU CAN AND WRITE—

WHAT WE'D GIVE TO HEAR FROM OUR OWN KIND . . .

FIFTH IMMIGRANT:
BOAT ACROSS THE OCEAN DIDN'T KILL ME.
SLUMS OF THE CITY DIDN'T KILL ME.
JOURNEY WEST, THE COLD AND NO FOOD
DIDN'T KILL ME.
SO I SHOULD FEEL NO LITTLE DISAPPOINTMENT IN DYING NOW
    WE'RE HERE.

VOICE:
CAUSE THERE'S GOLD IN THE RIVERBEDS.

VOICE:
SILVER ON THE PLAINS.

VOICE:
SALT INSIDE THE MOUNTAINS.

VOICE:
AND DIAMONDS IN THE RAIN.

ALL:
ALL THAT POSSIBILITY
RUNNING TO THE SEA.
AND NOT ANOTHER HOMESTEAD
BETWEEN THAT SEA AND ME. (*Last verse repeated by all a cappella.*)

Immigrants slowly disperse, as:

SIXTH IMMIGRANT:
WHY DOES WINTER COME
WHEN IT'S NOT WANTED HERE AT ALL.
NO ONE EVER PRAYED FOR ICE
OR NEEDED SNOW TO FALL.

SEVENTH IMMIGRANT:
AND WHY DID I COME HERE
WHEN IT'S TOO HARD TO BE ALIVE?

BECAUSE I'M JUST AS CRUEL AS WINTER
TOO COLD NOT TO SURVIVE.

SCENE TWO

Music Cue 3—Wind Music

Winter—a drastic change. Alexandra drives the wagon through the lonely cold. Carl appears on the horizon and hails her from a distance.

CARL: Alexandra! Alexandra! (*She pulls the horses in.*)

ALEXANDRA: Carl! What are you doing in town?

CARL: I came in to help my father. But I told him I might ride back with you.

ALEXANDRA: Yes, of course, come on! (*He climbs into the wagon and they take off. They regard each other shyly.*)

ALEXANDRA: Cold!

CARL: Yah! (*Pause.*)

ALEXANDRA: Colder tomorrow!

CARL: Yah! (*Pause.*)

CARL: Not as cold as yesterday, though.

ALEXANDRA: No! (*Pause.*)

CARL: What brought you all this way?

ALEXANDRA: I had to see the doctor.

CARL: About your father?

ALEXANDRA: (*With difficulty.*) Yah . . .

CARL: Is he going to be alright?

ALEXANDRA: No. (*Pause. Alexandra sits up straighter.*)

CARL: I'm sorry, Alexandra. (*She nods.*) What are you going to do?

ALEXANDRA: I wish we could all go with him and let the grass grow back over everything.

CARL: Does he know?

ALEXANDRA: I think he does. He lies alone in bed all day and counts what he has . . . what . . . he's leaving us . . .

CARL: Maybe I could come over soon and visit him. Help him take his mind off things.

ALEXANDRA: Would you?

CARL: Why, sure, I . . . I'll bring my magic lantern.

ALEXANDRA: You got it?

CARL: Right here! And I figured out a way to paint my own pictures for it so I don't have to buy them.

ALEXANDRA: Pictures of what?

CARL: Oh, Germany, near where I grew up, mostly. That's the only way I'll ever be able to see it again. You can let me off right here. (*Alexandra reins the horse in.*)

ALEXANDRA: When will you come see us?

CARL: Whenever you want.

ALEXANDRA: Tomorrow.

CARL: Tomorrow, then. (*He jumps down and lights her lamp for her.*)

CARL: Whatever happens, Alexandra, you can always count on us. (*He turns and runs off, calling to her as he disappears in the distance and she drives on alone into the dark, lit only by the lamp. Wind music crescendoes and stops abruptly.*)

SCENE THREE

Out of the utter darkness comes a voice:

FATHER: Daughter! Daughter! . . . (*A shaft of light appears. Alexandra stands as if in a doorway. Mother and Emil are in background "kitchen".*) What is happening now?

ALEXANDRA: Mama is fixing a rabbit for dinner. The boys are outside, cutting wood. A window has cracked.

FATHER: Come here. (*She wipes her hands and moves to him. Light comes up a little.*) You will have to do the best you can for your brothers. It will all fall on you now.

ALEXANDRA: Don't talk like this, Papa.

FATHER: Teach your brothers. They are not as smart as you. Don't let them get discouraged and go off. You have to keep this land.

ALEXANDRA: You need another blanket.

FATHER: Listen to me. You are old enough now to understand. My father, your grandfather, was not an honest man. We had to leave Stockholm and come here. We had no choice. You can't go back.

ALEXANDRA: I understand.

FATHER: Alexandra . . . don't let all this have been for nothing. In eleven long years I have made not one solid mark on this land. Only mistakes. But they are a kind of soil too. You can make things grow from them. (*Lou and Oscar enter the house, stomping their boots, cold.*)

FATHER: What is happening now?

ALEXANDRA: Lou and Oscar are coming in from the barn.

FATHER: Call them in here. Call them. (*She goes to the light, beckons them in. They shuffle in solemnly, stand stiffly by.*)

OSCAR: You want something, Papa?

FATHER: I want you all to listen to me now. So long as there is one house there must be one head. Alexandra is the oldest. She knows my wishes. I want you to be guided by her. (*Boys look at each other a moment.*) The next few years you will have it hard. Alexandra will manage the best she can. But you must all keep together. And you must promise me one thing: you will never give up this land.

LOU: But Papa—

OSCAR: We promise, Father. It would be so without your asking.

FATHER: Alexandra? . . . Alexandra?

ALEXANDRA: I promise.

FATHER: Good. That is good. You boys, go and get your supper. (*They move off.*) What is happening now?

Music Cue 4

ALEXANDRA: Water is coming to a boil on the stove. The cattle are moving up close to the house.

FATHER: How many head of cattle?

ALEXANDRA: Two.

FATHER: How many hogs in the pen?

ALEXANDRA: Three hogs.

FATHER: Five hens—

ALEXANDRA:—and seven chicks—

FATHER: Go on.

ALEXANDRA: Three cherry trees, two pear . . .

FATHER: Go on . . . Blackberries,

ALEXANDRA AND FATHER: Chokecherries, dandelion, milk-weed, cattails, buffalo-grass, (*He stops. She goes on.*)

ALEXANDRA: Linden, cedar, cottonwood, oak—(*Alexandra looks at Father. He's gone. Family gathers around a grave.*)

OSCAR: Only through death can heaven be attained. This hard and sorrowful life is the trial we stand that will determine our places there. And so we consecrate this body to the cruel earth which is the stuff of this body, ashes and dust, ashes and dust. (*All disperse except Alexandra. She stoops and fingers the earth. Throws it down with hate. Leaves.*)

SCENE FOUR

Alexandra works earth with hoe. Sun grows gradually bigger in the sky. Emil plays in the dust with his friend, Marie. Oscar and Lou work in a field upstage.

Music Cue 5—Drought Song

APRIL ONE: NO RAIN.

APRIL SEVEN: NO RAIN AGAIN

APRIL TWENTY: STILL NO RAIN.

> SUNRISE COMES
> AND THE STARVING EARTH LIES DRY
> AND THE CORN IS TOO WEAK TO FEED
> ALL OF US, ALL OF US.

> DAYLIGHT COMES
> AND THE DYING RIVERBED CRACKS

ALL ACROSS AND LIKE MY HANDS
BLEEDS RED, BLEEDS RED.

THERE IS NOTHING YOU CAN DO ABOUT IT.
THERE IS NOTHING YOU CAN DO.

BUT I AM SMILING.

MAY ELEVEN: SOW WHEAT.

DARK WIND BLOWS
AND THE SUN BEATS DOWN
AND THE FLOWERS I PLANTED BURN AND BREAK
INTO DUST, INTO DUST.

BUT I AM SMILING.
THERE IS NOTHING YOU CAN DO ABOUT IT.
I AM SMILING.
THERE IS NOTHING YOU CAN DO.
SUN KEEPS RISING.
THERE IS NOTHING YOU CAN DO.
I AM SMILING.
FOURTH OF JULY: BROKE MORE LAND AND BROKE THE PLOW.
JULY SEVEN: ALL THE CROPS DEAD ANYHOW.
WHERE DO WE GO?

BUT I AM SMILING.
THERE IS NOTHING YOU CAN DO ABOUT IT.
I AM SMILING.
THERE IS NOTHING YOU CAN DO.
SUN KEEPS RISING.
THERE IS NOTHING YOU CAN DO.
STILL I'M SMILING.

Lou gives up in fury at the earth. Oscar keeps on, like an ox.

LOU: What are we doin' this for? Can you tell me that? (*Alexandra stops and looks at him. He indicates Oscar.*) Look at him. You point him to a plot of land and he works it. Don't matter to him if nothin' comes up. Well, it matters to me. I'm no fool . . . You're the one got us into this, Alexandra. What are we gonna do now? (*Pause. She considers.*)

ALEXANDRA: We're going to take the afternoon off.

LOU: What?

ALEXANDRA: Oscar! Get the wagon ready! We're taking the afternoon off. Emil, you and Marie can come too.

OSCAR: Where we goin'?

ALEXANDRA: We're going out to Ivar's place . . . to trade for a hammock. We'll pick up Carl on the way. Come on . . . Come on!

Music Cue 6

They all pile into the wagon. Lou shakes his head and joins the rest. They take off. Carl appears in a field. They hail him.

ALEXANDRA: Carl! Come on! Come on!

OSCAR: We're goin' to Crazy Ivar's! (*Carl jumps into the wagon.*)

LOU: I heard Crazy Ivar howls at the moon, Emil.

EMIL: He does?

ALEXANDRA: No, Emil.

OSCAR: But it's true!

ALEXANDRA: Don't believe a word they say.

LOU: I heard he runs all over the prairie at night, howling cause he thinks the Lord is out to destroy him.

EMIL: You boys are gonna watch out for us, aren't you?

ALEXANDRA: It's just that he speaks the old language, Emil. Even I can only understand him a little.

CARL: But he wouldn't hurt you. He came to doctor our mare once, when she had the colic. But he cured her, just by groaning like he had the pain himself.

OSCAR: He don't know the first thing about doctorin'! When the horses have distemper, he takes the medicine!

ALEXANDRA: Yah, but it works!

Music Cue

OSCAR: Whoa, whoa now! (*He reins the horse in.*)

EMIL: How come we're stopping?

ALEXANDRA: We're here! (*They all climb out except Emil.*)

EMIL: But there's nothing here! (*Suddenly, a door opens in the ground. Ivar pops out. He's an old man with long, gray hair, wearing traditional Norwegian dress and no shoes.*)

IVAR: No guns! No guns!

ALEXANDRA: No, Ivar, no guns!

EMIL: What's he saying?

OSCAR: Ask sister, I don't understand it. (*Boys go upstage and squat, glancing suspiciously over at the scene. Emil tries to follow them, but is collared by Alexandra. Carl stays with her. Marie goes right up to Ivar.*)

ALEXANDRA: Ivar, this is our little brother Emil. And this is his friend, Marie. We came to buy a hammock if you have one, Ivar, and to show the little ones your birds.

Music Cue

IVAR: Not many birds now, I'm afraid. A crane came by last week. A seagull passed through.

ALEXANDRA: He says a seagull came here.

MARIE: A seagull! (*She claps. Emil is morose.*)

EMIL: What's that?

IVAR: A big white bird belongs on water. Lost here for sure. You boys never shoot wild birds, do you?

LOU: What's he saying?

ALEXANDRA: He wants to know if you boys ever shoot wild birds? (*Boys look at each other and roll their eyes.*)

IVAR: Yah, I know, boys is thoughtless. Those birds belong to God, not you. God counts them every day. It says so in the New Testament. Well, come on then.

Music Cue

Boys shrug at each other. Marie, Carl and Alexandra follow Ivar to his door. Emil hangs back, Marie flops down and peers down into the hole.

MARIE: You live here? (*Ivar pops his head up.*)

IVAR: Yah! (*He pops down again.*)

CARL: But where do you sleep, Ivar? (*A heap of rainbow-colored hammocks flies out of the earthen house. Ivar follows.*)

IVAR: Hammock!

Music Cue

Marie and Emil roll in the hammocks. Alexandra pulls Ivar to the side.

ALEXANDRA: Ivar, I really came here today because I need your help.

IVAR: I figured.

ALEXANDRA: I've made a terrible mistake. I put all my fields in corn this year but the soil is so poor the stalks dry up before they have a chance to stand. If we lose this crop we'll lose everything and I'm to blame. It's all on me and I don't know what to do.

IVAR: You think too much of yourself, little sister. You didn't keep the rain away. God did. This drought's been coming on for years now. You'd have known that if you hadn't been so scared of knowin' it. There's nothing you can do. The land will come around again. It's people who give up. Plant potatoes.

ALEXANDRA: Thank you, Ivar. That's just what I'll do.

Music Cue

Boys stand. Ivar growls at them. They jump and he laughs. All get into the wagon.

LOU: Yup, he's crazy alright.

OSCAR: He don't even work his land.

LOU: He's gonna lose it, he don't watch out.

CARL: He never has gotten used to it over here.

LOU: We wouldn't listen to a thing he says, sister.

ALEXANDRA: You didn't understand a word of it.

OSCAR: We still wouldn't listen to him.

ALEXANDRA: Yes, boys.

Music Cue

They drive on away.

SCENE FIVE

Music Cue 7—LOCUSTS

A few months later. Alexandra works in the garden, digging up potatoes. Carl comes up behind her as she stares off for a moment.

CARL: Alexandra . . .

ALEXANDRA: Oh! I didn't hear you come up.

CARL: Yah, well . . . hot.

ALEXANDRA: Hot, yah . . .

CARL: Hotter than yesterday, even. (*She looks at him. He avoids her. She stands up.*)

ALEXANDRA: What's the matter, Carl?

CARL: We've finally made up our minds. We're leaving.

ALEXANDRA: It's settled?

CARL: My father's heard from St. Louis. He can get his old job back.

ALEXANDRA: But what about you?

CARL: I'm going to learn engraving there. There's a future in it, in the cities. And it's good to have a trade. You have a trade, you can get a job anywhere. It's not enough for me to dig in the dirt in the middle of nowhere. There's so much that I am missing . . . It seems like we're leaving you to face the worst of it. But we never were good neighbors. Father was never meant to be a farmer, that's for sure. And I hate it. I want to be good at what I do.

ALEXANDRA: Lou and Oscar will be so unhappy when they find out.

CARL: What about you?

ALEXANDRA: This has been harder on them than it's been on me. Lou, he wants to marry Annie Lee, and he can't until things get better.

CARL: Do you ever think of marrying, Alexandra?

ALEXANDRA: I don't have time to think about it, there's so much work to do. (*She shows him the potatoes.*)

ALEXANDRA: Look at these. Everything around here is drying up and dying and these just grow that much stronger. (*Pause. Locust increases.*) What am I going to do without you? (*She starts to cry. Carl feels terrible.*)

CARL: You don't need me. I'm just a fool out here.

ALEXANDRA: You're my best friend. You understand me.

CARL: What good is that?

ALEXANDRA: I suspect it's the only thing one person can really do for another.

CARL: I can't stay here. I don't belong here. I want to go where I can do something you'll be proud of ... (*She turns away from him.*) Look at me. (*She shakes her head.*)

ALEXANDRA: You'll write to me, won't you?

CARL: Every day ... Alexandra—(*She rises abruptly.*)

ALEXANDRA: I better be getting back. Mother will want her potatoes. (*She runs off quickly. He stands a moment, looking after her. Then leaves.*)

SCENE SIX

Evening. Bergson family is gathered about. Alexandra turns to family.

ALEXANDRA: (*With difficulty.*) Carl Linstrum came by this afternoon. He had some news ... the Linstrums will be going back to St. Louis.

MRS. BERGSON: What?

LOU: See there? Everybody's leaving! They know when to quit!

ALEXANDRA: Where would we quit to?

LOU: Chicago. We could go to Chicago and work for Uncle Otto in the bakery. Steady jobs. A day off once in awhile.

ALEXANDRA: And dependent on somebody else for the rest of our lives.

LOU: I don't want to end up like Father, workin' himself to death early for nothin'.

ALEXANDRA: It wasn't for nothing.

LOU: Well it is now! Nothing is all that grows here!

ALEXANDRA: We just haven't figured out how to do it yet!

MRS BERGSON: You never used to fight like dis when your father was aroun'. (*Pause.*)

LOU: Percy Adams traded his land to Charley Fuller for a place down by the river. That's what we oughta do.

ALEXANDRA: That Fuller has a head on him. I wish he'd take me on for a partner. He's buying and trading for every bit of land he can get up here. Someday, he'll be rich.

LOU: He's rich now. He can take a chance.

ALEXANDRA: Why can't we? We're going to live longer than he is anyway. We ought to think like the rich ones, not like the poor.

LOU: You don't know what you're talkin' about. We've tried! We've tried and we can't make it here.

ALEXANDRA: (*Manipulatively.*) What do you think, Mama?

MRS. BERGSON: You go if you want! Me, I'll get some neighbor to take me in. I'm going to stay right here and be buried next to Father. I'm not leavin' him all by himself on the prairie for the cattle to tromp!

ALEXANDRA: You don't have to do anything you don't want to do, Mama. A third of this place belongs to you and we can't sell it without all our consent. That's American law. You know that, don't you?

MRS. BERGSON: I think I heard it once. But I knew I wouldn't understand it so I didn't listen.

ALEXANDRA: It was harder times than this in the early days, wasn't it, Mama?

MRS. BERGSON: Oh, worse, much worse. All we did was scratch in the dirt for food and try to keep warm. But we never quit! (*Mrs. Bergson gets up, blowing her nose, and leaves.*)

OSCAR: Maybe it's time we did.

LOU: It's no use hangin' on here just because of a promise. Everybody's gettin' out. All the Americans for sure. They're either goin' back East or down to the river.

ALEXANDRA: Then I'll go down to the river and take a look at what they've got.

OSCAR: What?

ALEXANDRA: Maybe you're right. If I find anything good, you boys can go down and make a trade.

OSCAR: Nobody'll trade you for this piece of desert.

ALEXANDRA: Maybe. (*Pause.*)

LOU: Don't agree to anything before we see it.

OSCAR: Don't let on that we can't make it here.

ALEXANDRA: Yes, boys. (*She seizes Emil's hand and they run off.*)

SCENE SEVEN

MUSIC CUE 8

Alexandra and Emil walk along the river.

EMIL: Look, sister, a wild duck!

ALEXANDRA: The water is so still it looks like there are two of her. But she doesn't know that. She doesn't know age or change. She is so free that everything fulfills her. She could fly away forever right now . . . but only one of her could go . . . (*The duck flies off.*) There's nothing for us down here, Emil. Oh, there are a few fine farms but they're owned by the rich men in town. We could always scrape along down here but we'd never be able to do anything big. Down here, what they have is certainty. But up where we are, there is a very big chance.

SCENE EIGHT

Alexandra stands before the boys.

ALEXANDRA: The thing to do . . . is to sell our cattle and the rest of the corn and buy the Linstrum place. Then we'll take out two loans on our half-sections and buy Peter Crow's place. Raise every dollar we can and buy every acre we can.

LOU: What? . . .

OSCAR: Mortgage the homestead?

LOU: I won't do it! I won't slave to pay off another mortgage ever again! You're gonna kill us with your crazy schemes!

OSCAR: How you gonna pay off these mortgages?

ALEXANDRA: We borrow the money for six years. With the money, we buy a half-section from Linstrum and a half from Crow and a quarter from Struble, maybe. That will give us upwards of 1400 acres. We won't have to pay off our mortgages for six years. By that time this land'll be worth thirty dollars an acre. It'll be worth fifty, but we'll say thirty. Then we can sell a garden patch anywhere and pay off our debts.

LOU: What about the taxes and interest?

OSCAR: Yah!

ALEXANDRA: I'm worried about that. We'll have to strain to make the payments. But as sure as we are here tonight, we can sit down ten years from now independent. Not struggling farmers anymore! I want to send Emil to school. I want to give him what I . . . what we missed.

LOU: But how do you know the land is going to come up?

ALEXANDRA: I can't explain it. I just know. When you ride over the country you can feel it.

LOU: Feel it! You're bettin' our lives on a feelin'?

OSCAR: We can't work so much land. We can't even begin to.

ALEXANDRA: Oh, Oscar. You won't have to work it. All we have to do is sit back and own it. Just like the men in town.

LOU: Everybody's gonna think we're crazy. We must be, otherwise everybody'd be doin' it.

ALEXANDRA: That's just it. When I was down on the river I met a man who was growing a new clover called alfalfa. He put in fields of it and everybody thought he was insane. He said the right thing is usually just what everybody won't do. (*Pause. Lou and Oscar move angrily away. Lou plays his harmonica, Oscar storms out. Alexandra follows him.*)

Music Cue 9—Harmonica/Cricket

Oscar sits glumly with his head in his hands.

ALEXANDRA: Don't do anything you don't want to do, Oscar.

OSCAR: I dread signin' my name to them pieces of paper. All the time we were kids we had a mortgage hangin' over our heads.

ALEXANDRA: Then don't sign. I don't want you to, if you feel that way.

OSCAR: No. We're in so deep we might as well go deeper. But it's hard work pullin' outa debt. 'S like pullin' the thresher outa the mud. It breaks your back. But I can see that at least there's a chance your way.

ALEXANDRA: I don't want you to have to grub for every dollar all your life.

OSCAR: Maybe it'll come out alright. But signin' papers is signin' papers. Ain't no maybe about that.

Music Cue 10—Land Music

Alexandra walks upstage. At the hands of the Immigrants, who enter as well, the land transforms from a desert to a lush green place. Alexandra trades her rags for better clothes. Emil and Marie grow up. Music rises and ends.

SCENE NINE

Sixteen years later.

Music Cue 11—Telephone Wires

Father climbs out of the grave, long-haired, barefoot, wild. He blinks, looking around. Recognizes nothing. Ivar comes along, picking up the litter of abandoned homesteads: a shoe, spoon, half a cup, a horseshoe . . .

IVAR: Make a joyful noise unto the Lord, all ye lands. Serve God with gladness. Come before God's presence with singing.

Know ye that—(*He spies the ghost, who wanders to a pole. He follows him.*) Telephone pole. They're all over the place now. No privacy for them as has 'em. (*Ghost picks a leaf.*) Alfalfa. She put it in, oh, maybe twelve, fourteen year ago. Everybody thought she was crazy. Now they're all growin' it. (*Ghost stares into distance.*) That's your old place now. You don't recognize it, do ya? See the new house there and all the little outbuildings . . . She done pretty good with those. But it's with the soil she done the best. (*Ivar leads the ghost back to his grave.*) Make a joyful noise unto the Lord . . . Know ye that God made you and not you yourself . . . (*He goes off.*)

SCENE TEN

Ivar is fixing a harness in the barn. Alexandra comes in.

ALEXANDRA: Do you have everything you need, Ivar?

IVAR: Don't need anythin'.

ALEXANDRA: I want you to be as comfortable here as you were at your old place.

IVAR: My old place was cold and damp and flooded most o' the time. Fitting pennance for a life full of errors.

ALEXANDRA: You're sure you're warm enough out here?

IVAR: Plenty warm. (*Pause.*)

ALEXANDRA: Maybe you ought to come up and live in the house.

IVAR: Too many temptations in the house.

ALEXANDRA: But you're strong enough to resist them, aren't you?

IVAR: I am . . . But my body is not. I give in to my body, my mind'll go next. I do give in to the desires of the feet, however. The feet are free members. I indulge them. But feet wash clean quicker than the soul.

ALEXANDRA: Well, then, unless there's something on your mind, I'll just go back up—

IVAR: I heard some talk!

ALEXANDRA: Talk? About what?

IVAR: About sending me away! To the asylum!

ALEXANDRA: Nonsense. Where did you hear that?

IVAR: Your brothers said it. The night Emil come home from that university where they teach him how to leave us all behind.

ALEXANDRA: You know I would never consent to sending you away.

IVAR: You can't prevent it if your brothers complain to the authorities.

ALEXANDRA: They have no power over me.

IVAR: You didn't hear 'em, Mistress. They despise me because I don't look like them. Because I have visions. Back home, where we all come from, there were a lot like me. People let us alone. But here, suddenly everybody forgets. They put us in the asylum. Look at old Peter Kralik. I knew him when he was a boy. He drank out of a creek one day and swallowed a snake. And always after that he could only eat such food as the creature liked because, if it didn't get what it wanted it would gnaw him from the inside out. The only thing that would keep it quiet was alcohol. That was the only way he could ever get any rest. He could work as good as any man when his head was clear, but they locked him up for being different in his stomach. Only your prosperity has protected me in America. If you had had misfortune, they'd have taken me away long ago.

ALEXANDRA: I'm sure they'd like to take me away too, for putting up that silo. You and I can go together. But till then, I need you here. I'm grateful you came to me when you lost your place. Don't worry about my brothers. I'll take care of them.

IVAR: You know what they got down to Lou's now? A big white tub, like a horse's trough, to wash yourself in. I was over dere the other day and old Mrs. Lee showed me the thing. Terrible, horrible. In so much water you can't make a suds. When they send her in there to wash at night, she makes a splashing sound. Then, when everybody's asleep, she scrubs herself in a little wooden bowl she hides under the bed.

ALEXANDRA: Maybe we ought to start our own asylum.

IVAR: Yah! I got a lot of friends to put in it.

ALEXANDRA: So do I . . . You're sure you're warm enough out here, now?

IVAR: Don't matter. Too many temptations in the house. Too soft chairs.

ALEXANDRA: Well, good night, then . . .

IVAR: Make sure you tell that Emil to stay off the bay mare. She's got a sore shoulder and needs the rest.

ALEXANDRA: I will.

SCENE ELEVEN

In the house, Signa helps Alexandra undress and change into a long white nightgown. She goes and Alexandra settles into a chair. Her loneliness overwhelms her. She looks for something to do, picks up an old letter to read. Falls asleep.

Music Cue 12—Transformation Song

THE YEARS PASS BY MORE PEOPLE COME.
WHEAT AND CORN MAKE A CHECKERBOARD
OF THE LAND THAT ROADS RIDE OVER.
THE YEARS PASS BY THE WINDMILLS SPIN
FROM ONE WEEKS' END TO ANOTHER
AND THE BROWN EARTH SURRENDERS TO PLOWING.
PLEASE, GOD, DON'T MAKE US BE POOR AGAIN.
WE PROMISE TO LIVE AS HUMBLE AS YOU.
PLEASE, GOD, DON'T MAKE US BE POOR AGAIN.

MY VOICE CARRIES A HUNDRED MILES
OVER WIRES STRUNG FROM TREE TRUNKS.
I CAN CALL MY AUNT IN LINCOLN.
I WANT TO BUY A GRAMOPHONE
IT WILL MAKE ME FEEL LESS ALONE
WHEN THE TELEPHONES GO DOWN IN WINTER.
THANK GOD, NOTHING WILL STOP US NOW.
WE CAN WITHSTAND WHATEVER BEFALLS.
THANK GOD, NOTHING WILL STOP US NOW.

Music Cue 13—I Call Your Name Instrumental

In a dream, a young man appears. He picks her up and carries her across the fields. She slides from his arms to the floor and wakes there. She's shaken. She rushes to a washbowl, takes down her nightgown and scrubs herself brutally.

SCENE TWELVE

Signa and Ilsa, two young housekeepers, set the table for Sunday dinner.

Music Cue 14—Tablesetting Song

SERVIETTEN VANSTER OM GAFFEN GAR OCH
SKEDEN TILL HOGER OM KNIVEN SA
(NAPKIN GOES TO LEFT OF FORK AND
SPOON GOES TO THE RIGHT OF KNIFE.)
LU-LU-LU-LU-LA-LA-LA
DINGA DINGA DINGA KGA.

OCH SATT TALLRIKEN MELLAN SILVRET
GLOM INTE SMORETSOM GAR TILL HOGER
(PUT THE PLATE BETWEEN THE SILVER
BUTTER DISH GOES UP AND OVER.)
LU-LU-LU-LU-LA-LA-LA
DINGA DINGA DINGA KGA.

SATT DU GLASET OVER KNIVEN
KAFFE KOPPEN BREVID SKEDEN
(PUSH THE CHAIRS UP TO THE TABLE
PLACE THE ROLLS AND SALT WHERE ABLE.)
LU-LU-LU-LU-LA-LA-LA
DINGA DINGA DINGA KGA.

Emil comes on pursued by Alexandra.

EMIL: Not another Sunday dinner! Please, Alexandra!

ALEXANDRA: But, Emil, I need you! And besides, they've hardly seen you at all since you got back from school.

EMIL: I don't have anything to say to them!

ALEXANDRA: Neither do I! But they never notice!

EMIL: They won't notice me sneaking out the back, either.

ALEXANDRA: Why don't you go and see Marie, then?

EMIL: Another time.

ALEXANDRA: I know Marie would be glad to see you. I think it gets a little lonely over there. Her husband is not . . . very happy.

EMIL: Maybe in a few days.

ALEXANDRA: Well you'd better get going. They'll be here any minute.

EMIL: Thanks, sister. (*He runs off. She turns to girls.*)

ALEXANDRA: What are you two standing around for? There's work to do! (*Girls hurriedly finish their work and go off.*)

GIRLS: SEDAN NAR SLUTET PA MIDDAGEN NARMAR

KAMMA HARET RATA PA FLATEN

(AS A FINAL TOUCH TO DINING

FIX YOUR HAIR IN THINGS THAT'S SHINING.)

LU LU LU LU LA LA LA

DINGA DINGA DINGA KGA. HIE!

(*Alexandra's family appears. Mrs. Lee is with them, dressed in her old-world clothes. The rest, however, are modern Americans now.*)

ANNIE LEE: I just love what you've done with the house, Alexandra! So many fancy things!

ALEXANDRA: I don't care for them at all. But they seem to put other people at ease.

LOU: And where is Emil?

ALEXANDRA: He had some business to attend to, Lou.

LOU: He's not coming to Sunday dinner?

ALEXANDRA: He's very sorry, Lou, he wanted very much to be able to come, but—

OSCAR: You let him off the hook again.

ALEXANDRA: No, Oscar, don't be silly—Shall we all sit down to eat? (*They do. Ivar enters, gets a plate and serves himself from the table, much to the guest's annoyance. He flirts with Mrs. Lee.*)

ANNIE LEE: (*Trying to smooth things over*) Did Lou tell you he's running for County Clerk?

IVAR: He has not got a fox's face for nothing. (*Mrs. Lee snorts with laughter.*)

ANNIE LEE: Mother! . . . What did he say?

ALEXANDRA: Ivar says congratulations, Lou.

ANNIE LEE: Why, thank you, Ivar, yes, we're pleased. Milly, dear, be careful now. Don't drop anything on Mother.

IVAR: What's that she's done with her hair?

LOU: (*Losing patience.*) What's he sayin'?

ALEXANDRA: He says please pass the preserves.

ANNIE LEE: (*Trying to calm him.*) Pass the preserves, Lou, dear.

IVAR: She don't watch out a buzzard's gonna nest in it. (*Mrs. Lee snorts again.*)

ANNIE LEE: Mother! (*Alexandra gets the preserves and shoves them at Ivar, who takes them quizzically.*)

ALEXANDRA: (*Warningly.*) Ivar!

IVAR: It's the house. The house makes me say things. (*He returns preserves to Alexandra and departs. She passes preserves back down table.*)

LOU: I was in Hastings last week. Went to a convention there.

ALEXANDRA: Hastings. How interesting.

LOU: Drove by the asylum and talked to the superintendent about the old man.

ALEXANDRA: Please pass the preserves. (*They pass them down to her again.*)

LOU: He says Ivar is a dangerous case. Says it's a wonder he hasn't done anything violent up to now. (*Mrs. Lee, irritated, starts mumbling irritatingly.*)

ANNIE LEE: Oh! My!

ALEXANDRA: Is that so?

LOU: That's what he says.

ANNIE LEE: Well! I guess he ought to know.

ALEXANDRA: Ivar has more sense than half the hands I hire. I am lucky to have him here.

LOU: The doctor was mighty surprised at how you'd put up with the old man. Mighty surprised. It seems he's likely to set fire to the barn any minute.

ANNIE LEE: No!

LOU: That's a fact. Or take after you and the girls with an axe!

ANNIE LEE: Dear Lord! (*Ilsa and Signa burst out laughing.*)

LOU: It's only necessary for one neighbors to make a complaint, you know. Then he'll be taken by force.

ALEXANDRA: Well, Lou, if any of the neighbors try that, I'll have myself appointed his guardian and take the case to court. That's all.

ANNIE LEE: Will you pass the preserves back this way, Lou, dear? (*He passes them furiously.*) You know, Alexandra, he is a disgraceful-looking object. And the place is fixed up so nice now.

ALEXANDRA: I'll see from now on that he stays on the property and doesn't bother people. So don't you trouble yourselves anymore about him. I hear you bought a bathtub, Lou. How is it working? (*Mrs. Lee snorts raucously. Lou drops his fork.*)

ANNIE LEE: Well, I can't keep him out of it! He'd run his business from there if I let him. You really ought to get one, Alexandra. I don't know how we ever lived without one!

ALEXANDRA: I think I will get one. I'll put it in the barn for Ivar. That will ease people's minds.

LOU: You can't just put aside what we're sayin' here, Alexandra!

OSCAR: You're ruinin' the help just like you ruined Emil, sendin' him off to that college, there. You don't watch out, it will all come back on you!

ALEXANDRA: Well! Don't we all get more like ourselves every year! Come on, Milly. Let's go for a walk. I'll tell you more about the good old days!

Music Cue 15—In The Field

Alexandra and Milly come downstage as the scene behind them dissolves. They walk hand in hand, looking out over the fields. A stranger appears on the horizon. He carries a suitcase and approaches. Alexandra spies him and sends Milly home. She eyes him warily.

CARL: Don't you know me, Alexandra?

ALEXANDRA: I'm afraid I . . . Carl? Carl Linstrum? Is it really you?

CARL: Are you glad to see me?

ALEXANDRA: I can't believe it!

CARL: I'm on my way out west. But I couldn't pass through here without getting a look at you.

ALEXANDRA: You've changed!

CARL: And you're just the same.

ALEXANDRA: Well I hope you're going to stay with me. (*She picks up his suitcase. He grabs it from her.*)

CARL: I'll get that.

ALEXANDRA: See there? I have only women come and visit me. I don't know how to behave!

CARL: I can only stay a few days.

ALEXANDRA: After all this time?

CARL: I'm going to Alaska.

ALEXANDRA: Alaska! Are you going to engrave the Eskimos?

CARL: I'm a fortune hunter now. I had to give up engraving. The only thing I cared about was wood engraving and that went out. Everything's cheap metalwork now, touching up bad drawings and ruining good ones. I'm sick of it. What a wonderful place you have made of this. I would never have believed it could be done. I'm disappointed in my own imagination. (*Lou and Oscar come up.*)

ALEXANDRA: Oscar! Lou! Look who's here! It's Carl Linstrum! They don't believe it either! Come, boys, it's our old Carl! All the way from New York City! (*They keep their distance.*)

LOU: Good to see ya.

OSCAR: How d'do.

ALEXANDRA: Carl's on his way to Alaska.

LOU: That so?

OSCAR: Terrible cold winters up there, I hear.

LOU: Quit your job, did you?

CARL: Engraving is a fine profession, but a man can't make any money at it. I'm going to the gold fields.

OSCAR: Ever done anythin' in that line before?

CARL: No. I'm going to try my luck.

ALEXANDRA: You always were a dreamer.

LOU: New York, eh? What do you New Yorkers think of William Jennings Bryan?

CARL: Well, Lou, there are about as many opinions in New York as there are people.

LOU: I guess we gave your Wall Street quite a scare in '96, alright.

CARL: I guess you did.

LOU: And we ain't afraid to do it again. You fellas back there must be a tame lot. You had any guts, you'd march right down to your Wall Street there and blow it up.

CARL: They'd just rebuild it somewhere else. But what are you complaining about? You folks are as rich as barons.

LOU: We got a good deal more to say than when we was poor, that's for sure. (*Annie Lee rushes up, dragging Milly.*)

ALEXANDRA: Carl, you remember Annie Lee, don't you?

CARL: Of course I do.

ANNIE LEE: How nice to see you again, Mr. Linstrum. You really ought to have called before surprising us like this. I must apologize for the dress I'm wearing, I don't usually look this plain. Have you met my oldest daughter yet? Milly! Come here, darling! Milly plays the piano, don't you, Milly? And the organ! And she paints, and sews and does pyrography. That's burnt wood, you know. You won't believe what she can do with her poker!

CARL: I'm sure she's a very clever girl.

ANNIE LEE: Well, you'll have to wait a few more years for her!

MILLY: Mother!

CARL: Does Milly run barefoot all over the countryside like you and Alexandra used to?

ANNIE LEE: Oh, my, no. Things has changed since we was girls. Milly will be going out into company, soon as we rent our place and move into town. Everybody's doing that here now. Lou's quitting farming and going into business.

LOU: That's what she says.

ANNIE LEE: I am so interested in New York City and how they do things there. Why haven't you married yet? And at your age, too. Or is that one of those eastern things we haven't heard about yet, way out here?

LOU: You go and get your things. It's time to leave.

ANNIE LEE: Please come over and visit us, Mr. Linstrum. Just make sure you telephone first. Lovely dinner, Alexandra.

LOU: Bye, now.

OSCAR: Be seein' you. (*All go except Carl and Alexandra.*)

CARL: Up and coming in the cornfields, eh, Alexandra? (*She laughs. He offers her his arm and they go off.*)

SCENE THIRTEEN

Music Cue 16—Carl's Song

Carl and Alexandra walk in the garden at night.

CARL: Lou and Oscar certainly have done well. But I think I liked the old Lou and Oscar better. They probably feel the same way about me.

ALEXANDRA: They've become just the same as the people we came to this country to get away from.

CARL: If you don't mind my saying it, I liked the old land better too, when it was still wild . . . How strange things work out . . . I've been away engraving other people's pictures, and you've stayed home and made your own. How did you do it?

ALEXANDRA: The land did it. It had its little joke. It pretended to be poor because nobody knew how to work it right. Then, all at once, it woke up out of its sleep and stretched itself, and it was so big and rich that we suddenly found that we were rich, just by sitting still. But I really built this place for Emil.

CARL: Will he farm here with you?

ALEXANDRA: He'll do whatever he wants. (*Pause.*)

ALEXANDRA: Would you like to go and see your old place tomorrow?

CARL: I guess I ought to.

ALEXANDRA: Don't you want to?

CARL: I'm a bit of a coward when it comes to things that remind me of myself. I wouldn't have come back here at all if I hadn't 've wanted to see you.

ALEXANDRA: Why are you so dissatisfied with yourself?

CARL: You always were direct, Alexandra . . . All the way out here I planned to make you think I had made something of myself. I waste a lot of time pretending to people and the joke of it is, I never fool anybody. By your standards here, I'm a failure. I couldn't buy one of your cornfields.

ALEXANDRA: I'd rather have had your freedom than my land.

CARL: I don't know. Here, you're needed. You're an individual. In the cities there are thousands of people like me. Whenever one of us dies, the only folks who mourn are the landlady and the delicatessan man. We leave nothing behind us but a coat and a pile of papers. Maybe a canvas or two. All we ever managed to do was pay our rent. Exorbitant rent that one has to pay for a few square feet of space near the heart of things. We live in the restaurants and look about at the hundreds of people all around us who are just like us, and we shudder.

ALEXANDRA: Still, I would rather have Emil grow up like you than like his two brothers. If the world were no wider than my cornfields, if there were not something besides this, I wouldn't feel it was much worthwhile to work. It's what goes on in the rest of the world that reconciles me to this one.

Music Cue

They walk slowly off under the moon.

SCENE FOURTEEN

Graveyard

Music Cue 17—Emil's Dream

Emil moves downstage by degrees, scything hard. He stops to rest. Lies down and puts his hands behind his head.

Emil's Dream:

Frank Shabata, dressed like a dandy, swaggers onstage. Marie, in a group of girls, watching him devoutly. A group of guys stand off to the side, watching him too. Purely for Marie, he pulls a silk handkerchief out of his pocket and the girls nearly faint. Marie approaches him.

MARIE: I'm sorry, but I could never stand to be courted by you, Frank Shabata.

FRANK: I hadn't thought of asking you, Marie.

MARIE: Well, good, because I wouldn't be able to stand it . . .

FRANK: And why is that?

MARIE: Because I get so happy whenever I see you. And I couldn't bear feeling that happy all the time.

She strides off. Frank pauses, then pursues her, scooping her up off her feet. She squeals with delight as he carries her about and then off. Emil awakes in pain. Then rises and starts back to work, trying to shake the dream from his head. He works harder than ever. The present Marie appears, dressed in a cloak and straw hat, older. She watches him awhile before speaking.

MARIE: Almost through, Emil?

EMIL: Yes. (*He halts, stricken. Turns.*) Marie . . .

MARIE: (*Laughing.*) Yes . . . (*Pause.*) It's so good to see you. It's been so long.

EMIL: Yes.

MARIE: You must have done well at school.

EMIL: I'm not exactly sure why I went, now that I'm through.

MARIE: I didn't think you were ever coming back.

EMIL: Well, I did.

MARIE: Yes . . .

EMIL: Yes . . .

MARIE: Yes . . . Well . . . You'll have to meet my husband, Frank. He was a city boy. But my uncle gave us the money to buy the Linstrum place and Frank's been a farmer ever since . . .

EMIL: That must have been a big change for him.

MARIE: Yes . . . I was going to offer you a ride up, if you were through. But it doesn't look like it.

EMIL: I am! Almost. I've finished my mother and father, but now I feel obliged to the others. Will you wait?

MARIE: Yes . . . (*He scythes furiously.*)

EMIL: Look. Here are the Kourdas. Remember them? They were Bohemians. Why aren't they in the Catholic graveyard?

MARIE: Free Thinkers.

EMIL: I met a lot of Free Thinkers at the university.

MARIE: Did they teach you that you Swedes would all be heathens if it weren't for us Czechs?

EMIL: We might've been better off that way.

MARIE: What religion were the Swedes before they were Christians?

EMIL: Something like the Germans, I think.

MARIE: We Bohemians worshipped trees. There were good luck trees and bad luck trees.

EMIL: Which are the lucky ones, I'd like to know.

MARIE: I don't know all of them, but lindens are. I'm a good Catholic, but if I weren't, I could go for loving trees, if I hadn't anything else.

EMIL: That's a poor saying.

MARIE: Why? If I feel that way, I feel that way.

EMIL: You don't have to love only trees.

MARIE: You always were so serious . . . I wish I had an athlete to mow my orchard. Frank won't do it. He's mad at me again. And I get wet to the knees whenever I go pick cherries.

EMIL: You can have one any time.

MARIE: (*Laughing.*) Can I?

EMIL: Yes.

SCENE FIFTEEN

Music Cue 22

Carl and Alexandra make their way in bright sunshine to Marie's.

ALEXANDRA: See here? We kept up the path. It's been good having a friend at the other end of it again.

CARL: Well, I hope it hasn't been quite the same.

ALEXANDRA: Marie could never take your place, if that's what you mean.

CARL: Alexandra, wait. Look at me. Are you at all disappointed in seeing me again?

ALEXANDRA: Why would I be? Is something wrong?

CARL: It's so easy to be frank with you about everything under the sun except yourself.

ALEXANDRA: Are you afraid of hurting my feelings?

CARL: No! I'm afraid of giving you a shock!

ALEXANDRA: Are you angry with me?

CARL: I'm trying to tell you something! I've been trying to tell you for days now!

ALEXANDRA: Well, go ahead.

CARL: You astonish me.

ALEXANDRA: Oh.

CARL: You must sense it when people admire you.

ALEXANDRA: I felt that you were happy to see me.

CARL: And you can feel it when other people are happy to see you?

ALEXANDRA: The men at the bank always seem happy to see me. It's always pleasent to do business with someone who's clean and healthy.

CARL: Oh, it is now.

ALEXANDRA: I think so. . . . Don't you love this weather? Not a cloud in the sky! (*She runs ahead of him.*) Mariiiie! Mariiie! (*Marie appears, running toward them. She jumps into Alexandra's arms, hugging her.*)

MARIE: Oh, I'm so glad to see you! I thought you'd never come! Mm! You smell so good! You put rosemary in your drawer like I told you to! It's so good to have you here, Mr. Linstrum. Let's go up to the house!

ALEXANDRA: Oh, let's sit in the orchard! Carl wants to see it. He planted all these trees himself.

MARIE: That reminds me! I want to show you something! (*She runs off. They fall to the grass.*)

ALEXANDRA: Isn't she amazing?

CARL: Yes, but does she always run like that? Doesn't she ever walk?

ALEXANDRA: Never. I don't know what I would have done all these years without her. She makes me laugh. (*Marie runs back on with a tree branch.*)

MARIE: Did you plant these too? They're so beautiful!

CARL: Yes, I believe I did. We left when they were so young, I never knew what they would look like.

MARIE: I remember you. I thought you were very romantic.

CARL: You were always playing with a little doll—a Gypsy doll with a yellow turban on her head. (*Frank appears, morose.*)

MARIE: Frank! Look who's here! This is Mr. Linstrum! He grew up on our place. This is my husband, Frank.

FRANK: I had to drive old woman Hiller's hogs outa my wheat. I take dat woman to court if she ain't careful, by God.

MARIE: But Frank, she has no one to help her. She does the best she can.

ALEXANDRA: Why don't you just go over there and hog-tie her fence?

FRANK: I keep my hogs at home, she can do the same.

ALEXANDRA: Sometimes it pays to mend other people's fences.

MARIE: I'll speak to Mrs. Hiller again. I'll see what I can do.

FRANK: You tink I can't take care of dis myself?

ALEXANDRA: We'd better get going. Come and visit us soon, Marie.

MARIE: You're not going already! I haven't even shown you the house yet!

ALEXANDRA: Another time, alright?

MARIE: It was so good to see you. I'm sorry.

ALEXANDRA: Good-bye. Good-bye Frank.

MARIE: Good-bye. Thank you for coming. (*They go.*)

FRANK: We have so much work and you just quit what you're doing and run off with your friends. They all know it too. They know you don't care.

MARIE: They only came to visit.

FRANK: They can afford to visit. We can't.

MARIE: But Frank—

FRANK: Don't matter. I don't care what you do.

MARIE: You've got a headache, haven't you? Let's go up to the house. I'll make you some coffee.

FRANK: I work so hard. Just as hard as she does. She has so much and she only gets more . . . All I get is dis. Dis is what I work myself to death for?

SCENE SIXTEEN

Music Cue 23—Scything

Emil scythes furiously. Marie runs on with bucket, wearing huge rubber boots.

MARIE: Oh, don't mind me. I'm just going to pick some cherries. Isn't everything beautiful after a rain? Just smell the wild roses. You're not going to mow the roses, are you? I couldn't stand it if you did. Well, you could mow some of them. But not all of them. If I see a snake, I'll call you. (*He reacts as if she's crazy.*)

EMIL: What's the matter with you?

MARIE: Nothing . . . What do you think of Mr. Linstrum?

EMIL: He's alright, I guess.

MARIE: Alexandra certainly thinks so.

EMIL: They're old friends. (*Marie laughs.*)

MARIE: That's not all they are!

EMIL: What do you mean? Alexandra? Never! All she knows about is crops and seasons. She doesn't understand a thing about people, or love.

MARIE: If you had any eyes, you'd see what was going on. Mr. Linstrum appreciates her more than any of you. It would serve you all right if she just ran off with him.

EMIL: I appreciate her. I appreciate him too. He's been telling me about New York.

MARIE: You're not thinking of going there!

EMIL: Why not? I have to go somewhere.

MARIE: Why?

EMIL: Because there's nothing for me here.

MARIE: Alexandra hopes you'll stay on here.

EMIL: Then Alexandra will be disappointed. She can run the farm alright without me. I want to do something on my own.

MARIE: There are so many, many things you could do. You can do anything you want!

EMIL: And there are so many, many things I can't do!

MARIE: Why does everything I say always make you angry? (*He grabs her arm.*)

EMIL: I can't play with you like a little boy anymore! If that's what you want then you'll have to get another little boy to play with! And you're not helping things by pretending you don't understand me!

MARIE: I don't want to understand you!

EMIL: Why?

MARIE: If I understand you then we can never be alone like this again. If you were only a Catholic then you would understand me. And it wouldn't be so hard on you. You could pray.

EMIL: What good does that do?

MARIE: You wouldn't feel so bad about things that can't be changed.

EMIL: I won't pray to not get what I want.

MARIE: Then all of our time together is over, don't you see Emil?

EMIL: Then all of our time together is over. (*Marie runs off. Emil stands alone.*)

Music Cue 23—Scything

SCENE SEVENTEEN

A baseball game in the French country. Everyone plays.

Music Cue 24—My Life Is a Field (Baseball Song)

THERE WAS A DREAM HERE
MY PARENTS DREAMT AWAKE.
THEY DREW IT ON THE EARTH
AND PASSED IT ON TO ME.
AND SO THE DREAM REMAINS
BUT NOW THERE ARE NO EMPTY PLAINS.

MY EYES ARE A PLOW.
MY MIND IS A SCYTHE.
MY HANDS ARE OXEN IN HARNESS.
MY SOUL IS THE GROUND.
MY HEART IS THE WEATHER.
MY LIFE IS AN OPEN FIELD.

I DON'T KNOW WHAT I WANT
BUT I KNOW IT ISN'T THIS.
MY PARENTS' DREAM COMES BACK TO ME
LIKE MEMORY, AND HURTS
BECAUSE IT'S ALL BEEN CHANGED
TO A DREAM OF EMPTY PLAINS.

MY EYES ARE A PLOW.
MY MIND IS A SCYTHE.
MY HANDS ARE OXEN IN HARNESS.
MY SOUL IS THE GROUND.
MY HEART IS THE WEATHER.
MY LIFE IS AN OPEN FIELD.

All disperse except Emil, Amedee, Marcel and Angelique. Marie stands aside. Carl watches a moment, then leaves.

EMIL: You're hitting better than you ever have, 'Medee. If you'd gone to the university you'd have made the team for sure.

AMEDEE: Sure! A married man don't lose his head no more. Hey, Emil, you wanna get married right away. It's the greatest.

EMIL: Can't get married without any girl.

MARCEL: There are plenty of girls around!

AMEDEE: That's right. Marcel is right. There's Severine.

MARCEL: Augustine,

AMEDEE: Ernestine,

MARCEL: Sondrine,

AMEDEE: and my cousin,

BOTH: Evangeline!

AMEDEE: I could love any one of those girls. Go after one of them!

MARCEL: Get yourself a French girl!

AMEDEE: They're the greatest! Or are you too stuck up? You wanna be a priest, maybe?

EMIL: No.

AMEDEE: Me neither. I bring a whole lotta Catholics into this world. That's my contribution to the church! Honest and true, Emil, ain't there any girl you want?

EMIL: Maybe.

AMEDEE: Bah! I think you got a rock in there! I can jump higher than you anyday. (*He smacks Emil in the chest.*)

ANGELIQUE: Amedee can do everything better than anybody!

EMIL: Oh he can, can he? (*He picks her up and races around with her. Marie watches sadly.*)

ANGELIQUE: 'Medee! 'Medee! (*Emil deposits her in Amedee's arms.*)

EMIL: There! I don't have the heart to take you away from him. (*Angelique sticks her tongue out at him as Amedee parades around with her.*)

AMEDEE: Everybody gotta get married right away! It's the greatest! (*They all go off. Emil watches, turns, sees Marie, heads off. She turns the other way and goes.*)

SCENE EIGHTEEN

Music Cue 25—Clock Chimes

Alexandra does the books at her desk at night under a single lamp.
Lou and Oscar enter the dark room.

LOU: You are alone?

ALEXANDRA: Yes, come in . . . What brings you two out so late? (*They look at each other.*)

LOU: When's he leaving?

ALEXANDRA: Not for a long time I hope.

OSCAR: We thought we oughta come by and tell you that people begun to talk.

ALEXANDRA: What about?

OSCAR: 'Bout you. Keepin' him here so long. Looks bad for him to be hangin' on to a woman this way. People think you're getting taken in. They think you're gonna marry the fella.

ALEXANDRA: Let's not go on with this. We won't get anywhere. I know you mean well. But if we continue with this now, there'll only be hard feelings.

LOU: Maybe you oughta think about your family, then. You're makin' us all look ridiculous.

ALEXANDRA: How is that?

LOU: He's just after your money! Can't you see that? Wants to get taken care of!

ALEXANDRA: And what if I want to take care of him? Whose business is it but my own?

LOU: He'll get hold of your property.

ALEXANDRA: He'll get hold of what I want to give him. I'll do exactly as I please with my land.

OSCAR: Your land!

LOU: That land came out of the homestead! It was bought with money borrowed on the homestead! Oscar and me worked ourselves to the bone payin' interest on it!

ALEXANDRA: And when you got married we divided the land and you were satisfied.

LOU: That's what comes of letting a woman meddle in business.

ALEXANDRA: Don't talk wild, Lou. I've made more on my farms since I've been on my own than when we all worked together.

LOU: Everything you've made came out of the original land that Oscar and me worked. It belongs to us!

ALEXANDRA: You're not making sense. Go down to the County Clerk and ask who owns my land. I own it, not you.

OSCAR: Property of a family belongs to the men of the family. It's the men who're held responsible. It's the men who do all the work.

LOU: Except for Emil. He's never done a thing around here.

ALEXANDRA: What about my work?

LOU: You liked to manage around so we thought, why not give her something to do? But the real work always fell on us. Good advice is alright, but . . .

OSCAR: It don't get the weeds outa the corn.

ALEXANDRA: No, but it keeps the fields for the corn to grow in. Why, Lou, I remember when you and Oscar wanted to sell this place and go down the river. If I'd consented, we'd have scraped along on poor farms all the rest of our lives.

LOU: Just like a woman. She tells you to do something and she thinks she did it.

OSCAR: Don't care how hard it is on us.

ALEXANDRA: I wasn't hard on you. Conditions were hard. And I didn't choose to be the kind of person I am. You take a vine and you cut it back again and again, it grows hard like a tree.

LOU: You can't expect us to sit back and watch you done out of the property by some loafer who just happened to come along.

OSCAR: Everybody's laughin' at you. And at your age too.

ALEXANDRA: That doesn't concern anybody but me. Go to town and ask your lawyers what you can do to restrain me from doing what I want with my property. And I advise you to do what they tell you. Because the authority you exert by law is the only authority you will ever have over me. I would rather not have lived to find out what I have tonight. (*They back out. As they go:*)

LOU: You oughtn't to have said that about her age.

OSCAR: I only meant she was gonna get married, she ought to have done it long ago. Not go makin' a fool of herself now.

LOU: Can't do business with women. (*They go off. Alexandra goes to her chair, sits, cries. Emil enters. She covers up her feelings.*)

EMIL: What's the matter with them?

ALEXANDRA: Where is Carl? Didn't he come back with you after the game?

EMIL: He was right behind me. (*She starts out after him.*) Alexandra, I have to speak to you.

ALEXANDRA: Can it wait, Emil?

EMIL: No it can't! . . . I can't. (*She stops. Turns.*) I don't want to go to law school. I don't know what it is I want to be yet. It's easy to rush into a profession and hard to get out of it if you don't like it. That's what Carl says, and I think he's right.

ALEXANDRA: I imagine he is. It will be wonderful having you here all winter. Just like old times.

EMIL: I'm restless. I want to go to a new place.

ALEXANDRA: Well.

EMIL: I want to go to the City of Mexico. I can get work on an engineering site down there with a friend of mine. I want to go as soon as the harvest is over. I guess Lou and Oscar will be pretty sore about it.

ALEXANDRA: They won't be coming back anymore, Emil. They're very angry with me.

EMIL: What about?

ALEXANDRA: They think I'm going to marry Carl and give all my property to him.

EMIL: That's nonsense.

ALEXANDRA: It is?

EMIL: Well . . . I guess not . . .

ALEXANDRA: Do you think I'm ridiculous?

EMIL: Well I don't exactly see why you'd want to do it.

ALEXANDRA: You do, don't you?

EMIL: It's really none of my business.

ALEXANDRA: I thought that at least you would understand me . . . I've had a pretty lonely life, Emil. Besides you and Marie, Carl is the only friend I've ever had.

EMIL: Then do what you want. (*Pause.*) Marie said it would serve us all right if you just ran off with him.

ALEXANDRA: Thank God for Marie, she would say that. (*Carl enters.*)

EMIL: I guess I'll go upstairs and get these boots off. (*He leaves. Pause.*)

CARL: I just met your brothers outside . . . It's your fate, Alexandra, always to be surrounded by little men. I'm no better than the rest. I'm too small to face the criticism of even smaller men than me. I can't ask you to promise me anything until I have something to offer you.

ALEXANDRA: But I don't need anything!

CARL: Alexandra—

ALEXANDRA: I need you! Everything else I can get for myself! I need you! Why have I been allowed such success if it's only to have the people I love taken away from me?

CARL: I'm going away because I have to. I need something to show for myself. To take what you would give me, I'd have to be either a very great man, or a very small one. I'm somewhere in the middle class.

ALEXANDRA: But you've been happy here with me. You may never be this happy again. It's always easier to lose than to find. What I have is yours if you care enough about me to take it.

CARL: I can't. I'll be leaving first thing tomorrow morning. I'll go north right away. Give me a year, Alexandra.

ALEXANDRA: You won't come back. Something will happen to one of us. Or both.

CARL: I have to go.

ALEXANDRA: I know you do. I know. I understand . . . I am just so tired of understanding . . .

SCENE NINETEEN

Alexandra's second dream: She is standing in a white nightgown. Sees the young man. Tries to get away from him. He seizes her up in his arms. She struggles. He lets her down. She falls to the ground, shivering. He leaves. Snow begins to fall.

Music Cue 26—I Call Your Name

I CALL YOUR NAME

AND THE LARK ANSWERS BACK

AND THE WIND SIGHS A SLOW SAD SIGH

AND DIES.

I CALL YOUR NAME

AND THE CLOUDS UTTER RAIN

AND THE WIND TAKES MY SOUND AWAY

AND STAYS. AND STAYS.

BUT STILL

YOU COME TO ME

WE CROSS THE SEA OF WILD PRAIRIE

IN THE LITTLE BOATS

OF OUR SOULS . . .

END OF ACT 1

SCENE TWENTY

Snow keeps falling. Marie sets up her kitchen. Pots of geraniums are in bloom and tea boils. She looks out the window as the song goes on.

Music Cue 27—Roll Over Me Snow

ROLL OVER ME SNOW.

BURY ME DEEP AND I'LL GO TO SLEEP

WAKE ME WHEN IT'S TIME TO GROW, OH

ROLL OVER ME SNOW.

ROLL OVER ME SNOW.

KEEP ME INSIDE WHERE MY HEART CAN HIDE

AND MY SORROW NO ONE WILL KNOW, OH

ROLL OVER ME SNOW.

ROLL OVER ME SNOW.

WEIGH ME DOWN, HOLD MY FEET TO THE GROUND

SO THAT I MAY NEVER GO, OH

ROLL OVER ME SNOW . . .

Alexandra and old Mrs. Lee arrive for a teaparty.

ALEXANDRA: Here we are!

MARIE: Mrs. Lee!

MRS. LEE: Hallo hallo hallo! . . . Is he around?

MARIE: (*Laughing.*) No, Mrs. Lee, Frank won't be home till later.

MRS. LEE: Then it be yusta like old times! (*She takes off her boots and relishes her bare feet. Then she whips out an apron with a flourish, clears her throat obviously and puts it on.*)

MARIE: Oh, isn't it beautiful? I've never seen this one before, have I, Mrs. Lee?

MRS. LEE: Nope. Yusta las' night I make.

ALEXANDRA: Nobody does things like this anymore.

MRS. LEE: See dis thread? From Sweden! Vera strong! No wash out, no fade. (*She plops in a chair.*) Oh, looka dese plants! Sucha much flower! How you keep from freeze?

MARIE: I keep the fire going all night. Frank laughs at me for fussing, but when they don't bloom he says, what's the matter with the darned things? (*She offers a plate of rolls.*) Would you care for an apricot roll, Mrs. Lee?

MRS. LEE: I tink dey stop my yaw from ache no more! (*She weighs them in her hand.*) Yusta like fedders! (*She spices them up with brandy she sips from her own flask.*)

MARIE: Have you heard from Carl, Alexandra?

ALEXANDRA: He got to Dawson before the river froze. I won't know anything more until spring. But I've heard from Emil. I brought his letters for you. (*She gives the bundle to Marie who stares at them.*)

MRS. LEE: I tink I take anudder on of dese here, tankya. (*Mrs. Lee takes a few rolls. Marie opens a letter.*)

MARIE: Dear Sister, I am sitting in an Italian cafe beside a German couple in the heart of Mexico City. There is a band playing on every corner and I have been to the bullfights twice now. This morning, as I walked past the cathedral, I met a blind shoeshine boy who could play every song I asked for by dropping the lids of the polish tins on the stone steps of the church. There is a flower here that blooms only at night. I go to the *zocolo* to watch it every evening, then to the cafes to drink until sunrise a kind of liquor made from cactus which is the same color as the dawn. I am learning to play the guitar . . .

ALEXANDRA: Out of all my father's children at least now there's one fit to cope with the world. That's what I've worked for all these years. (*Marie starts to cry.*) What's the matter? Did I say something wrong? (*Marie shakes her head.*) Snap out of it, Marie, you have guests . . .

MARIE: More coffee, Mrs. Lee?

ALEXANDRA: I'll get it. (*Alexandra goes to the table, sees a photograph of Frank.*) Don't tell me this is Frank!

MARIE: I found it in the attic just this morning. That's how he looked before we were married.

ALEXANDRA: You don't mean he used to dress like this?

MARIE: I guess he did look pretty silly. Poor Frank. He was so happy then. And now he's so . . . unhappy. So little that's new ever happens here. Things just keep repeating themselves: the weather, the crops, the people. It's hardest on those who don't feel a part of it. But maybe people always get what's hardest for them.

ALEXANDRA: Nonsense.

MARIE: Is it? Frank would have been alright in the right place with the right sort of wife. I know just the kind of wife he ought to have had. She should have been shy and not mind being alone and she ought not to care about another living thing in the world but him. The trouble is, you have to marry a man before you can find out what kind of wife he needs and what if it's not the kind of wife you are?

ALEXANDRA: You get along with Frank as well as anyone could.

MARIE: No. I'm spoiled. I always do what I want and say what I'm thinking and it always makes him angry. I've ruined his life. I should never have married him.

ALEXANDRA: No good ever came out of talking about such things.

MARIE: No. I suppose not.

ALEXANDRA: And besides, if you get down-hearted, Marie, what will become of the rest of us?

MARIE: I try not to. (*Frank enters. He carries a gun and a bucket and stomps the snow from his boots. Mrs. Lee wakes with a start.*)

MUSIC CUE 28

FRANK: Snowing again. That makes eight days running it snows. Pretty soon we won't be able to get out our own door. (*He spies the picture where Alexandra left it. Picks it up.*) . . . I hate dis country. (*He throws the picture down. He goes off through the house. The women avoid looking at each other. Marie goes to the window.*)

MARIE: Look how the currents of snow are swirling over the orchard. How could Spring survive under the weight of all this snow?

SCENE TWENTY-ONE

Music Cue 29—The Fair

The stage transforms into the Catholic Fair. Marie works in a fortune telling booth, dressed exactly as her old doll. Other booths are set up, hawkers sell their games. Alexandra enters with Emil on her arm. She pulls him to Marie's booth.

ALEXANDRA: Look who's home! Can you believe it? Hasn't he changed? (*Marie squeals with delight. Grabs his hat.*)

MARIE: Oh, Emil, was everything in Mexico as beautiful as this? How could you ever come back here? (*Emil backs away.*)

EMIL: Excuse me. (*He goes off. Marie turns her back. Alexandra is completely confused.*)

ALEXANDRA: What in heaven's name is the matter? (*Amedee grabs Emil.*)

AMEDEE: Emil! Emil! Where you been, man? You're home two days and you don't even come to see my new son!

EMIL: I'm awful glad it was a boy, 'Medee.

AMEDEE: Not just any boy. My boy . . . Emil, you gotta get a baby right away! It's the greatest! (*He pulls Emil aside.*) Listen, at eleven o'clock we gonna play a little trick on the girls. You in with us?

EMIL: Sure.

AMEDEE: Good. We gonna pull off all the lights and everybody gonna get a chance to kiss their sweetheart. Only problem is, Marie got a candle in her tent. We gotta put it out. Since you got no sweetheart, maybe you do dat for us, no?

EMIL: I'll do it.

AMEDEE: Good! Now you dance with my cousin, Evangeline!

Music Cue 30A—Dance

He pushes Emil into the dance. All dance raucously. Marie tries to get Frank to dance with her, but he won't. Dance ends. She turns immediately to her booth.

MARIE: Fortunes! Fortunes told! (*Priest hobbles up.*) Father Duchesne! I see a long journey across water for you. I see an old lady with a white cap and you very happy where you go.

PRIEST: Mais-oui! c'est L'Isle-Adam, chez ma mere. Vous etes tres savante, ma fille. Venez donc, mes garcons! Il y a ici une veritable clairvoyante!

AMEDEE: Hey, Frank, you wanna get a fortune right away, eh?

FRANK: She tell my fortune long ago. Bad enough.

AMEDEE: Me then! I want my fortune!

MARIE: Amedee. You will have twenty children! (*Angelique nearly faints.*)

MARIE: Nineteen of them will be girls! (*Loud laughter.*)

Music Cue 30B

People gather into groups as Emil goes to Marie.

EMIL: Do you think you could tell my fortune?

MARIE: Not since you walked away from me the way you did.

EMIL: I'm sorry.

MARIE: Then give me your hand. (*He does.*)

EMIL: My luck hasn't changed any. It's still the same . . . (*Lights go out. Screams. Emil kisses Marie as he douses her candle.*)

Music Cue 31A—The Kiss

Lights up: Emil is across the room with men, Marie is alone and stunned. Frank stares at her. Alexandra rushes to her.

ALEXANDRA: Marie? Are you alright? (*Marie draws away from her as if burned and runs out. Emil, watching, runs after her.*)

SCENE TWENTY-TWO

Music Cue 31B—Far Away Party

Emil chases Marie outside in the dark.

EMIL: Marie, wait . . . wait! . . . (*Finally, she stops.*) Do you know how unhappy I am?

MARIE: If I were big and free like you, I wouldn't let anything make me unhappy. I'd take the first train out of here and go off and have all the fun there is!

EMIL: I did that. The nicer the place was, the more I wanted you. (*Pause.*) Why did you do it, Marie? Why did you run away with Frank?

MARIE: Because I was in love with him.

EMIL: No you weren't.

MARIE: Yes! I was! I was the one who wanted to run away! And now I've got to remember that. Frank is just the same now as when I married him. It's just that then I only saw him as I wanted him to be, not as he was. And now, I'm paying for it.

EMIL: You're not the only one who's paying.

MARIE: That's just it! When you make a mistake, there's no telling where it will stop. Now I've passed mine on to you. But you at least can go away. You can leave all of this behind you!

EMIL: Come with me.

MARIE: How can you say that to me?

EMIL: Look at me, Marie. Look at me, no one can see us! (*She turns.*)

MARIE: I thought it would be alright when you came back. Oh, Emil, what am I going to do if you don't go away? I can't go, and one of us has to!

EMIL: On my honor, Marie, if you will tell me that you love me, I'll go away. (*Pause.*)

MARIE: How could I help it? Didn't you know? (*Slowly, Emil backs, turns and goes.*)

SCENE TWENTY-THREE

Morning. A few days later. Alexandra sits sewing a shirt for Emil. He enters and flops into a chair.

ALEXANDRA: Are you finished packing already?

EMIL: Alexandra, was our grandfather really as crooked as they say?

ALEXANDRA: He married an unscrupulous woman. Well, that's not fair. Yes, I guess he was crooked.

EMIL: I don't remember our father very well. He must've had a hard fight here.

ALEXANDRA: He did. But he also had hope. He believed in this place.

EMIL: If Father had lived, all of this would have meant something, then, wouldn't it?

ALEXANDRA: It has meant something, Emil. It means that after all these years there is finally one member of our family who can choose what he wants to do with his life. Nothing will ever hold you back.

EMIL: I wish something would, sometimes.

ALEXANDRA: Don't say that.

EMIL: But Lou and Oscar would be better off if they'd stayed poor.

ALEXANDRA: No one is better off poor.

EMIL: But then maybe they wouldn't be so bigoted and self-satisfied.

ALEXANDRA: Maybe not. But I have great hopes for their children.

EMIL: I don't know. It seems to get worse every day. The Swedes are never willing to find out how much they don't know. Bohemians are different. The Germans. The French. At least they know how to have a good time.

ALEXANDRA: Don't go back on your own people, Emil. Not all of us are conceited. Father wasn't. Even Lou and Oscar weren't, when they were young.

EMIL: Do you remember the wild duck?

ALEXANDRA: Of course.

EMIL: That was good. That was good then. (*Pause. He rises.*) Goodnight, sister. I think you did pretty well by us. (*He goes. Alexandra sits still in the lamplight.*)

SCENE TWENTY-FOUR

Music Cue 32—Thresher

Amedee's fields, day. Amedee and Marcel work behind the machine. Emil approaches them, shouting over the machine. Marcel is practicing his Gloria *as he works.*

AMEDEE: You wanna talk to us, you gotta work with us! Hey, Raoul! Right! Turn right! (*He gestures wildly to the driver offstage. Emil joins in.*)

EMIL: That's some work song you've got there, Marcel.

MARCEL: There's a big confirmation Sunday! I got to practice all day!

AMEDEE: That's all he thinks about dese days, the confirmation. He sure don't care about my wheat.

MARCEL: I care about your wheat. The thresher, she keeps time for me.

EMIL: I came to say good-bye, Amedee.

AMEDEE: Good-bye! Again? No! (*He makes a gesture and grips his side suddenly with pain.*) Owww . . .

EMIL: What's the matter?

MARCEL: He's had a stomachache all day and half the night. Won't go to the doctor cause he don't trust us with his new machine!

AMEDEE: That's cause none of you knows how to work it!

MARCEL: He's right, there.

AMEDEE: I got no time to be sick! This thing cost me $3,000 and the wheat's so ripe it's fit to burst!

MARCEL: Where you goin', Emil?

EMIL: Omaha, to read law for awhile. Then Michigan for school.

MARCEL: Michigan! . . . Out east, huh?

EMIL: Yeah! Out east!

AMEDEE: Aw, don't go, man! Stay here and get old with us!

EMIL: I've got to start my life!

AMEDEE: There's a whole lotta lifes around here too.

EMIL: I've got to make good for Alexandra! I can't do that here!

AMEDEE: Ah, you gotta rock in there! (*He smacks Emil on the chest.*)

MARCEL: Ay, what's he doin' with your machine?

AMEDEE: Hey, Raoul! Where you goin', man? Hey! (*Amedee begins to run but falls, clutching his side.*)

EMIL: Amedee! You alright?

AMEDEE: I'm alright! I'm alright! I just gotta rest a minute . . . See? I'm all better! (*He collapses. Emil and Marcel pick him up and carry him off. BELLS.*)

SCENE TWENTY-FIVE

Music Cue 33—Gloria And Ave Maria

Church. Funeral and Confirmation take place at the same time. Half the congregation is in white, the other in black. Emil stands beside Angelique. Frank stands in back.

PRIEST: We are gathered here today to commit to the earth the body of Amedee Chevalier. When the body of our earthly dwelling lies in death, we gain an everlasting home in heaven.

BISHOP: By baptism, God, our Father, gave these adopted children new birth to eternal life. Do you reject Satan and all his empty promises?

CHILDREN: I do.

PRIEST: Amedee Chevalier is not dead! In Jesus Christ the dead rise to life again.

BISHOP: Do you believe in the Holy Spirit, the giver of Life, who comes to you today in the sacrament of confirmation?

CHILDREN: I do.

PRIEST: This is our faith!

BISHOP: This is the faith of our church. And we welcome you now as soldiers to the armies of Christ.

PRIEST: And we join the angels in a hymn of unending praise. (*Marcel comes up, dressed in his farming clothes, hat in hand, and sings his heart out finishing the music. Emil is overcome by the music until he can no longer stand it and runs out. Alexandra tries to stop him. Lets him go. Light changes.*)

Music Cue 34—The Hunt

In the orchard, Marie wanders. She lies down under a tree sorrowfully. Emil appears at her house. Calls her name. She's not there. He goes down to the orchard, forgetting his scarf on a chair.

EMIL: Marie! . . . Marie! . . . (*He finds her in the orchard.*) I came to say good-bye. (*They fall into an embrace, make love. Frank comes home. Finds the scarf. Grabs his gun and goes out to the orchard. He finds them. He raises his gun in sudden rage, then lowers it, confused, hurt. Then raises it again and fires two shots. Emil and Marie fall away from each other. His hand clutches at the dirt. Marie stands. Walks toward Frank, takes her hand from her breast and sees blood on it. Falls and crawls back to Emil, and lies in his arms. Frank drops the gun. Frank runs off screaming:*)

FRANK: Marie! . . . Marie! . . . Marie! . . . (*He falls and runs, falls and runs till he's gone. Lights go down. Slow dawn. Ivar comes along picking up litter. Stumbles onto the bodies. Falls to his knees and screams. Alexandra appears. Stands over the bodies.*)

ALEXANDRA: (*Awed.*) They're so perfect, Ivar . . . Look . . . The wild roses have bloomed! (*She staggers, steadies herself and does not cry. Lou and Oscar come downstage and pick the bodies up. Carry them off.*)

SCENE TWENTY-SIX

Music Cue 35—Wind

In a high storm, Alexandra lies on Emil's grave. Ivar comes up.

IVAR: What are you doing out here? Eh? You're soaked clear through! Everybody worries about you! Nobody knows where you are!

ALEXANDRA: Why didn't they come to me, Ivar? Why?

IVAR: Let's go home.

ALEXANDRA: How could I have been so blind? If I had just seen what was happening . . . I could have stopped all this.

IVAR: Don't talk like dis, mistress, it's not good.

ALEXANDRA: Why didn't I see it? Why didn't I see? (*Ivar kneels beside her, takes one of her hands and pours dirt into it.*)

IVAR: Look. Look how lucky we are. The earth will give them back to us. Come home, mistress. Come home now. (*She allows him to lead her away.*)

SCENE TWENTY-SEVEN

Signa helps Alexandra into her dressing-gown.

ALEXANDRA: Do you think he was afraid that night? Do you think he knew he was going to die? How terrible it would be to lie there alone and know . . .

SIGNA: That's all over now, Mistress. All he feels now are the old things, maybe, before he was born. He don't remember no pain at all. He don't even feel the rain.

ALEXANDRA: I am so tired of having a body. So tired of washing it and dressing it and carrying it around all day. It just gets heavier and heavier . . . I don't have the strength for it anymore. (*She settles back in her chair. Signa shakes her head.*)

SIGNA: I can't believe you've come to this. Of all the people in the world . . . (*She goes. Alexandra falls asleep.*)

Music Cue 36—I Call Your Name

I CALL YOUR NAME
AND THE SOUND HITS THE GROUND
AND THE WIND PICKS IT UP AND SENDS IT FLYING HIGH.

I CALL YOUR NAME
AND MY VOICE COMES BACK ALONE.
MY VOICE COMES BACK ALONE BUT CHANGED.
BUT CHANGED.

AND THEN YOU COME TO ME
WE CROSS THE SEA OF WILD PRAIRIE
IN THE DARK BOATS OF OUR SOULS . . .

During the song, Alexandra dreams. Young man appears, dressed in a winter cloak that hides his face. Death. He beckons to her. She faces him and walks away.

ALEXANDRA: I know who you are . . . I know who you are now . . . (*He disappears. She wakes standing.*)

SCENE TWENTY-EIGHT

Morning. Signa brings coffee and rolls to Alexandra, who sits up, clear now.

ALEXANDRA: Signa!
SIGNA: Drink dis.
ALEXANDRA: Signa, please, I'd like you to pack a bag for me.
SIGNA: Yah, sure. Eat dis.
ALEXANDRA: What is this, it's terrible!
SIGNA: It's good for you.
ALEXANDRA: Would you also ask Ivar to get the horses ready for me?
SIGNA: You're not goin' anywhere.
ALEXANDRA: I'm going to Lincoln.
SIGNA: I was in Lincoln for an hour once. Terrible place.
ALEXANDRA: I have to see Frank Shabata.
SIGNA: Let me feel your forehead. You're not talkin' sense.
ALEXANDRA: Frank did what he had to do. That is the way he was. Marie knew him. She knew what he would do. Why did such

good people have to die, and fools like Frank and me be the ones left to go on? I have to see him.

SIGNA: I'm callin' the doctor. You're not goin' to Lincoln. You're not goin' to Lincoln!

SCENE TWENTY-NINE

Music Cue 36—Jail Music

Prison. Alexandra sits in the visiting room. Frank is brought in by a guard, haggard, sick-looking. He won't look at her.

ALEXANDRA: Hello, Frank. (*No answer.*) Are you getting along alright? (*No answer.*) Is there anything you need? Perhaps they'll let me send you something . . . (*No answer.*) Do you know, that in all these years, I have never been to Lincoln? (*No answer.*) Frank, I came to see you because . . . I understand now . . . why you did . . . what you did and I . . . I didn't come here to blame you . . . I think they were to blame as much as you . . . and so was I . . . I could have stopped all this, but I . . . I didn't want to see what was happening. I didn't want to think . . . it might be true . . . I hope you can forgive me . . . (*Pause.*)

FRANK: Dey cut my hair. . . . I no can tink widout my hair.

ALEXANDRA: I know you didn't mean to hurt Emil or Marie.

FRANK: I near to forget her name, even.

ALEXANDRA: Perhaps I shouldn't have come here. (*She rises. He grabs her arm and holds on hard.*)

FRANK: I don' wanna kill nobody! I never woulda done it I ain't had dat gun! She always say I'm not dat kinda man oughta carry a gun. If she been in dat house where she oughta been . . . but das a foolish talk. I never wanna do noting to dat woman or dat boy . . . dey was the bes' around . . .

ALEXANDRA: Marie showed me an old picture of you once. You looked so fine then. So happy. I don't understand how you ended up like this . . . or how someone as full of life as Marie could have brought about so much destruction . . . so much sorrow. That is the strangest thing of all. Is there something so wrong with being so alive? But there is Emil in the graveyard back home, and here . . . here you are. I can't do anything for them now. But I can help you. I'm going to get you pardoned. I'll never give the Governor a moment's peace. I want to get you out of this place, Frank.

FRANK: I get out of here, I go back where I came from. Never make you any trouble again . . . Alexandra . . . you don't tink I used dat woman awful bad before—(*She pulls away from him.*)

ALEXANDRA: No . . . let's not talk about that. (*She goes.*)

SCENE THIRTY

Music Cue 39—Carl's Song

Alexandra returns from Lincoln with her suitcase. She's greeted by Ivar and Signa, who rush to take her things. She turns to find Carl standing there. She runs to him and they embrace. For the first time since the tragedy, she cries.

CARL: I came as soon as I heard the news. I figured I could reach you as fast as any letter. I figured you needed me.

ALEXANDRA: Oh, Carl, why couldn't it have been someone else? Why did it have to be my Emil?

CARL: He was the best. They both were the best there was around here.

ALEXANDRA: Are you going to stay with me now?

CARL: Yes. I'll have to go back up north in the spring to see to things. Perhaps you'll go with me then.

ALEXANDRA: You would never ask me to go away from here for good, would you?

CARL: I know how you feel about this country as well as you do.

ALEXANDRA: I have lived here a long time . . . This is what peace is, Carl. And freedom . . . Suppose I did leave all this to Lou and Oscar's children? What difference would it make? I might as well will the sunset to them. Those who love and understand this

country are the only ones who ever really own it. For awhile . . .
Getting chilly.

CARL: Yah. (*He puts his arm around her.*)

ALEXANDRA: Warmer tomorrow, though.

CARL: Yah . . . (*He kisses her face and her eyes and they walk off. Ivar comes along, looking after them.*)

IVAR: Fortunate country. Someday you'll receive their hearts into yours. And then you'll give them back again in the billowing wheat, and the bursting corn, in the wet green leaves and the eyes of the young . . . (*Slowly, the old immigrants and rest of cast make their ways to the stage.*)

Music Cue 40—End Song

MAN
AND THE OWL FLIES LOW IN THE SKY,
WE TAKE THE OLD ROAD HOME.

WOMAN
NOW THAT YOU'VE COME, UNTIL I DIE
I'LL NEVER BE ALONE.

(MORE JOIN IN)
TWELVE YOUNG HORSES GALLOP BY
THE PRAIRIE MOVES IN WAVES . . .

(MORE JOIN IN)
LET'S GO UP TO THE HOUSE WE BUILT
AND WATCH THE END OF DAY.

(MORE JOIN IN)
WHY DOES THE SUN SET SLOWLY?
WHY DOES THE MOON FLY PAST?

(MORE)
WE'D BETTER DO NOW WHAT WE CAN DO:
THESE LIVES WE HAVE DON'T LAST.

ALL
I'M NOT AFRAID OF DYING CAUSE
I KNOW WHERE I WILL BE:
IT WON'T BE MY LOVE OR MY BROTHER
BUT THE LAND THAT WILL BURY ME.
IT WON'T BE MY LOVE OR MY BROTHER
BUT THE LAND THAT WILL BURY ME.

Lavonne Mueller

VIOLENT PEACE

Author's Introduction

I have always been interested by what I call the invented family. The family we are born with has never interested me as a writer; it is too ordained. Rather, I am intrigued by that family that we must *create* in order to get through a very difficult situation—fellow workers in a factory who entertain and protect each other to get through a meaningless day as in my play, *Killings on the Last Line;* or a group of mothers in Argentina who unite to protest the disappearance of their children in my play, *The Mothers.* I think such bonding of people is the one essential mystery. Other things may be mysterious, but the basis of the invented family involves operational illusion; it is a marker of time. We have two real families: before our birth and after our life is done. These are the public families, but perhaps the real family is the one we invent, the one we live daily, which we imagine.

It took me ten years to write this play because I am often haunted by mothers, perhaps because I never had one. Yet I feel that if I were a theologian, happily, I'm not, I'd find an argument in favor of being motherless. Because something must surely take its place (for Kim it's Mark and thus a secret island). Motherless has a peculiar horror to it, to Kim, and to me. Motherless, that tiger of the dream.

Violent Peace was produced by the Women's Project & Productions under the directorship of Julia Miles at the Apple Corps Theatre, New York City from February 20–March 11, 1990. It was directed by Bryna Wortman with the following cast:

KIM   Jenny Robertson
MARK   Dennis Parlato

Set design by James Noone
Costume design by Mimi Maxmen
Lighting design by Victor En Yu Tan
Casting by Elissa Myers

Production stage manager   Linda Carol Young
Sound designer   Bruce Ellman

Violent Peace is supported in part by grants from the National Endowment for the Arts and the New York State Council on the Arts.

TIME

1988

PLACE

A hotel room in Kansas City

CHARACTERS

KIM, the general's daughter, age 22
MARK, the general's aid, age 44

ACT ONE

At rise: Kim is wearing a prim, basic, black dress with pearls. Her hair is elegantly up. A vase of double-daisies is on the dresser. Knocking is heard on the door, each knock is getting progressively more and more impatient. Kim ignores the knocking until Mark pushes open the door. Mark enters; he wears a class-A uniform with a light top-coat over it. A beat as Mark stares at Kim.

KIM: New shoes, soldier? (*Mark kicks the door shut.*)

KIM: You can ruin new French Shriners that way. (*Mark stares at her. Then he turns to the door to leave.*)

KIM: You leave, and I'll call your wife. (*He stops. His back is to her.*)

KIM: (*Goes to phone:*) My hand's on the phone. (*As he puts his hand on the doorknob, she picks up the phone.*)

KIM: I mean it. (*He turns to face her, then goes to her and knocks the phone out of her hand and sits down in agitation.*)

KIM: That's right. Sit down. (*Mark now stands very stiff and straight.*)

KIM: At least take off your coat. (*Mark now buttons the last and top button of his coat.*)

KIM: I like you hot. (*He now takes off his coat and roughly flings it on the chair. We see that he is wearing a black arm band on the sleeve of his uniform.*)

KIM: When did you start wearing Class A uniforms? (*Silence.*)

KIM: I love you in fatigues.

MARK: That's why I wear full dress.

KIM: You said full dress made you feel geeky.

MARK: Not now, friend. (*A beat.*)

MARK: Let's get this straight. I stay now. Until 0600. Tomorrow.

KIM: Right.

MARK: And then you'll never. . . . I repeat, never bother me, call me . . . speak to me, acknowledge me, ever again.

KIM: That's correct.

KIM: After 0600 tomorrow, it's all over.

MARK: What time is it?

KIM: 1815.

MARK: That's all?

KIM: That's all.

MARK: God.

KIM: Time flies when you're having a good time.

MARK: I should have brought my supply requisitions.

KIM: Requisitions not allowed.

MARK: Do you know how much work I have piled up on my desk?

KIM: How could I know that when I haven't seen you in over a year?

MARK: I got a man A-W-O-L. Papers to fill out that weigh more than he does.

KIM: Let some second lieutenant do it. That's what you always did before—when you had work and came to me instead. (*Mark glares at her and stands.*)

KIM: Going? So soon? (*Mark walks to the door.*)

KIM: Would you like to hear my message to Louise? I wrote it down . . . so if I called, I wouldn't forget anything. (*Mark is still facing the door.*)

KIM: (*Reads from a slip of paper:*) Hello . . . Louise . . . this is Kim Denton. I'm calling to tell you what a beautiful fuck your husband is. (*Mark turns abruptly from the door and goes to her and tries to grab the paper. She pulls back.*)

KIM: Not what you want to tell somebody's forty-year-old wife pregnant for the first time. (*She opens a bedside table drawer and takes out the Bible.*)

KIM: "Thy. . . . . rod. . . . . and thy *staff* shall comfort thee." (*She puts the paper in the Bible.*) (*Mark tries to get the paper, but she holds up the Bible as if fending off Dracula.*)

KIM: (*Still holding up the Bible:*) Later on . . . I use the word copulate. It has such a nice old fashion sound, don't you think? (*A beat as they glare at each other. Then he sits down.*)

MARK: You're bluffing. (*A beat. She takes out the paper and hands it to Mark.*) (*Mark takes out his reading glasses from his jacket pocket and looks at paper.*)

KIM: When did you start wearing glasses?

MARK: (*Sternly. Not looking up.*) Probably the same time you stopped.

KIM: I got contacts now. (*Mark looks up angrily. He takes off glasses and puts them back in his jacket.*)

KIM: Believe me? (*He tears up the paper.*)

KIM: The Army brought me up good. I do everything in triplicate. Two more nice clear copies in my purse. (*A beat.*)

MARK: What time is it?

KIM: Fifteen minutes later.

MARK: God. (*A beat.*)

MARK: Kim, this is blackmail. (*Silence.*)

MARK: I'll stay two hours. (*Silence.*)

MARK: Four hours. (*Kim shakes her head "No."*)

MARK: I'm not the kind of man who begs. (*Silence.*)

MARK: You know what we tell men when they're captured? Defiance. Always defiance. (*Silence.*)

MARK: What the hell can you prove with a defiant man? (*They stare at each other.*) (*Mark begins to ask the time, but she cuts him off.*)

KIM: Five minutes later. (*Mark glares at her.*)

KIM: Do you tell your men how tedious defiance is?

MARK: We're wasting a perfectly good night.

KIM: Let's not call it a waste. Not yet.

MARK: I'll stay till 2200?

KIM: No.

MARK: Till 2300?

KIM: No. (*Silence.*)

MARK: Not a minute less?

KIM: That's right.

MARK: God, how much like him you are.

KIM: Sure I'm like him. What did you expect?

MARK: Selfish.

KIM: Don't forget arrogant.

MARK: Arrogant.

KIM: Your bad arrogant General.

MARK: That's right.

KIM: My bad selfish Daddy.

MARK: That's right.

KIM: Then why did you stay with him all these years?

MARK: He was a damn good Army man. Personally—a bastard. Professionally—we got along fine. And I always came back to him. I'm loyal. Honduras. Salvador. Nicaragua. Always came back to Headquarters Company.

KIM: I don't suppose I had anything to do with that?

MARK: You? (*A beat.*) The sub-human. Late for your own father's funeral this morning.

KIM: *He* was late.

MARK: They had to ship his body from West Point. (*A beat.*) Not even a tear.

KIM: How do you know? I was wearing sunglasses.

MARK: I've never seen you cry. Never. Just little gargoyle smiles. (*A beat.*) Now . . . dressed like that. Miss Proper. (*Mark pulls at her neckline.*)

MARK: So where's my dog tags? The ones you said you'd wear forever? (*A beat. Mocking.*) "I give her my personal own dog tags, and she says: "I'll never take them off."

KIM: (*Pulls at his neckline:*) And why don't you have some new ones? Army regulation, soldier.

MARK: (*Ignoring her question:*) Miss Civilian sure as hell chucked me out flank speed. For a string of cheap pearls.

KIM: Afraid dog tags will remind you of making love to me? Leaning over . . . the chain hanging down from your neck . . . the silver tags falling between my breasts.

MARK: Dog tags don't go nice with Civie-black. Right? They aren't the fashion in Oak Park. (*Mark pushes her down on the bed.*)

MARK: I don't know why I'm surprised. You never feel anything. Not for me. Not for the old man. (*A beat.*)

MARK: The doctor said . . . there was nothing left of his heart but dead tissue—spotted like an old leopard's hide.

LIGHT CHANGE/FLASHBACK

Mark takes a thermometer out from under Kim's tongue.

MARK: (*Looking at thermometer:*) Jesus, a 104. (*A beat.*) It's all right. You're gonna be fine. I'll just pat some water on you to bring the temperature down . . . I'll just swab you in a little water, that's all. (*Kim groans.*)

MARK: I'm here. I'm here. (*Mark gets a glass from the table and gives the water to Kim.*)

MARK: You got to drink water. We have to bring the temperature down. (*Kim shoves the glass away.*) (*Mark feels her forehead.*)

MARK: Damn. I've got to get this fever down. (*A beat.*) God, you're getting hotter. (*He lifts her up and tries to get her to drink more water.*) Drink. You've got to drink all this water. (*She drinks some then shoves the glass away.*) Come on. Come on. Cool off. (*Mark goes to the phone.*)

MARK: (*Into phone:*) Put me through to the C-O at Fort Sills. (*A beat.*) This is Captain Feeney, Headquarters, 1st Army. I have an emergency message for General Robert Denton. Tell him to call his home. Immediately. (*A beat.*) I don't care if he is on the parade field. Go out and get him. His three-year-old daughter is sick.

LIGHT CHANGE/END OF FLASHBACK

KIM: Well, the leopard's dead. (*Mark stands. He takes off his jacket and puts it on the back of a chair.*)

KIM: Where you going?

MARK: To the latrine. That *is* all right?

KIM: Even P-O-W's get to do that.

MARK: (*He turns left and goes by mistake into the closet. A noise of hangers falling.*) Damn. (*He comes away rubbing his head.*)

KIM: The bathroom's on the left.

MARK: And that's another thing. Every time I'm around you, I have accidents. (*He goes into the bathroom.*) (*Kim goes to his jacket and puts the sleeves of his jacket around her.*)

MARK: (*Calling from bathroom:*) Damn little bars of hotel soap. How the hell's a man supposed to wash his hands?

KIM: (*Calling to him:*) You used to think they were cute.

MARK: (*Calling back:*) I thought they were funny.

KIM: (*Calling to him:*) Big brave Colonel. Can't even hold on to a little bar of soap. Are those the hands that killed a thousand Sandinistas? (*She puts the ends of the sleeves of his jacket to her lips*)

MARK: (*From the bathroom:*) Go to hell. (*Kim puts the sleeve back down as Mark comes out of the bathroom drying his hands. He glares at her, then throws the towel at her.*)

KIM: (*About his hands:*) Are they bothering you again?

MARK: Don't worry about me. You're the last person I want worrying about me. (*Mark blows on his hands.*)

MARK: Ever since Nicaragua. I was fine till Nic. Jesus, I come back with my hands all fucked up.

KIM: You're blaming Nic? Not even a real war?

MARK: It's real, all right. (*He rubs his hands.*)

MARK: I never got a thing in Nic. Nothing. But these lousy hands soak up everything: tobacco, syrup from C-rations, pig guts, rifle oil, fermented hay, bore cleaner, stains from red coffee berries, odor of dead cows, rum, dust, wild yucca roots, blood, moss, powder burns. Everything goes in the pores and plugs up my skin. (*A beat as he looks at his hands.*) They're dirty, crusty gloves. (*A beat.*) Every damn soldier in the U.S. Army's got athlete's foot. Not me. My hands are festering.

KIM: (*Struggling with wine bottle:*) I can't open this.

MARK: Your party. Your problem.

KIM: I like a man to open wine.

MARK: So they tell me.

KIM: I take that to mean . . .

MARK: . . . . . you're not the type to sit around the house.

KIM: Are you telling me . . . . . me, the object of this disgusting evening . . . that I'm desirable?

MARK: Easy. The word's *easy*.

KIM: Easy for what?

MARK: For every man around.

KIM: Let's be specific. Would you mind listing these men—alphabetically. Last name first. First name last. Army roster style.

MARK: It made me sick to walk into the officer's club with you.

KIM: What made you sick?

MARK: The looks you got.

KIM: It made you feel old.

MARK: The end! I don't want to talk about it.

KIM: Then help with this. (*She tosses him the wine bottle.*) (*Mark catches the wine bottle.*) (*Kim sits on a chair across from him.*)

KIM: Whack it. Against the pelvis. (*She strokes the underside of her chair.*) (*He tosses it back to her. She catches it. She tosses it back to him.*)

MARK: Sure. Everything's a game to you.

KIM: Meaning?

MARK: Meaning life is one damn laugh after another. Keep the jokes rolling. Keep the good times coming. Bring on the wine. (*He throws the bottle to her.*)

KIM: I never cared where we were . . . if I could be with you. That's all that ever mattered.

MARK: Sure.

LIGHT CHANGE/FLASHBACK

MARK: You want me to pack this red sweater?

KIM: What red sweater?

MARK: The long sleeve one. (*Silence.*) The one with . . . "fall out." (*He picks fuzz off.*)

KIM: That's my best angora.

MARK: So. . . . does it go?

KIM: I've never been to Switzerland before. How should I know what to take? (*A beat.*)

KIM: Mark . . . what . . . what if I don't like it there? What if I'm . . . a flop . . . what if nobody likes me?

MARK: It's just like any other high school. Just in a different country, that's all. (*A beat.*)

KIM: Mark . . .

MARK: The Old Man give you some money?

KIM: (*Shakes her head "yes".*) Mark. . . . I'll miss you.

MARK: Where's the dictionary we bought you?

KIM: Mark . . .

MARK: With you gone, I'll be able to get a decent night's sleep. Jesus, I was born at reveille. I've been getting roused up ever since. Just once I'd like to see how long I can sleep.

KIM: When am I going to see you? (*He's busy getting things in order.*)

KIM: Will you sit? Talk to me. (*She gets him to sit next to her.*)

KIM: Mark. . . . I'm. . . . I'm scared.

MARK: Of what?

KIM: Kids. From real homes. What do civilians do all day, for godsakes? I mean, what do they talk about? (*A beat.*) I've never even had a girlfriend before.

MARK: You've got plenty of time for that. You're only seventeen.

KIM: Where do they hang out? How do they get it on?

MARK: Who? (*He begins rubbing his hands.*)

KIM: Kids that come from real homes.

MARK: You come from a real enough home.

KIM: I'm talking about normal people.

MARK: We're normal enough for anybody. And don't you forget that.

KIM: Do they dance? Do they drink? Do they smoke pot?

MARK: Stay away from people with pot . . . hear me!

LIGHT CHANGE/END OF FLASHBACK

MARK: Sure.

KIM: If I could be with you, that's all that mattered. I always wanted to be like them. The men you were pals with. Sitting around a campfire in green drawers and unlaced combat boots, drinking beer and laughing . . . like those basic training pictures you showed me on the kitchen table . . . when we drank black coffee after supper. (*A beat.*) Did it ever cross your mind to give me hot chocolate? (*A beat.*) I tried to be those pals . . . standing on a hill, watching the sky, mistaking birds that flew over my head for distant artillery. I still love the smell of oil from an M-16. I love the shiny barrel of a gun. I flirt with a hunter's eye, slightly closed, taking aim. Why do you think I always wanted you to take me hunting? You bought me my first gun. All I ever wanted was to hit something. To wound. I wanted some victim to close its heart like wings, spiralling from the sky. Then I'd hold up my skirt and catch it—like falling leaves, blood red from dying.

MARK: You knew how to kill, all right.

KIM: You were the expert.

MARK: Sure.

KIM: You were the pro.

MARK: Your "instinct", friend, was the pro.

KIM: That's not true.

MARK: You were born with a trigger finger. Aimed at me. Like a lizard's tail it's gonna jiggle after you're dead.

KIM: I loved you then. I love you now. (*She throws the bottle at the wall and smashes it.*) I christen that the truth.

MARK: That's your way of solving everything. Smash it.

KIM: Christening. A starting. Not an ending.

MARK: You only know how to *end*. (*Mark looks at her angrily, then stands, then abruptly goes to the bathroom and gets a towel and comes back in the room.*)

MARK: Let's get something straight. I don't want anything from you. I just want the hell out.

KIM: 0600. Tomorrow.

MARK: Right.

KIM: Drying your hands again?

MARK: Somebody's gotta clean up the mess. *Your* mess.

KIM: Why?

MARK: Sure. Let somebody else worry about it. That's the way you like it. Leave it to the other guy. (*He bends over and begins to mop up the glass.*) (*Mark brings the trash basket over and puts bits of glass in it.*)

KIM: You got most of it. Let it alone.

MARK: I'm in a place with a mess. I can't just sit there like you do. I gotta clean it up.

KIM: Good old Mark. Policing the area. R-A all the way.

MARK: You can make all the fun you want, friend, but you can't get to me. You just can't get to me anymore.

KIM: That's a very challenging thing to say to a woman. (*Points to some glass:*) Over there. (*He automatically goes toward the glass she is pointing to. Then:*)

MARK: Oh . . . damn . . . goddamn. Now you've done it.

KIM: Cut yourself. Right?

MARK: Happy?

KIM: They've got maids for this, you know.

MARK: Sure. Let the maid do it. Let some poor overworked old lady cut herself to death.

KIM: You're bleeding.

LIGHT CHANGE/FLASHBACK

Kim is eight

MARK: (*Rubbing his cheek:*) Just a little nick. From shaving.

KIM: (*Alarmed.*) You're cut.

MARK: It's o.k., Kimmy. (*A beat.*) Here . . . feel it.

KIM: No!

MARK: I'm all right.

KIM: (*Near tears.*) Don't do it anymore . . . o.k.? Don't do it anymore.

MARK: It was just an accident.

KIM: I don't want (*Starting to cry.*). . . . you to bleed any more . . . ever . . .

MARK: (*Takes out his handkerchief:*) Here . . . I have a whole package of combat-wound bandages. Nice biggies. (*A beat.*) Put one on Mark's chin . . . one on Mark's nose . . . one on Mark's mouth . . . (*He mumbles through his handkerchief.*)

LIGHT CHANGE/END OF FLASHBACK

MARK: (*He puts the handkerchief around the cut.*) I always bring a first-aid kit when I spend any time with you. (*Mark sits down stiffly in a chair. Then he is still.*)

KIM: That's a good soldier. Sit on the forward six inches of your chair. (*Mark moves back in the chair, slouching.*) (*A beat.*)

KIM: How about chow? (*Silence.*)

KIM: At first, good food made me sick.

MARK: Still stab the table with your fork?

KIM: You made the worst bread.

MARK: You ate it.

KIM: I can still hear you slapping dough like you were punishing it. (*Pause.*) I could never figure out why you liked to make bread.

MARK: My father was a baker. You haven't forgotten that?

KIM: Did he tell you it's the best way to clean your hands?

MARK: That man died from flour in his lungs. Don't you talk about my father.

KIM: But his hands were clean. (*A beat.*)

KIM: Aren't you hungry?

MARK: Yah. I'm hungry.

KIM: Why don't you call room service?

MARK: You're the C-O.

KIM: You don't like the "help" coming in and sizing us up. Remember?

MARK: You're in a room with an old dude. I don't care anymore if they size us up.

KIM: You're not an old dude.

MARK: Smack in the meridian, friend.

KIM: I like your meridian.

MARK: Sure!

KIM: You're the one hung up on age.

MARK: I'm twice as old as you.

KIM: Nobody talks about age anymore. You're the only man I've ever known still hung up on that.

MARK: It bothered me.

KIM: It never bothered me.

MARK: Nothing ever bothered you, friend. Nothing.

KIM: What are you talking about, now?

MARK: I'm talking about the way you conducted yourself on Post.

KIM: What about it?

MARK: You're a tease.

KIM: Really?

MARK: You work at it.

KIM: How do I do that?

MARK: The way you walk.

KIM: How do I walk, Mark?

MARK: You know how. I don't have to tell you. You're the expert.

KIM: Seems to me I walk like just about anybody else—one foot forward, one back.

MARK: I think . . . I really think in all seriousness . . . I really believe you'd like to take on every bastard in the U.S. Army.

KIM: Is that all?

MARK: Just about sums it up.

KIM: Most of the time, believe it or not, there was only one bastard I was interested in taking on.

MARK: It wasn't me. Don't you dare sit there and tell me it was me.

KIM: That's right. You.

MARK: Me. What a laugh.

LIGHT CHANGE/FLASHBACK

Kim is dancing.

MARK: (*He is sitting in a chair and writing a report.*) Turn that thing down.

KIM: It's Prince.

MARK: Turn him down. (*Kim still dances.*)

MARK: You have a test tomorrow.

KIM: I have a birthday tomorrow. Twelve. At last. (*She dances.*)

KIM: You and Daddy taking me to dinner this year?

MARK: Yep.

KIM: Off Post?

MARK: Yep.

KIM: Where?

MARK: The Pheasant House.

KIM: That dump? (*A beat as she dances.*)

KIM: Louise coming with us?

MARK: Sure.

KIM: It's not Louise's birthday. (*A beat as she dances.*)

KIM: Daddy said I could pierce my ears. (*A beat.*) Daddy said I could "double pierce" my ears.

MARK: (*Looks up at her disapprovingly:*) I told you. . . . turn that thing down.

KIM: Come on . . . dance with me. (*Mark gets up reluctantly from the chair and goes to the record player. He turns it off.*)

KIM: Why'd you do that? (*Mark goes back to his report.*)

KIM: I can dance without music. (*A beat.*) See? (*A beat.*) Look Mark . . . see anything different? (*Mark looks up.*)

KIM: See them? (*Dancing.*) I got tits now. Look at them jiggle.

LIGHT CHANGE/END OF FLASHBACK

MARK: Believe me, you can take my word for this. I do not, do not find you sexy in any way.

KIM: Want to dance? (*Silence.*)

KIM: (*She stands and holds her hands out to him:*) I knock off one hour if you dance with me. (*A beat.*)

KIM: You give me five minutes. I give you sixty big ones. (*Silence.*)

KIM: Whattaya say? (*Mark slowly stands.*) (*Kim starts dancing around him as he stands still.*)

KIM: Gotta move with me or it doesn't count. (*He continues to stand still.*) (*Kim holds out her hands to him. He just stares at her. She goes to a doorknob and holds it like a hand—dancing back and forth to it—moving the door and alternating with the inside doorknob and the outside doorknob.*)

KIM: This is how you told me to practice my dancing. With a door knob. Safer than using a horny young officer at the Club. Right? (*She dances over to Mark with her outstretched hands.*)

KIM: Got to touch me or it doesn't count. (*She keeps trying to grab his hand until he grabs her arm and angrily flings her against the bed.*)

KIM: (*She remains in a freeze the way she has been flung.*) Oh. We're playing "Swing the Statue." Like real old times.

MARK: What time is it?

KIM: Here we go again. (*Comes out of her statue freeze.*)

MARK: I asked you, what time is it?

KIM: I really wish you'd wear a watch.

MARK: You know I can't stand nothing next to my hands. (*A beat.*) Time?

KIM: Moving toward the bewitching hour. (*Puts up her hands and acts out a witch.*)

MARK: Come on. The time.

KIM: This is getting pretty tedious. I don't like the idea of giving you the time, hour by hour, minute by minute, all through the night.

MARK: We can take care of that. Say the word. Say the word and we can stop all this pretty damn fast.

KIM: (*She takes her watch off and holds it by the strap.*) This is what we're going to stop. (*She walks to the door.*)

MARK: What are you going to do now? (*Kim opens the door, looks both ways down the hall, then goes out for a few seconds and returns without the watch.*)

KIM: There. Taken care of.

MARK: What did you do?

KIM: I dropped my watch down the letter chute.

MARK: I don't believe it.

KIM: Yep. Time is gonna fly tonight. Air mail.

MARK: Yah. Let one of your daddy's flunkies buy you another one. Snap you fingers and one of Daddy's grunts will hop on down to the PX and buy his little girl a new watch.

KIM: The General's dead, remember.

MARK: That's right. I don't take your father's orders no more.

LIGHT CHANGE/FLASHBACK

Kim is two. Mark goes to the phone and dials.

MARK: (*Into phone:*) Mark Feeney. Sir. (*A beat.*) She's finally down. (*A beat.*) I know how important a nap is. I've been trying since noon, sir. (*A beat.*) First I brought Louise over to tell her some stories. That didn't work. Louise couldn't stay but thirty minutes anyway, because of the Officer's Wive's Lunch today. (*A beat.*) The thing is, I wore her out, sir. She finally knuckled under by the hickory tree near the front porch. (*A beat.*) We were using one of the branches for a parachute—that skinny one you want trimmed. Actually, you'd be proud of how she just kept dropping down like a plum. Every time. Down to the jungles in Jalapa. And . . . after about twenty jumps, she was wiped out. My guess is she'll be gone for at least two hours. I got Cpl. Flowers over here to sit. (*A beat.*) Yes, sir. OER's on your desk by 1800. Right, sir.

LIGHT CHANGE/END OF FLASHBACK

MARK: Ran right out in the hall.

KIM: Why not?

MARK: That's right. Why not. You get kicks that way, don't you? Thrills. With me sitting in here. . . . you out there . . . wearing cheap perfume.

KIM: It's not cheap.

MARK: You can dump the whole damn bottle on for all I care.

KIM: You used to buy those bottles. *White Shoulders.*

MARK: The smell of that stuff makes me sick.

KIM: You told me you got turned on every time you smelled it.

MARK: Now it's like field latrines.

KIM: Really?

MARK: Dog smells.

KIM: Nothing, huh?

MARK: Nothing.

KIM: Just plain old indifference.

KIM: It wasn't always like that.

MARK: Don't tell me about the past. I'm not interested in the past.

KIM: The past is interested in you.

MARK: Forget it. That's the best thing you can do. (*A beat.*) The time? Think you're going to cheat the hell out of me on that? Ditching the watch. No way. Call—double time. And have the operator ring here at 0600 tomorrow.

KIM: Mark, you don't trust me?

MARK: You don't know what trust is.

KIM: You used to trust me.

MARK: I used to be stupid, too.

KIM: Silly. Never stupid.

MARK: Call!

KIM: (*She calls the operator:*) Hello . . . operator? This is room 3801. Would you ring me at . . .

MARK: Tell her 0600. Sharp. Exactly.

KIM: (*Into phone:*) The stud in my room says 0600 sharp. Exactly. Thank you. (*She hangs up.*)

MARK: You always have to be a smart-ass. Why'd you do that?

KIM: Embarrassed? She can't see you. She doesn't know you're a big brave colonel who's been to Nic.

MARK: I don't know how he stood it. Beats the hell out of me. No wonder the man died. (*He gets up and goes to the door, opens it, and looks both ways down the hall.*)

MARK: Where is it?

KIM: What?

MARK: The letter-chute?

KIM: Are you sending me a love note?

MARK: Come on. Where?

KIM: On the left. (*Mark disappears down the hall, then returns after several seconds.*)

MARK: Nothing.

KIM: So what did you think you'd find?

MARK: I thought maybe it got caught on something.

KIM: When I mail a watch, I mail it right.

MARK: You don't have any respect. People. Things. It's all the same to you. (*A beat.*)

LIGHT CHANGE/FLASHBACK

Kim is sleeping. She is six. Mark goes to the closet and gets a coat hanger and takes it to use as a stick. He goes to the trash can and rattles the hanger inside the trash can.

MARK: On yer feet! Shake it up! (*A beat.*) (*Rattling stick.*) OK, soldier, time to get ready for school.

KIM: I don't wanna go to school.

MARK: (*Talks into the trash can:*) Orange juice. (*He puts trash can down by the bed as a little table.*)

KIM: Barf.

MARK: Gotta drink your orange juice.

KIM: You always get seeds in it.

MARK: You want it dumped on your head? (*A beat.*) One way or the other, friend, you're getting Vitamin C. (*A beat.*)

KIM: (*Pouting some orders:*) With a straw . . . on the rocks . . . with a swizel stick.

MARK: Right. (*He hands her the drink. She reluctantly drinks.*)

MARK: And hot oatmeal.

KIM: Daddy said I don't have to eat oatmeal if I don't want.

MARK: This isn't instant. I dirtied up a double-boiler, for god-sakes. (*A beat.*) Come on . . . like Mark had in Paw Paw, Illinois, when he was a boy.

KIM: It's got lumps.

MARK: Nope. No lumps. (*He dips spoon in bowl.*) That's . . . just a little potato-masher grenade. . . . (*He feeds her.*) . . . this . . . is a 105MM howitzer . . . (*Feeding her.*) . . . now we come to a silly one-shot bazooka . . . and here we are . . . a nice BX missile . . .

LIGHT CHANGE/END OF FLASHBACK

MARK: You were the meanest little kid I'd ever seen.

KIM: I was cute and you now it.

MARK: Demanding. You were worse than he was. I suppose if your mother had lived. . . .

KIM: I think about her a lot . . . what she must have been like.

MARK: I never saw the woman. People said she was nice. Good natured. Not like you, obviously. You. You take after him.

KIM: It was no picnic for me, you know, having my mother die when I was 6 months old.

MARK: I stayed with you the day of her funeral. (*A beat.*) Didn't know that, did you?

KIM: Daddy told me.

MARK: The day of your mother's funeral.

KIM: Daddy said you put black ribbons around the arms of all my teddy bears.

MARK: Here I was, a brand new adjutant. The post is in an uproar. The old man is half out of his mind. That's how I met him; his eyes all red. Orderlies standing around with their heads hanging down. Funeral arrangements being made. Doors slamming; windows shut. Disorder. Somebody hands me this baby I'd never seen before.

KIM: I put my face on your chest. I grew up thinking taupe was a mother's breast.

MARK: Chaos. Disorder like that on my first day.

KIM: Why didn't you just dump me and leave?

MARK: I follow orders. I do the job.

KIM: I'm glad you stayed around.

MARK: Sure. You had your own personal slave.

KIM: I wasn't so bad.

MARK: I was damn glad when the old man sent you to school in Switzerland. Hell, it was worth it. One less person to order me around.

KIM: I never ordered you around.

MARK: I had to drive you everywhere. The airport to get you off for that Swiss school. The airport to pick you up. The dentist to get your braces on. The dentist to get your braces off. The music store for your lessons. The dance hall for your dancing . . .

KIM: (*Amused.*) . . . dance hall.

MARK: I was always on the road with you. Ugly mean little thing that you were.

KIM: You know what they say about ugly little girls? (*She moves closer to him.*)

MARK: Keep your intervals, friend.

KIM: They grow up to be beautiful.

MARK: That's your side of it. I saw you *then*. I see you *now*. You ain't beautiful.

KIM: That so?

MARK: I'm talking about the soul. (*Puts hand inside his shirt on his heart.*) (*She walks over to him. She takes his hand and puts it on one breast.*)

KIM: I'm not beautiful . . . here?

MARK: (*Pulls his hand away.*) You . . . you . . . whore.

KIM: The whore survived.

MARK: Certain professions, friend, tend to preserve people. (*A beat. They look at each other in silence.*)

KIM: Want something to drink?

MARK: You killed it dead, remember?

KIM: Call room service.

MARK: Leave room service out of this.

KIM: Tell them to put it by the door.

MARK: Gotta sign for it. And there's no flunkie around to sign for supplies, Kim. No grunts to wait on you. Just me. And the man's not your slave. No more. The end.

LIGHT CHANGE/FLASHBACK

Kim is fifteen. Kim is holding her stomach. Mark takes a bag from the dresser.

MARK: I got the stuff. (*Kim ignores him.*)

MARK: I went all the way to Wallgreens. Your father called me off the rifle range to get this.

KIM: Ok . . . ok. . . . (*Mark throws a box of Kotex on the bed.*)

KIM: I told Daddy Tampex.

MARK: I'm not going back.

KIM: You get the Midols?

MARK: You know how hard it was for me to ask for just that? (*Kim throws Kotex on the floor.*)

KIM: I don't use those.

MARK: Friend, I was embarrassed in Wallgreens once today. No more.

LIGHT CHANGE/END OF FLASHBACK

KIM: You were no flunkie.

MARK: Sure.

KIM: I loved you.

MARK: Sure.

KIM: (*Says name tenderly:*) Mark.

MARK: (*Bitterly.*) You loved a lot of men.

KIM: Not like you.

MARK: Good. The kiss of death. Don't ever love anybody like me.

KIM: You taught me men had feelings. Yes. That's the truth. I grew up surrounded by soldiers . . . grovelling . . . quaking around my father. I never knew men had any sensibility. I thought they just jumped when you asked them to. That's what they did for my father all the time. And that's what they did for me. Later on . . . when I was older . . . well, they still jumped. Sometimes they got erections, groaned, sighed a little, wiggled in a moment of pleasure, and then snapped back to attention. And then. . . . when we made love for the first time. . . . when I got back from Switzerland. On my eighteenth birthday. That night at the Officer's club. You danced with me . . . and I knew then . . . I knew that night how much you wanted me. You were wearing tropical dress. Stiffly starched and dazzlingly white. The creases so sharp it was hard to lie down. Those little gray hairs over your ear were marked blue from your pen. You wanted to rub the blue off, but I wouldn't let go of your hand. I told you how the amazons in mythology defeated the enemy. They raised their skirts and showed their genitals. The other side ran in fright. You shook more. I drew a bead on you as you lay there. Powerless. I knew the rules. My training's along thin, light, quick-hitting lines. I must go deep. I made you cry. (*Pause.*) I never knew a man felt pain.

MARK: Oh, I was a good study in pain, all right.

KIM: You were happy, too, damn you. I know. I felt your heart pounding against me. I felt your mouth here. (*She rubs her breast.*)

MARK: Go to hell.

KIM: Oh, I know that much about you.

MARK: You got all the answers.

KIM: I got the answers from you.

MARK: Good old Mark. Taught you everything. Well, it was just one of those things, friend. (*Pause.*) So skip it. Skip the whole damn thing. And keep your intervals. (*Mark suddenly begins to do standing bends by his chair. She watches silently for several seconds.*)

KIM: What's all that?

MARK: (*Exercising.*) Just . . . keeping . . . the blood . . . going.

KIM: Keeping fit as a prisoner.

MARK: Right.

KIM: P-O-W style?

MARK: Right.

KIM: Don't deteriorate. Keep natty. Fit. Honor in the face of adversity. Defiance over the enemy.

MARK: Right. (*Mark stands erect and begins to do full breathing exercises. He then goes to the drapes at the window, fumbles.*)

MARK: Where's the damn cord?

KIM: Leave them open.

MARK: And have everybody looking in?

KIM: Whose gonna look in? We're on the thirty-eighth floor.

MARK: Copters look in.

KIM: This isn't Managua. (*Mark finds the drape cord and pulls it vigorously. It breaks.*)

KIM: We're not in the barracks. You don't have to yank that thing like it's made for a squad of recruits.

MARK: (*Throws broken drape-cord at her.*) What the hell do you know about recruits?

KIM: Just about as much as you do. (*Throws drape cord on the floor.*) (*Mark yanks the drapes with his hands. One side of the drapes comes off.*)

MARK: Damn!

KIM: Try not to dismantle the room. It doesn't belong to me.

MARK: Recruits! The woman never saw a recruit in her whole life.

KIM: That's news. You just told me I *took on* the whole U.S. Army.

MARK: Would like to. It may come as a surprise, Kim, but there's probably a few men out there who really wouldn't give a shit how you walk in front of them. Wouldn't want to "take you on" no matter what.

KIM: You know, huh?

MARK: I see things.

KIM: You do?

MARK: I've been around.

KIM: To all the best places.

MARK: That's right.

KIM: Honduras. Costa Rica. Salvador. Nic . . .

MARK: That's right.

KIM: Mark, you're really going to have to come up with some better wars . . . cause I'm having one hell of a time working up any kind of enthusiasm for Low Intensity Conflicts.

MARK: L-I-C, friend, is worse than a fuckin' war. Let me tell you, we aren't sitting around in nice little trenches. With atomic missiles. And it's not like WWI when the Americans went to France and the people cheered and threw apples at them. Nic is mind control. Without the all-out. The big Psyche Job. The only territory worth while is the six inches between the ears of the peasants, and that's Low Intensity Conflict.

KIM: Low intensity for you. High for the Nics.

MARK: We're just like the Lincoln Brigade. Fighting in Spain.

KIM: The Lincoln Brigade wasn't organized by the CIA.

MARK: We're the "private sector solution". Spain had contributions from their private sector.

KIM: But it wasn't tax-deductible.

MARK: Is that your "civilian" friend talking?

KIM: It's me talking.

MARK: Your civilian boyfriend making you a dove, Kim?

KIM: I'm too far gone to be a dove.

MARK: Tell the boyfriend . . . soon as we declare a liberated zone that the non-aligned countries can recognize, then aid will start coming into Nic. That's all we want.

KIM: You're beginning to sound like a training film.

MARK: Is that why your hair's up? Trying to look prissy like the boyfriend's mother?

KIM: There weren't too many role models on the Post, now were there?

MARK: Wanna be Miss Country Club?

KIM: His mother kisses my cheek . . . and I don't feel any stubble. I can't tell you how amazing that is for me. (*Mark goes to her and pulls at her hair clip. Kim takes her hair down.*)

KIM: There. Just the way you like it. (*Mark ignores her. He sits down and takes off his shoes.*)

MARK: I'm gonna jog in place. (*A beat.*) I jog every night around the Post. (*A beat.*) I'm in damn good condition for my age.

KIM: You're in good condition for any age.

MARK: You should know. You have all those men to compare me with. (*Mark jogs in place for a few minutes. Then he suddenly jogs to one end of the room and lifts up his foot in pain.*)

KIM: You stepped on the drape cord.

MARK: (*Picks up drape cord and flings it on the floor.*)

KIM: Your foot all right?

MARK: My foot's just fine.

KIM: Mark, sit down. You just get careless.

MARK: Don't tell me . . . I know how to take care of myself.

KIM: Will you sit?

MARK: What the hell kind of place is this with a crummy floor that sneaks up on you? Sandinistas do that. Wearing their damn grass-soled sandals. (*Pause.*) Things like this don't happen to me when you're not around. Do you know that?

KIM: How can I know that since I'm not there when I'm not around?

MARK: Things go smooth at Headquarters. I'm agile. I'm efficient. I'm not West Point, but I can handle things pretty goddamn ok.

KIM: Are you speaking of Daddy's West Point?

MARK: I'm talking about West Point. You know what I'm talking about. (*A beat.*) The old man strutting around with his ring . . . wearing that West Point ring.

KIM: He was laughable.

MARK: Ring knockers. All of them. Every West Point officer, tapping those over-sized rings on the desk so we could see and hear. So we couldn't forget where they went. Well, in a nun-killing regime, nobody gives a damn about the Point. Can you carry out aerial reconnaissance. That's what you have to know. How to get a C-2 through Nic airspace from Panama or Honduras.

KIM: Right. And you were the one who knew that.

MARK: You'd think they were the only damn soldiers in the world. A second-class Army man if you didn't make the Academy. Old Man wanted to run the whole Central America operation like it was a West Point plain.

KIM: You ran it with good Paw Paw, Illinois, common sense.

MARK: I see all kinds of soldiers in Nic. All kinds. I see this Lieutenant in a fought over camp near the Mosquito Indian territory. Some border area in a volcanic valley. He picks up a grenade and the damn firing pin falls out. Grenade has a three second fuse, so he figures to pitch it—Army football style. . . . lifts his arm to throw it..whamo! Blew his hand right off. (*A beat.*) Howling in pain, and he grubs around for the hunk of mangled hand to get his fuckin' West Point ring back.

KIM: God.

MARK: You think I didn't want the Point?

KIM: (*Disgusted.*) God.

MARK: The old man had West Point. Christ, he was there. Right there where the Greats started. The warriors of W-W-II. (*Pause.*) You don't think I wouldn't give my soul to have been in the West Point class of 1915 . . . Eisenhower . . . Bradley . . . Van Fleet . . . the class the stars fell on.

KIM: Too bad the whole damn sky didn't fall on them.

MARK: You think I didn't want the Point!

KIM: It's a stupid fantasy.

MARK: Easy enough for you to say. What do you know?

KIM: Nothing.

MARK: That's right. Nothing.

KIM: Forget it.

MARK: What do I get? Shake-n'bake Officer's Candidate School at Fort Dix. (*A beat.*) You and the Old Man . . . both of you. What do you care? West Point . . . Switzerland . . . you were both too damn important for Fort Dix. (*A beat.*) Lucerne, Switzerland. That was you territory. Mark, pick up Kim. Mark, take Kim to the airport. Mark, do this. Mark, do that. I got tired of it all. You were always leaving. But you never had the decency to stay away. You came back. Stepping off the plane in that blue and white school uniform. That funny book-bag on your arm. I'd see ten girls getting off that plane, all with the same identical Academy uniforms. But you . . . you always fucked yourself up. Blouse collar all rolled up. A tie on backwards. Your hat in your eyes. You always had to come out different.

KIM: Your wife . . . Louise . . . wore her apron like a real soldier's wife. She wasn't different.

MARK: Leave Louise out of this.

KIM: Louise respected Ft. Dix.

MARK: I said . . . leave Louise out of this.

KIM: The perfect wife.

MARK: She did for herself. She didn't make demands on my time. She let me get my work done. A good wife's right there on an Officer's Efficiency Report. That woman only helped me.

KIM: One way *I* helped you—got you to start wearing sleeveless undershirts. So I could see the gorgeous hair on your chest. (*Pause.*) Of course you can't cover up those pects no matter what you wear. (*A beat.*) What kind of undershirt are you wearing now? (*Kim moves toward Mark.*)

MARK: Hold your position.

KIM: I remember when you liked me very close.

MARK: Things are a hell of a lot different now.

KIM: Is that so?

MARK: You're disgusting to me. Disgusting!

KIM: That's pretty strong.

MARK: It gets stronger. You wouldn't want to know how damn sick I am at the sight of you.

KIM: Times have changed.

MARK: Yes.

KIM: I'm disgusting.

MARK: Yes.

LIGHT CHANGE/FLASHBACK

Mark goes to the phone.

MARK: (*Into phone:*) Kim. . . . Kim. . . . I know you're there. I can hear you breathing. Don't hang up on me. . . . Tell me what's wrong. Why won't you see me? I deserve an explanation. Jesus, you owe me that. Just talk to me. . . . give me one minute. That's all I'm asking for. . . . .one minute. I'm not a man who begs. . . . . . . .after all these years. . . . .please. . . . (*Kim has hung up. He slowly puts down the phone. Mark sits down slowly, stunned. He sees the trash can by his chair that used to wake her up. He picks it up slowly in his arms, rocking it . . .*)

MARK: Oh, god. . . . . . . god. . . . . . Kimmy. . . . .

END OF ACT ONE

ACT TWO

Time: A few minutes later
At Rise: Mark is staring at Kim.

MARK: First thing. . . . I step on the base . . . first day . . . I'm no sooner there and somebody hands me a strange baby I've never seen before. Somewhere a mother I don't know from nothing is dying. The old man is bleary-eyed. My first look at him and I see that. My commander—demoralized. And here I am holding a baby that I get stuck with for the rest of my military career. Day in. Day out. (*A beat.*) Even Father Lewis . . . even Lewis says: "That kid's so mean I don't think she's been baptized cause she's gotta have the devil still in her." A chaplain. A U.S. Army chaplain who's been to Central America said that.

KIM: Father Lewis never said that. He liked me.

MARK: He couldn't tell you the truth. He couldn't yell at the General's daughter.

KIM: Priests can yell. They get dispensations.

MARK: Everywhere but the U.S. Army. (*A beat.*) Ever see a chaplain pull KP? It's pitiful.

KIM: Come on, I wasn't that bad.

MARK: I got you through the double-headers. I got you through tonsillitis and mumps and God knows what else. And where was the old man? At a retirement parade. I think every officer in the U.S. Army retired when you were growing up. I used to wonder who the hell was left to run the Army.

KIM: Mark . . .

MARK: I had more rest in Honduras.

KIM: Mark . . .

MARK: I didn't have combat that bad in Nic.

KIM: Mark . . .

MARK: I got better treatment from the Sandinistas.

KIM: Mark . . . remember your systolic pressure.

MARK: (*Points to his neck:*) See this! See it! You can take my pulse here. That's what you did to me. (*A beat.*) I gave up peace and quiet because of you. I gave up my family because of you.

KIM: I never asked you to give up your family.

MARK: You think I didn't feel bad about leaving Louise alone so much?

KIM: Why did you then?

LIGHT CHANGE/FLASHBACK

Kim is six.

MARK: A lot of people think foot soldiers are old fashioned, Kimmy.

KIM: I wanna see. I wanna see.

MARK: Just plain old infantry. That's all.

KIM: Can I stand on the Jeep, Mark?

MARK: Look at that. Those are wild magnolia blossoms. (*A beat.*) I love the smell of magnolia . . . and the sun on vegetables . . . palm oil . . . sandlewood and copra . . . dried fish.

KIM: I wanna stand on the Jeep.

MARK: Here. I'll help you up. (*A beat.*) Now can you see?

KIM: What's that?

MARK: Where?

KIM: (*Pointing.*) That!

MARK: Some cows.

KIM: They don't look like cows.

MARK: Cause you've never seen cows.

KIM: I have, too. On T V (*Pause.*) Those are funny looking.

MARK: That's cause they're dead.

KIM: How did they get dead?

MARK: Stray bullets. (*A beat.*) Dead cows . . . fall on their backs . . . and then their stomachs get all bloated from the heat.

KIM: What's bloated?

MARK: All puffed out.

KIM: Like what's carried over there.

MARK: Why don't we pick some magnolia . . .

KIM: Is that bloated?

MARK: Come on, let's smell some flowers.

KIM: Where's that going?

MARK: It's a sick man. The medics are going to fly him to a hospital at Chinandega.

KIM: Oh . . . now I can see . . . there's an arm . . . and part of a leg . . .

MARK: He's all twisted up . . .

KIM: Like the cows?

MARK: Yes. And the medics are having trouble fitting him on the stretcher.

KIM: Cause he won't fit. Right? Cause everything's all going a different way . . .

MARK: Just look at the mountains, Kimmy. There's always one more mountain . . . and higher. If you ironed Nic flat, it would cover the whole world . . . (*Pause. He looks around.*) Kimmy? Jesus, Kimmy . . . where are you? Kimmy!

KIM: I'm over here, Mark.

MARK: Get away from that stretcher, hear me? Don't look at that man, for godsakes. Don't touch him!

LIGHT CHANGE/END OF FLASHBACK

MARK: I couldn't stand to see you waste away like a barefoot urchin on a chicken farm in Matagalpa.

KIM: I was no barefoot urchin on a chicken farm.

MARK: Like those beggar kids I'd seen sleeping in the streets of Managua.

KIM: Nobody asked you to sleep with the beggar kid.

MARK: I was seduced.

KIM: Tell that to Louise.

MARK: (*Scratching his hands.*) Don't think I don't feel bad about Louise. Don't think I didn't get ulcers looking into her trusting face day after day. Don't think I don't realize how I neglected a wonderful decent women for..for a selfish, demanding weirdo.

KIM: But did you love her?

MARK: You bet I loved her. I love her. To this day.

KIM: Especially to this day.

MARK: Oh, it wasn't just me you ordered around.

KIM: To hear you talk, the whole post was standing around waiting on me.

MARK: Just about it, friend. Just about. (*Pause.*) I watched you in the Mess Hall . . . turn over a mug of milk so one of the nice Privates could clean it up. That was your fun. Your personal game. Drop your clothes on the floor. Turn over your trike. Throw all your dolls down the stairs so Kimmy can watch Daddy's nice Privates hop-to and pick them up.

KIM: I told you, Mark. I thought they didn't feel anything. I thought they never got tired. You could knock them over cause somebody would just set them right back up and their arms and hands would keep moving . . . like in the *Nutcracker*.

MARK: You were the most insensitive little brat I'd ever seen.

KIM: My father treated men that way. He talked to them like they had small hollow heads. What else was I supposed to think?

MARK: You two were a pair. A couple of Neanderthals . . . warmed-up left-overs from the Dark Ages. (*Mark picks up the phone.*) Time please. (*A beat.*) Thank you. (*He hangs up.*) Things are looking good.

MARK: Where the hell did you get those scars under your chin? (*He goes to her and pulls up her chin.*)

MARK: These!

KIM: I'm not a masochist. Nobody hits me.

MARK: Nobody did that?

KIM: Just a big bad toaster oven. (*A beat.*)

KIM: Every time I lean down to check a frozen pot pie, my chin gets burned. (*A beat.*) Well, you never taught me to cook.

MARK: You could be locked in a mess full of canned goods and a can opener and you'd still starve to death. (*A beat.*) This man cooked you more meals. Fed you. Wiped up after you. (*A beat.*) But I learned. You know what slavery is? Feeding people. I'll never cook again. For nobody. I won't even feed a guppy now. I don't even water grass. (*A beat.*)

KIM: It hasn't been all that easy without you.

MARK: Good.

KIM: But I'm getting pretty independent now. (*Pause.*) First winter I haven't lost my gloves. (*Holds out her arms:*) I have bruises on my arms from hanging my own drapes. (*Pause.*) And I just got a driver's license.

MARK: Any license from the boyfriend?

KIM: We're talking about it. (*Silence. Mark sits down on a chair.*)

MARK: I bet he wears little understated rep ties . . .

KIM: Only on Sundays.

MARK: . . . thin leather jackets and silk socks.

KIM: As a matter of fact, most of the time he wears florescent striped surfer jams, op art boat shoes, no socks, and a Cubs baseball cap.

MARK: And you're the one who says military men don't know how to dress out of uniform.

KIM: And . . . he wears sleeveless undershirts. So I can see his biceps.

MARK: The woman says *we* look like thugs and busboys in civies. (*Silence.*)

MARK: He's why? (*Silence.*)

MARK: For "surfer jams" . . . you just go. No goodbyes. No letters. No phone calls. Bam! A whole year of silence.

KIM: I wanted to start clean.

MARK: (*Knocking ashtray off desk:*) That's clean. (*Rips drapes off window:*) That's clean.

KIM: I made a mistake. I didn't mean to hurt you.

MARK: Some mistake, friend. You know what you did to me? (*A beat.*) You knifed me. Left me for dead.

KIM: For once . . . I wanted to be with someone who didn't know the Old Man.

MARK: Sure. And somebody who didn't know me.

KIM: I wanted a civilian.

MARK: Just like that! She wants a civilian.

KIM: I wanted to . . . go to a restaurant where a Private didn't park the car.

MARK: God!

KIM: I wanted somebody all mine.

MARK: I was sure the hell full time.

KIM: You had Louise.

MARK: Louise has nothing to do with this.

KIM: The hell she doesn't.

MARK: Louise . . . never bothered you.

KIM: She bothered me.

MARK: The woman was an Army wife.

KIM: What does that mean?

MARK: It means she knows enough to do for herself. She knows my career comes first.

KIM: I hated her. She got you all to herself on vacations.

MARK: There were few vacations with you around, friend.

KIM: She got to wear your ring.

MARK: The ring through my nose was yours.

KIM: I wanted you every minute.

MARK: That's right.

KIM: I couldn't stand for her to have you . . . even for a second.

MARK: You don't have to tell me.

KIM: Well, I did you a favor. (*A beat.*) I left. Then you had to go home to your wife every night. (*A beat.*) That's why she's pregnant now, isn't it? (*A beat as he stares at her.*)

MARK: You think I didn't make love to Louise when you and me were together? (*Silence.*) Every day, friend. Sometimes twice a day.

KIM: I don't believe that.

MARK: I can never get enough of her. Not then. Not now.

KIM: (*Shaken.*) I don't believe that.

MARK: Never.

KIM: You're lying.

MARK: With Louise. . . . it was pure love.

KIM: You mean like . . . pure mathematics.

MARK: I mean like pure normal. (*A beat.*)

MARK: You were too experienced. Always one step ahead of me. Anticipating. Friend, you don't have to please a man to please a man. Louise had all the surprises. From her innocence. You . . . I always knew you'd pull something quirky. I always knew you'd figure out what I wanted. Well, you don't just win a battle by taking the high ground. Just cause it's high doesn't mean you win.

KIM: You told me . . . I was the best.

MARK: You thought I said that. You wanted me to say that.

KIM: I . . . felt you. I heard you.

MARK: I faked it. (*Silence.*)

KIM: Some things you *can't* fake.

MARK: Some things you can.

LIGHT CHANGE/FLASHBACK

Kim is ten.

KIM: (*Singing.*) I can't take this tension, it's too much to mention. I can't take this tension, man, it's too much to mention . . . Where's the enemy?

MARK: A long way from here. You know that.

KIM: Where Daddy is?

MARK: Around there. Yah. We're just doing reconnaissance here. Safe stuff.

KIM: Boring.

MARK: (*A beat.*) You want to stay home?

KIM: No.

MARK: Your father and me went to a lot of trouble to bring you with us.

KIM: I know. I know.

MARK: You're better off with us even if its Nic rather than stateside without your family.

KIM: OK, OK.

MARK: Do your homework. I gotta call battalion. (*He talks into the radio:*) "Tacos . . . tacos . . . this is Enchilada."

RADIO: Enchilada, this is tacos. Wait one. Wait one. (*A beat.*) Major Feeney?

MARK: Right.

RADIO: Call Division, Major.

MARK: Roger that.

KIM: Is that Daddy calling us?

MARK: We'll see. (*Into radio.*) "Tequila . . . Tequila . . . this Enchilada." (*Static is heard over radio.*)

MARK: I can't hear you. I can't hear you. What? The general called? (*Static.*) General Denton? (*A beat.*) Tequila . . . Tequila . . . there's ground static. (*Radio dies.*) What is this, a Mexican restaurant or Nic?

KIM: Daddy's really going to be mad if he can't get us.

MARK: At least we know he's all right. If he's calling, he's all right.

KIM: (*Singing:*) I can't take this tension, it's too much to mention. I can't take this tension . . .

MARK: You know something else?

KIM: I'm hot.

MARK: Look at you! A rash on your neck. I told you, we got to keep checking each other's skin . . . to see if we turn red or blistery.

KIM: Am I all right?

MARK: You're okay.

KIM: I'm thirsty. The water stinks here. I want a Pepsi.

MARK: Just keep on with your schoolwork. (*Pause.*) Know what? Father Lewis is here in these mountains somewhere. Saying Mass.

KIM: Really?

MARK: And a lot of your friends from the Post back home are out here, too.

KIM: Yah?

MARK: I'll try the radio again.

KIM: I want to. Can I? Can I, Mark? Daddy always lets me. (*He gives her the radio.*)

KIM: (*Into radio.*) Tequila . . . Tequila . . . read me. Read me.

KIM: I'm going to call again. (*Into radio:*) Tequila . . . Tequila . . . this is Enchilada.

RADIO: Enchilada, this is Tequila. Roger that. Wait one. General Denton for Major Feeney. (*Mark takes the radio from Kim.*)

MARK: (*Into radio:*) Sir, we're fine here. Glad to know you're likewise. Kim doing her homework . . . then we're going into town later for chow . . . (*Firing is heard.*)

MARK: My God . . . get the hell down, Kim. (*Into radio:*) We're taking sniper fire, sir. Jesus, we need help. (*Into radio.*) Tacos, get the fuck some support for us. I got a little kid here! Do you read me. Support!

LIGHT CHANGE/END OF FLASHBACK

MARK: Something abnormal about you, friend. Never crying. Never afraid. Never letting anyone else take over . . . not even for a second.

KIM: I don't want to hear it.

MARK: You're gonna hear it, all right. (*Kim covers her ears.*)

MARK: You wore the old man's rank in bed. (*Mark yanks her hands away from her ears.*)

MARK: Your MacArthur. To my Private E-1.

KIM: That's not true.

MARK: Your fingers pumping in my ears. Your mouth on my nipples. Your tongue curled like a spoon around the end— hard against my jaws. Always in a hurry. Always fast. Take. Take. Take.

KIM: Did you ever think about how you sounded? I was a little girl playing by the kitchen table when you and Daddy were talking: Getting in . . . pulling out . . . holding on . . . taking the breast of a hill . . . squeezing off a shot . . . getting on top . . . pump the old M-16 . . . forward thrust . . . blasting off . . . I grew up thinking women were the enemy. I was twenty before I found out love didn't look and smell like war.

MARK: We didn't know you were listening . . .

KIM: I was listening.

MARK: Louise heard stuff, too. And she gives and takes.

KIM: Louise was a woman.

MARK: Louise grew up Army.

KIM: She didn't grow up Army with you.

MARK: It's all water under the bridge, friend. Cause you did me a favor. With you out of the picture, I learned to slow down. My wife and I know how to be long and slow. It was good before. Now it's great. That's why Louise is pregnant. (*Mark sits down on a chair across from the bed and stares at Kim.*)

MARK: I can leave. Just say the word. (*Silence.*) *Kim is slumped over from the pain of his words.*)

MARK: Can't take it, can you? (*A beat.*)

MARK: Miss Civilian can't take it. (*Mark goes to her and rips the neckline of her dress.*)

MARK: Best thing you did for me was to chuck my dog tags. You're not fit to wear them. You're not the pearls type, either. (*He rips the pearls off her neck.*) (*Mark goes back to his chair and sits down.*) (*A beat.*)

MARK: So why the hell do you come back now! Why! (*A beat.*) And don't tell me cause the old man died.

KIM: Cause the old man died.

MARK: You never cared a damn for him.

KIM: I never saw him that much to care a damn. Why do you think I tried to shave my hair off when I was three? (*A beat.*) So I could be bald. Like Daddy. (*A beat.*) Why do you think I wore brass on my snowsuit and made everybody salute me? (*A beat.*) So I could be like Daddy. (*A beat.*) After a while, he faded out. And it was only you. Then . . . I didn't give a damn about him.

MARK: The man lost his wife. He had to take care of a kid. All by himself.

KIM: He had to order somebody all by himself to take care of a kid.

MARK: He did what he could. (*A beat.*)

MARK: He would have been different if his wife had lived.

KIM: I don't believe that. The man was an egomaniac. He only cared about himself. That Christmas he made his fourth star, he let the Cadet Choir change all the words and sing carols about him. (*Mock singing:*) "Joy to the General, the star has come."

MARK: Do you know what four stars mean to a man?

KIM: The lord only had one.

MARK: The man was West Point. He . . . couldn't operate like other men.

KIM: I deserved a normal life.

MARK: That's enough.

KIM: Enough's never enough.

MARK: What the hell was I supposed to do?

KIM: I wanted to play tambourines and wear little black aprons for painting like other kids.

MARK: Where was I supposed to find tambourines and little black aprons in the mountains of Rio Blanca?

KIM: That's just it! What the hell was a child doing in the mountains of Rio Blanca?

MARK: You think we didn't worry? Didn't agonize over how to bring you up? (*A beat. He sits on a chair.*) (*Kim sits on the bed and pulls the covers up to her neck.*)

KIM: How about turning off the lights?

MARK: Oh, no.

KIM: Don't trust me in the dark?

MARK: Don't trust you in the dark. In the light. Don't trust you.

KIM: That's not fair.

MARK: It's safe.

KIM: Please . . . turn off the light. (*A beat.*) I promise to be good. I'll stay here. I won't bug you. Code of the Point. Duty . . . honor . . . country.

MARK: The last thing I'd ever do is believe something you told me.

KIM: You used to make a tent out of the bed covers . . . so I could go to sleep. (*She pulls the blanket over her head.*)

KIM: I loved those tents. (*Mark goes to her and throws off the blankets.*)

MARK: You're out in the open now, friend. For everybody to see. For what you really are. Selfish. Unfeeling. . . .

KIM: I come by it naturally. Runs in the family.

MARK: Nothing wrong with your family. Say what you want, but the old man was pretty damn distinguished.

KIM: He didn't make "distinguished" decisions.

MARK: Like what?

KIM: Sending me to school in Switzerland. I had to spend my last year before college with a lot of strangers. (*Mark takes a stick of gum out of his pants pocket and begins chewing.*)

MARK: That's all C-2 needed—somebody like you in Switzerland messing up a neutral country.

KIM: At least I came back from Lucerne a woman.

MARK: That's a laugh. (*A beat.*) Ah . . . ah . . . (*He makes a face.*) God!

KIM: What?

MARK: I lost a filling. See what happens. Around you and it's instant 4-F.

MARK: You were intolerable after Lucerne. Making everybody call you *Kimberly*. Kimberly wants this. Kimberly wants that. (*A beat.*)

MARK: The old man was no better. Making us call him "mi commandant." Yelling about "hard currency" support for Nic.

KIM: I thought you *loved* his theory.

MARK: But he never stuck to theory. He wanted to drive all over the Jinotoga Province in a Toyota jitney with his Browning 9mm pistol in a Marlboro bag from the Miami airport duty-free shop.

KIM: They should have buried him in a great big Marlboro duty-free bag.

MARK: Don't talk like that.

KIM: Why not?

MARK: For godsakes, the man just died. (*A beat.*) You think I didn't feel guilt.

KIM: For loving me?

MARK: (*Scratching his hands.*) The man gave me his child. In trust.

KIM: You didn't make love to the child. You made love to the woman. I gave you the *woman*.

MARK: . . . . .always wondering if he knew. . . . .having to face him day in and day out. . . . .

KIM: He never knew.

MARK: The man wasn't stupid.

KIM: He didn't know. And if he did, he wouldn't have cared. Not then. Not when I was grown up. Not when I grabbed for love like some kind of wild thing. (*A beat.*) You both created the savage. (*Kim goes to her overnight case and takes out a silk cloth with something inside. She slowly unwraps the silk and we see four large magnetic stars.*)

KIM: From Daddy's coffin. Four stars. All that's left of him. (*She slaps the four stars—one by one—on the headboard of the bed as she sings:*)

KIM: I wish you a merry star. . . . I wish you a merry star. . . . I wish you a merry star and a happy new year. (*A beat.*)

KIM: A pretty pathetic monument for his daughter who learned everything about women from men's girlie magazines. (*A beat.*)

KIM: And from mortar shells I looked at in the skies of Jalapa. (*A beat.*) Some shells flirt and whimper . . . like little girls. Others crack bright and loud—like Mae West setting up for her lovers. Some shells explode like wild sperm leaking across the sky in silvering milk. (*A beat. She gets a grenade from her overnight case.*)

MARK: What the hell is that in your hand?

KIM: Don't you know a grenade when you see one?

MARK: Where'd you get that?

KIM: From Daddy's personal effects.

MARK: Hand it over.

KIM: No way.

MARK: Kim . . . don't do anything stupid.

KIM: You taught me everything I know, remember?

KIM: (*Takes pin out.*) Don't . . . rattle me, Mark. (*After three seconds she puts the pin back in.*)

MARK: You nuts or something? If you release the handle, there's a five-second fuse; put the pin back in.

KIM: Just stand back.

MARK: Gonna kill me twice?

KIM: L.I.C., Mark.

MARK: What you did to me, friend, was not Low Intensity Conflict.

KIM: L.I.C. . . . . a state of "violent peace". Isn't that what you always said?

MARK: What are you calling "violent peace". You just went. And left me nothing but my own life. In bandages. Shoved back at me.

KIM: What do you think we're doing now?

MARK: What the hell are we doing now?

KIM: Facing it!

MARK: I ain't facing anything but a weirdo and a grenade.

KIM: Forgive me.

MARK: Just like that.

KIM: Right here.

MARK: The hell I will.

KIM: Cause I forgive you.

MARK: She forgives me!

KIM: I'm waiting, Mark. Say it: "I . . . forgive . . . you . . ."

MARK: The pain you caused me, friend, ain't ever gonna let me forgive you.

KIM: I'm waiting.

MARK: That thing's a dud.

KIM: It's real.

MARK: You're bluffing.

KIM: You already accused me of bluffing once tonight. (*A beat.*)

MARK: There's no powder inside that thing.

KIM: There's powder.

MARK: Go ahead. Blow us up.

KIM: And leave Louise behind? And the baby? Just like that? (*Silence.*)

KIM: Want to miss knowing about my baby, too?

MARK: What the hell are you talking about?

KIM: I'll tell you why I left. (*Silence.*)

KIM: I lost your baby. (*Silence.*)

MARK: If it was true, you would have told me. When it happened.

KIM: There I was doubled up in some doctor's office on the South Side. . . . with a miscarriage.

MARK: You'd never go through something like that by yourself.

KIM: . . . in pain. For hours. The baby didn't want to let go of me . . . for hours. The only record of our son is here. (*Pats herself.*) (*Silence.*)

KIM: If I release the handle we have five seconds. My father's dead. My baby's dead. You're all the family I have left. (*A beat.*) You got five seconds, Mark. To forgive me. To hold me. Cause I'd rather blow us both up than . . . be an orphan.

MARK: That's why you left me? A miscarriage?

KIM: Yes.

MARK: That's why you walked out on me?

KIM: Yes.

MARK: I could have been there with you.

KIM: I was too ashamed.

MARK: Why didn't you let me share the pain?

KIM: I never wanted to see you again.

KIM: I stared at this little thing the doctor lay gently in a pan . . . I stared at what was pulled from me in agony . . . yanked out of me bloody and hurt . . . smelling of our seed . . . strings of wet blood around his neck . . . I've got to start over. (*Mark goes to Kim and carefully grabs her hand holding the grenade. Kim struggles against Mark's hold. There should be moments when the audience thinks the grenade will go off. Finally Mark firmly and cautiously guides her hand with the pin back into the grenade—and safety.*)

MARK: Where is he? (*Silence.*)

MARK: Where the hell is he?

KIM: I had him cremated. Along with dozens of daisies. His ashes scattered into the lake. Thrown into the water . . .

MARK: Like nothing? Jesus . . . no grave . . . no name . . . god . . . god . . .

KIM: He has a name! That's where your dog tags are. Wrapped around his caved in little chest. I had your dog tags cremated with our baby. (*A beat. Mark takes Kim in his arms and begins to rock her. After a beat he half sings the following children's ballad—he continues to rock her.*)

Hush-a-by
don't you cry
go to sleep
little baby.
When you wake
you shall have
all the pretty
little horses:
black and bays
dapples and grays
coach and six little horses.
Hush-a-by
don't you cry
go to sleep, little baby.

KIM: I feel like ten men. Yessir . . . I feel like . . .

MARK: . . . ten men.

KIM: Nine dead . . .

MARK: . . . . and one in the hospital. (*A beat.*)

MARK: God, my hands are like a baseball glove . . .

KIM: . . . fought over by two pit bulls.

MARK: I'm like some old farmer who gets a child bride . . .

KIM: . . . through a newspaper ad.

MARK: When kids played soldiers in war . . .

KIM: I wanted to be "the war." (*A beat.*)

KIM: Every time we moved, you wrapped my play dishes.

MARK: One whole sheet of newspaper for each dish.

KIM: You always slept on your back.

MARK: Like I was swimming in the ocean.

KIM: I cried cause my eyelashes weren't as long as yours.

MARK: I still have the pair of break-dancing gloves you gave me on Mother's Day. (*A beat.*)

KIM: Were you really poor when you were a kid?

MARK: Everybody was poor in Paw Paw, Illinois.

KIM: You had to decorate your Christmas tree with cigarette butts.

MARK: And chestnuts from the back yard.

KIM: You went rabbit hunting for supper. Every night.

MARK: I had an old twelve-gauge Fox. Every time I shot, it came apart in my hands.

KIM: The stock took off one way . . .

MARK: . . . the barrel the other. But it always shot good before it broke.

KIM: If you don't get a rabbit with the first shot, he gets to escape. (*A beat.*)

MARK: This guy you love . . . is he here? In the city?

KIM: Yes.

MARK: Waiting for you?

KIM: Yes.

MARK: When you leave this room?

KIM: Yes. (*Pause.*)

MARK: Have you heard? I'm thinking about retiring.

KIM: I heard.

MARK: So what do you think?

KIM: I think it's great.

MARK: All those peasants have left of their country is dirt. They're carrying it around on their face and hands. They've buried their own dead people on themselves. And I'm tired of looking at the face of graves. (*A beat as they stare at each other.*) (*Mark goes to the mirror on the dresser and looks at himself.*)

MARK: What's left? (*Pause.*) What's left of me? (*Pause.*) My hair's coming out in the brush. Teeth rotting on me. I'm forty-four years old. I look in there when I shave . . . and you know what I see? I see . . . the last one in the platoon. Fired on. Shelled. Everybody wiped out. But me. I'm coming down from the hills—the last man left. And there's no troops to hook up to. Nobody. (*He puts his face in his hands.*) (*Kim goes to the night table and returns with a glass of water for Mark. She also holds out a bottle of aspirin.*) (*Mark takes the aspirin and drinks.*) (*A beat.*)

MARK: First time the woman's ever gotten me anything. First time . . . she's handed me so much as a glass of water.

KIM: You've got somebody to hook up to. You and Louise have a baby . . . due in two months. (*A beat.*) A new beginning. Just like me.

MARK: I hope it doesn't look like you. You were the ugliest little kid I ever saw. (*A beat as he looks at her tenderly.*)

MARK: I never wanted you in the first place.

KIM: You know what they say . . . some people are born to love, others just have love thrust upon them.

MARK: Somebody hands me this strange baby I'd never seen before.

KIM: That's the breaks, friend.

MARK: I loved you when nobody loved you.

KIM: That's the way the old orders fall.

MARK: I saw you get off the plane after Lucerne . . .

KIM: That's right . . .

MARK: . . . short skirt . . .

KIM: Yep.

MARK: . . . those legs lean and naked . . .

KIM: Yep.

MARK: Your breasts bouncing . . .

KIM: All two of them.

MARK: I had such a longing.

KIM: An honest longing. (*A beat.*)

MARK: Kim . . .

KIM: Yes, Mark.

MARK: Kimmy . . .

He holds out his arms to her. Kim answers by taking the stars from the headboard of the bed, wrapping then and putting them in Marks's hat. A beat as they stare at each other. Then Kim notices the light coming through the window.

MARK: What's wrong?

KIM: It's starting to get light. (*A beat.*) Do we have to leave each other at six o'clock?

MARK: Yes we do. You know we do.

KIM: 6:30.

MARK: No.

KIM: 6:15.

MARK: No.

KIM: 6:10

MARK: 6 am and then it's over.

KIM: Over. (*Lights fade as Kim and Mark embrace.*)

Susan Yankowitz

NIGHT SKY

Perhaps someone with expert knowledge of the human brain will understand my illness, discover what a brain injury does to a man's mind, memory and body. . . . I know there is a great deal of talk now about the cosmos and outer space and that our earth is just a minute particle of this infinite universe. But actually, people rarely think about this; the most they can imagine are flights to the nearest planets revolving around the sun. As for the flight of a bullet, or a shell, or bomb fragment that rips open a man's skull, splitting and burning the tissues of his brain, crippling his memory, sight, hearing, awareness—these days people don't find anything extraordinary in that . . .

—L. Zazestsy, wounded in the head
during the battle of Smolensk, 1943.

Author's Introduction

As a writer, I am almost always drawn to the drama of people in extreme situations, people pushed by fate, or accident, or character to the edge of some abyss, either personal or political. When Joseph Chaikin asked me to write a play about his own extreme condition, aphasia, or speechlessness, it coincided with a nightmare of my own and one, which I believe I share with many others.

Six years ago, during open heart surgery to replace a defective valve, Joe suffered a massive stroke that rendered him aphasic. At the beginning he was able only to speak gibberish and a few isolated words. He couldn't read or write. His memory for names, places, and numbers was impaired; abstract thought, which had always been an essential element in his intellectual life, eluded him. During a long and arduous recovery, he began to assemble a vocabulary and finally, an original means of expression—a language without conventional syntax, often missing connective words, like prepositions, but nonetheless comprehensible, even poetic—if one listens.

Night Sky is about listening and language, about inner and outer space, about a medical condition, a family's ordeal, an individual triumph. But most of all, it is about communication. It is inspired by Joe and written for him with infinite love and respect.

Night Sky was produced by the Women's Project & Productions under the directorship of Julia Miles at the Judith Anderson Theatre, New York City, from May 14 to June 9, 1991. It was directed by Joseph Chaikin with the following cast:

DANIEL	Edward Baran
BILL	Tom Cayler
ANNA	Joan MacIntosh
SPEECH THERAPIST AND OTHERS	Aleta Mitchell
APHASIC PATIENT AND OTHERS	Paul Zimet
JENNIFER	Lizabeth Zindel

Set design by George Xenos
Lighting design by Beverly Emmons
Costume design by Mary Brecht
Sound design by Mark Bennett
Stage management by Ruth Kreshka
Casting by Susan Haskins

Author's Acknowledgments
I wish to express my gratitude for the invaluable support and collaboration of the many organizations and individuals who helped in the development of this piece. A grant from TCG provided the means for a stimulating workshop in A.C.T.'s Plays-in-Process series. A Playwrights' Center McKnight fellowship enabled a fruitful collaboration with The Illusion Theatre in Minneapolis, MN, under the sensitive direction of Martha Boesing. New Dramatists supplied much-needed space for early explorations and a reading. Dr. Martha Sarno at The Rusk Institute assisted with medical information. William Alschuler was a bountiful resource in the area of astronomy. Of the others, too numerous to mention, whose talents and insights contributed to the work's creation, I especially would like to thank Joyce Aaron, Noreen Barnes, Lillian Butler, Shami Chaikin, Bill Coco, Ed Gueble, Tori Haring-Smith, Irene Kling, and the people at San Francisco State University.

THE SET

Encompassing both naturalistic and abstract elements, the set for *Night Sky* needs to be imaginatively reconceived for each individual theatrical space. The play takes place, sometimes simultaneously, in various rooms of a middle-class home, on the street, in a classroom, a hospital, a school gymnasium, and conference hall. These should be suggested and defined by lighting and well-chosen objects rather than by any attempt at verisimilitude. Fluidity of movement from scene to scene is far more important than furniture. Platforms and levels can add to the desired flexibility.

THE COSTUMES

Because several actors play many roles and because characters move quickly from one scene to another, costumes also need to be adaptable. Each performer should have a basic outfit to which accessories—somewhat stylized, in keeping with the tone of the play—can be added as needed. The play should always feel contemporary.

CAST OF CHARACTERS

ANNA, an astronomer, 40
DANIEL, a baritone, 35
JENNIFER, Anna's daughter, 14
BILL, an astronomer, 30–50
SPEECH THERAPIST and other female roles
APHASIC PATIENT and other male roles

SCENE ONE

Everywhere, encompassing and unifying the audience and perfor-
mance area, is the vivid, star-filled night sky. Anna too stands within
it, on a podium, completing a lecture to her class.

ANNA: . . . But do you realize that what we see represents only
ten percent—possibly only one percent—of what exists? Most of
the universe is hidden, invisible to us still, a mysterious absence.
We know very little. Even the most basic insights elude us. How
many stars are there, and how do we know there aren't more?
Why do the planets spin, and if they didn't spin, where would they
go? Are we one of many universes, or is there only this one universe? If a black hole is truly black, and if it really is a hole, how can
we be sure it's there? And within all that dark matter, somewhere,
does life exist? *(Pause.)* Please consider these questions for your
next class. Oh, that reminds me: the word "consider" means
literally "with the stars." Study the language. You probably don't
know that people in the seventeenth century died in droves from
a disease called "planet." Or that when you miss a class because
you have the flu —influenza—your illness derives from the Italian
for "astral influence." And if your friend calls you a "schlemazel"
for spilling ink on your exam, are you aware that's Yiddish for
someone born under an unlucky star? Then there's a word your
generation uses every day—"disaster!"—and what does it actually
mean? Bad star! *(Steps down from the podium.)* Dismissed! *(The stars*
go out; the stage goes black. Lights up in Anna's living room. Daniel,
Anna's man, is playing solitaire. Jennifer, Anna's teen-aged daughter,
is eating candy and reading an Archie comic book.)
ANNA: *(entering; to Jennifer.)* That's dessert!
JENNIFER: I had a sandwich.
ANNA: And what about me?
JENNIFER: Chill out, ma. There's plenty of peanut butter left.
ANNA: Well. Thanks very much. *(Pauses near Daniel, who con-*
tinues playing cards.) No word of greeting?

DANIEL: Hi.

ANNA: No dinner?

DANIEL: You're late.

ANNA: You mean a working woman doesn't deserve to eat? (*Daniel makes a sheepish gesture.*) On my late days you could cook a little something . . .

DANIEL: You don't like scrambled eggs.

ANNA: You could read a recipe. . . . ! What did you do all day? (*Daniel looks at her directly for the first time.*) Ohhh. . . . City Opera. (*Moving close to him.*) You didn't get the role?

DANIEL: No.

ANNA: Weren't you in good voice?

DANIEL: I was in divine voice! (*Slumps on sofa.*) I thought so, anyway.

JENNIFER: Mom, who would you rather be, Betty or Veronica?

ANNA: I'd rather be me.

JENNIFER: You would? You'd rather be you than really nice *or* really rich? God, mom, you're weird!

ANNA: Don't you have homework?

JENNIFER: Tons.

ANNA: Hop to it. (*Jennifer hops, exits; to Daniel.*) Are you sure they didn't like you?

DANIEL: I must be the oldest promising baritone in the business . . . I can't take it.

ANNA: Maybe it's the way you present yourself. Why don't you take some acting lessons? When you go into an audition you have to radiate confidence . . .

DANIEL: Like you.

ANNA: I'm not trying to put you down.

DANIEL: You don't have to. I'm already down. You're kicking me.

ANNA: If I don't kick you, you'll stay down. (*As he picks up the cards, shuffles, starts to deal again.*) Listen, honey. You're giving a recital this weekend. People are coming—maybe important people. This could be your big chance.

DANIEL: You know, when you're not being a tyrant, you're a goddam optimist!

In her room, Jennifer begins to practice her French conjugations, continuing under the scene.

JENNIFER: Je parlerai. Tu parleras. Il/elle/on parlera.
Nous parlerons. Vous parlerez. Ils/elles parleront.
Je mangerai. Tu mangeras. Il/elle/on mangera.
Nous mangerons. Vous mangerez. Ils/elles mangeront.
Je comprenerai. ETC.

ANNA: But it's true. You never know which concert will be the crucial one. You have to sing your heart out every time. You have to be superb!

DANIEL: Maybe I should give up.

ANNA: Maybe you should just rehearse.

DANIEL: You're right. I will. Later. (*Starts playing again.*)

ANNA: Later? Later? Oh god, Daniel, I don't know what to say to you . . . !

DANIEL: Don't say anything.

ANNA: And watch you play cards? Waste yourself? I can't! (*She sweeps his cards off the table.*) I love you, idiot! Don't shut me out!

DANIEL: I knew this would happen. I saw the whole scene flash before me on my way home. (*Gets up; brings her a wrapped present.*) I picked up my apology in advance.

ANNA: I'm speechless.

DANIEL: Well, that's a new one! (*Nuzzles her as she opens the gift; a moment of intimate feeling.*) Sorry about dinner. Sorry about my gloom and doom. I do adore you, you know.

ANNA: (*Takes out a string of colorful beads.*) Oh Daniel. They're beautiful. (*She puts them on.*) I'll wear them to your concert.

DANIEL: I'll sing like an angel. My voice will be celestial. For you. For us.

ANNA: It can be. It will be. I know it.

DANIEL: Thank you, darling. (*Kisses her.*) And so ... (*Sings.*)

ANNA: Just toss me an apple. (*He does, then exits to vocalize and rehearse his aria. Anna eats the apple and starts working on her lessons. Jennifer continues her conjugations. It's noisy and chaotic. The telephone rings.*) Hello? Oh Bill. No, I can't talk now. I'm over my head. Out of my head, if you ask Daniel. Yes, you're teaching the next class. Basic, basic, sub-basic. Get down, as they say—meaning, I guess, down to their level. They don't know anything. Some of them thought they were registering for *astrology!* Pull out all your tricks. I'll see you in the observatory on Friday night. And don't forget Daniel's concert Saturday. We've got to fill the hall. Tell everyone in the department, will you? Thanks. 'Bye. (*Anna hangs up just as Jennifer runs in.*)

JENNIFER: Au secours, maman! Francais. Examen. Demain. Demain est la futur. Examen dans la tensê futur. Je suis perdu.

ANNA: Pardon?

JENNIFER: The future, mom, dig? Like, I don't know it.

ANNA: Well, who does?

JENNIFER: In French, mom! I've got an exam tomorrow, you know. In the future tense. You've gotta help me!

ANNA: Now? Why do you always wait till the last minute? I've got a paper to finish, classes to prepare ... !

JENNIFER: Well, why do *you* always wait till the last minute!

ANNA: Watch your tongue, young lady.

JENNIFER: Come on, ma, I'm gonna fail! I am really stressed out!

ANNA: Stress is a part of life. Just keep at it; you'll do fine. Go on. Drill yourself. But quietly, please.

JENNIFER: I will be. Je serai. You will be. Tu seras. He will be, she will be, one will be: il/elle/on. ... sera? Is that it? Sera? No, that's Italian. Or is it Spanish? "Che sera, sera, whatever will be will be. ..." Do you know that song, ma? (*Anna nods.*) So do you think it *is* sera? The same in Spanish and Italian and French? It could be, couldn't it?

ANNA: See if Daniel can help you.

JENNIFER: He doesn't know French.

ANNA: Yes, he does. He knows whole operas in French.

JENNIFER: He knows the words but he doesn't know what they mean.

ANNA: That's ridiculous. He couldn't sing them if he didn't know the meaning.

JENNIFER: He's got a translation that gives him the gist; but word for word, like, he doesn't have a clue. Anyway, he doesn't have time either.

ANNA: Why don't you just use your textbook?

JENNIFER: I forgot it.

ANNA: What?!

JENNIFER: Yeah, I know, like, I'm brain-dead. I left it at school . . .

ANNA: Then call one of your friends. (*Daniel's voice is becoming very loud.*) Daniel, can you tone it down a little?

JENNIFER: You don't care if I fail, do you?

ANNA: Haven't you heard of the Copernican Revolution, young lady? For your information, the earth does not revolve around you.

JENNIFER: Right. It revolves around *you!* (*Exits, upset.*)

Anna settles back to work. Daniel's voice sings out, more and more powerfully. She tries to blot it out but can't.

ANNA: Daniel, you're too loud! (*He keeps singing.*) Daniel, I can't hear myself think! (*He keeps singing; she flings down her pen, moves closer to his space, yells.*) Daniel, I am going out of my mind!

DANIEL: (*Entering.*) Were you calling me?

ANNA: You're too loud.

DANIEL: What do you expect me to do? Mouth the words?

ANNA: Are you going to keep it up all night?

DANIEL: First you complain that I don't rehearse. Then you complain that I do. Give me a break, Anna.

ANNA: You sound like Jenny.

DANIEL: Jenny's crying in her room.

ANNA: She's impossible.

DANIEL: She's your daughter. Can't you help her out?

ANNA: And who's going to help me out? Don't I exist? That paper I'm writing—the one I want to read at the conference—I gave you a draft two weeks ago! You still haven't read it!

DANIEL: I tried. I did. What can I say? It's . . . Greek to me.

Jennifer storms into the room and dials the phone.

ANNA: But you understand your own languages, don't you? That Pascal or Turbo you use when you free-lance. Your roulades and tussateras!

DANIEL: Tessaturas! And do you understand them? No. Have you tried? No. Do you have any interest? No.

JENNIFER: Nina? Like, I really messed up! I left my French book in school and my conjugations suck!

DANIEL: You think my work is shit.

ANNA: No. Just your vocabulary.

JENNIFER: . . . You will. Great, Nina. Thanks.

DANIEL: You turn everything around.

ANNA: Not your career.

DANIEL: You know, Anna, you're a bitch.

ANNA: You know, Daniel, you're a loser. (*Dead silence.*)

JENNIFER: J'aimerais. Tu aimeras. Il/elle/on—oh no, I've lost it. What is it? Aimera? I know; I'm just so spaced out . . .

ANNA: I'm sorry. (*No response from him.*) I said I'm sorry. (*Again.*) You don't realize how much I have on my mind.

DANIEL: Your mind, your mind! That's all you think about!

ANNA: Is that so? The greatest philosophers have brooded endlessly on whether it's possible for a mind to think about itself and—(*Snaps her fingers.*)—bingo! *you* solve the conundrum of centuries.

DANIEL: This is your favorite activity, isn't it? Brainstorming with yourself.

ANNA: What choice do I have? There's no other brain here to storm with.

DANIEL: You drive me up the wall! You always need to have the last word!

JENNIFER: (*Continuing on the phone.*) Je parlerai. I will speak. Je mangerai. I will eat. J'irai. I will go. J'aurai. I will have. (*Etc.*)

ANNA: I don't even have the first word! Look at this! I haven't written a thing! It's chaos in here. Physicists say that chaos is a higher form of order—but they haven't visited our house!

DANIEL: (*Exploding.*) And they won't! Keep them out of my life! I am going to rehearse at the top of my voice so that I can be superb! And you, hot shot, you can take your physicists and your stars and your brainstorms and go to hell! (*Slams out of the room.*)

ANNA: All right, I'm going! (*Slams out of the house and lights go out.*)

In the darkness:

JENNIFER: Je ferai. I will do. Je verrai. I will see. Je lirai. I will read. Je dirai. I will say. (*Etc.*)

She continues her conjugations; Daniel practices his aria. Suddenly, two bright headlights pierce the darkness. There is the screech of brakes and the thud of a body; all the sounds are amplified and jumbled together, as Anna is hit by a car. In the light shed by the headlights, Anna's beads, the string broken on impact, roll and scatter everywhere, a visual replica of what is happening to her speech. Over the rolling beads, soon overpowering and obliterating both the aria and the French drill, the doctor's words are heard.

DOCTOR: (*Into a dictaphone.*) . . . severe insult to left hemisphere of brain between primary auditory cortex and angular gyrus . . .

Dimly visible in the background, an Aphasic Patient sits in a wheelchair, picking up isolated phrases of the Doctor's report—a speech anomaly called echolalia—and functioning throughout the play as a kind of Greek chorus.

APHASIC PATIENT: Anger guy yes.

DOCTOR: (*Picking up the scattered beads and depositing them in a lab jar.*) . . . Profound injury to the language center and all language functions, including:

APHASIC PATIENT: Lewwwwd.

DOCTOR: ... anomia, alexia, agraphia, impaired syntax and verbal retention span, reduction of functional vocabulary ...

APHASIC PATIENT: Fuckyouvery.

DOCTOR: ... disturbances in decoding, manipulation and encoding of symbols ...

APHASIC PATIENT: Sin balls.

DOCTOR: ... damaged comprehension of verbal information, especially abstractions and words pertaining to time and positions in space ...

APHASIC PATIENT: (*With longing.*) Spaaaaaaaaaace ...

DOCTOR: (*Putting last bead in jar and screwing on lid.*) ... memory loss, disorientation, and multiple deficits of perception common to aphasia ...

APHASIC PATIENT: Aphasia, aphasia, aphasia. (*Daniel and Jennifer, holding bouquets, enter.*)

DANIEL: Aphasia?

DOCTOR: From the Greek, meaning "without a language," or "speechlessness" ...

APHASIC PATIENT: ... lessness. ...

In the glare of headlights, a hospital bed is carried on. Anna, her head bandaged, is sitting up against the pillows. Jennifer walks towards her.

JENNIFER: Hi, mom. (*Anna doesn't quite recognize her; stares.*) Hi, mom. (*Anna stares. Jennifer gives her the flowers—Asters, her favorite, named for stars. Anna looks at them and at Jennifer.*)

ANNA: Gee kidge syzzzz dibble dibble dibble ih.

JENNIFER: Mom?

DANIEL: Anna?

Anna doesn't know what is expected of her. She looks at the flowers— and begins to eat them. Jennifer and Daniel stare at her, shocked. At the same time: In another area of the stage, in the classroom, lights up on Bill, Anna's colleague, blowing up a balloon until it bursts: from inside, glittering paper stars spew out everywhere.

BILL: That's how it happened. Ten or twenty billion years ago, the universe suddenly exploded in the Big Bang, the greatest mystery we know, an incredible cosmic accident—and what had once been pure energy split into millions of bits and pieces spinning through space—an old order destroyed and everything beginning again, utterly strange and new. . . .

BLACKOUT

SCENE TWO

A series of vignettes, defined by lighting, each like an x-ray.

The Third Day

In the hospital: Anna, in bed, is trying out her voice.

ANNA: Gridge sac dibble foojimigu—(*As if she hears herself.*) Huh? (*Tries again.*) Ake dis looloo dibble—(*Hearing herself.*) Huh? Huh!? (*Again.*) I ghimma babba inbane—(*Desperate.*) Huh?! Huhh?! Huhhhhhhh??!!!

The Fourth Day

Daniel enters for his first visit. Whatever he does, she imitates. He smiles; she smiles in return. He takes her hand; she takes his hand. He pats her cheek; she pats his cheek.

DANIEL: How are you, sweetheart?
ANNA: I . . . I . . . I . . . glue.
DANIEL: I . . . glue?
ANNA: I . . . I glue . . . ue.
DANIEL: I glue. (*He starts to laugh; she starts to laugh.*) I glue you, too.

They laugh together. The laughter turns to tears. Only after they have been crying separately do they reach for each other.

The Sixth Day

Anna is slowly dangling her legs off the bed. The Aphasic Patient is seated in his wheelchair outside her room, practicing a sentence.

APHASIC PATIENT: Ame . . . isBoo
My . . . name . . . isBooBoooooce
Brame . . . BooBoor . . . (*Etc.*)

Anna slides off the bed. She doesn't yet realize how damaged her right side is. She takes a step or two and falls—right into the lap of the Aphasic Patient in his chair.

APHASIC PATIENT: Boo—Bruce!

The Eighth Day

In the hospital: Anna is working with the Physical Therapist, getting therapy for her weakened right arm and leg. At home: Jennifer is rehearsing for her first private visit with her mother; Daniel is playing Anna.

JENNIFER: So. Hi, mom.
DANIEL: (*Smiles, waves.*)
JENNIFER: How ya feeling?
DANIEL: (*Expression becomes doleful.*)
JENNIFER: Not so hot, huh?
DANIEL: (*Utters a few garbled syllables.*)
JENNIFER: She can say more than that! She can say a few words. You told me she could.
DANIEL: Very few. . . . Hi.
JENNIFER: Hi. . . Oh god, I can't do it! I don't know what to say!
DANIEL: Talk about yourself. What's going on. Be natural.
JENNIFER: Natural! Get real!
DANIEL: I hate to say it, Jen, but this *is* real. She needs you, honey. Come on. Try.
JENNIFER: Okay. . . . Hi, mom. . . . Guess what? Big news! We're having a dance at school. Finally! Like, it's for Valentine's Day, you know, boys—

DANIEL: Slow down. The doctor said she can't absorb the words if we talk fast.

JENNIFER: (*More slowly.*)—Valentine's Day, boys and girls, music. They're even gettin' a band. It's gonna be awesome. Don't worry, there'll be chaperones, some teachers, a few mothers . . . What do you think?

DANIEL: . . . Mo-ther.

JENNIFER: Pardon?

DANIEL: . . . Mo-ther. Me.

JENNIFER: You don't know what she'd say. You're just making it up.

DANIEL: Right. I'm using my imagination. All I know is, you've got to listen to her. Really listen.

JENNIFER: Oh yeah, right. Since when are you an expert on listening?

DANIEL: Since this week. Your turn. Communicate!

JENNIFER: All right, all right. God, this is worse than French! . . . Mother. You said mother. . . . I know you're my mother, mom. Like, what about it?

DANIEL: . . . Dance. Mo-ther.

JENNIFER: You want to come to the dance? (*Daniel nods, smiles.*) Like, be a chaperone, you mean? (*Daniel nods again. Jennifer goes into a panic.*)

JENNIFER: She can't do that. She can't. It'd be gross. Everyone'll think she's a retard. She can't come to the dance. I'd die. (*Daniel's face gets tearful.*) You're not going to cry . . . ?! Daniel, why are you doing this? You're supposed to be helping me!

DANIEL: I am helping. I'm your mom now. You just told me you're ashamed of me, that you don't want me at your dance. I get the picture. Maybe I can't talk, but I can feel.

JENNIFER: This is really freaking me out! What am I going to do if she cries?

DANIEL: What does she do when you cry?

JENNIFER: (*Considers; then puts an arm around Daniel.*) Mom, don't cry. I'm sorry. Sure, you can be a chaperone if you want. Don't worry, mom. I love you.

In the hospital: Anna succeeds in lifting her right arm over her head.

The Tenth Day

The Speech Therapist is holding up a blackboard with the word "ANNA" written on it.

SPEECH THERAPIST: This is your name. Can you tell me what it is? (*Anna can't find it.*) Your name is . . . (*Anna can't find it.*) Your name is Aaaaa . . .
ANNA: Aaaaaa . . .
SPEECH THERAPIST: (*Pointing to the letters.*) Aaa . . . nnaaa . . .
ANNA: Naaaa . . .

The Therapist continues trying to get Anna to pronounce her name. Anna can only manage one syllable. At the same time: Bill is on the telephone with Daniel.

BILL: She can't speak clearly? Can't understand what's said to her? Can't read or write? Then what goes on inside her head?
DANIEL: I don't know.
BILL: Well, can she think?
DANIEL: Can a person think without words? I don't know, Bill. Why don't you go see her?
BILL: Well, you, you think in music, don't you? Maybe she's thinking in pictures, in star charts . . .
DANIEL: You're the one to ask her that.
BILL: Will she be able to teach again?
DANIEL: I don't know.
BILL: Is she the same person? I mean, do you think she's different on the outside but the same inside? Or different on the outside *and* the inside? Does she feel different to herself?
DANIEL: I told you, Bill, I don't know!!!

By this time, the Speech Therapist is erasing Anna's name from the blackboard.

The Twelth Day

Jennifer is sitting with her mother.

JENNIFER: . . . And that French test, mom? The one I thought I'd fail? I got an 87. An 87! (*Anna plants a kiss on her daughter's head.*)

ANNA: Elevator.

The Fourteenth Day

The sounds of an aria fill the air. Daniel is visiting, and has put on a tape of his concert.

DANIEL: The concert was great. I did three encores. You would have been proud of me. Just listen. (*Anna does. Then she starts humming along with the melody—perfectly in tune. He is elated, and runs to get the doctor.*)

DANIEL: Doctor. Listen. She's singing along with me. It's the aria I was rehearsing before the accident.

DOCTOR: The musical area of the brain is located in the right hemisphere. It's the left part that's damaged.

DANIEL: But she can remember . . . !

DOCTOR: I don't want you to have false hopes.

DANIEL: You mean she could be like this forever?

DOCTOR: Oh no. She'll change. . . . Just keep in mind that there are many ways of communicating. (*The doctor exits. Daniel assimilates the information, then adds his voice to the tape recorder's. He sings and sings at the top of his voice, passionately.*)

The Twentieth Day

Anna is playing chess with the Aphasic Patient and trying to explain the accident.

ANNA: (*Struggling for each word.*) Head fights. Car simin arrow me. Daarbyss. Anna cashimpa!

APHASIC PATIENT: (*Fluently.*) Oh, so that, why not, I know just how you want to everything and then, well, okay, it's like that and I stroke, rain mixed up all the time, sleeping English, and then go to possible, naturally, very good. (*They stare at each other, each with a strained false smile. Then the Aphasic Patient moves a piece.*) Heck!

The Twenty-Eighth Day

In the hospital: Anna is struggling to unwrap a gift box. In the classroom: Bill is standing beside a plain locked box. Almost imperceptibly, the box seems to move, as if something is inside it.

BILL: Keep your eyes on this box. Watch carefully. Now. Now. Are your eyes sharp? Did you see it move? Is something inside it? How can you know? You, my friends, are trapped in the famous paradox of Schrödinger's cat! Yes, I confess, a cat was placed in here twenty minutes ago. Aha! Now you think you might have heard a mew, or the sound of claws scratching against wood . . . But did you? Or is it in your imagination? Think hard now: we're talking life, we're talking death. Because inside this enigmatical box is a device which can release a noxious gas, killing the cat instantly. And what triggers the device? A random event, the spontaneous decay of an atom. Has the event occurred? Has the gas been released? Is the cat alive now, or dead? (*Pause.*) You can't say, can you? Because as long as we don't open the box, there's no way to know for sure, and the animal is neither alive *nor* dead, but exists in a third realm, on a different plane altogether, in a limbo of pure possibility that contains *both* extremes simultaneously: life and death, life and death, commingled. (*Pause.*) Now . . . should we open it? Are you curious? (*He starts to unlock the box, then stops.*) But we still wouldn't be sure, would we? You know what curiosity does to a cat.

Anna takes the gift out of the box. It is a large fluffy stuffed animal: a cat.

The Fortieth Day

Anna is sitting on a straight-backed chair, Opposite her, the Speech Therapist sits on another chair. Throughout, Anna struggles for even

*the simplest syllable. Elsewhere on the stage is the Aphasic Patient
who also responds to the questions but his language is limited to the
following expressions:*

"Yes yes yes yes yes"

"Help"

"Thassit"

"Wonderful"

"Shit!"

"Omigod!"

"No way"

*As before, this patient provides a kind of Greek chorus, another
variant of the effort to communicate. The responses should be worked
out in a precise, almost musical, counterpoint to the central scene.*

SPEECH THERAPIST: . . . Again, what is your name?

ANNA: Aaaaa—

SPEECH THERAPIST: Yes, yes. Aaaaaa—

ANNA: Aaa—starmer.

SPEECH THERAPIST: You're an astronomer, yes, but that's not
your name. Your name also begins with A. A for Aaaa—Aaaa—

ANNA: Aaaa—Aaaaa—na!

SPEECH THERAPIST: Anna! Right! That's wonderful. Now.
Answer these questions with yes or no. Listen carefully. Do children
cry?

ANNA: . . . No. Yes. Yes yes.

SPEECH THERAPIST: Do cats like milk?

ANNA: . . . Milk . . . yesmilk.

SPEECH THERAPIST: Excellent. Do dogs bark?

ANNA: Yes. No. Yes. Yes!

SPEECH THERAPIST: Good! Are you a dog?

ANNA: . . . No.

SPEECH THERAPIST: Right. Are you a man? (*Anna pauses;
thinks.*) Are you a man?

ANNA: . . . No.

SPEECH THERAPIST: Good. Are you a woman?

ANNA: . . . . Woman.

SPEECH THERAPIST: Are you a woman?

ANNA: . . . No. Yes. Yes. Woman.

SPEECH THERAPIST: And do you have any children?

ANNA: Woman. My. Wom . . . baby.

SPEECH THERAPIST: Your daughter?

ANNA: Yes!

SPEECH THERAPIST: What is her name? (*Anna can't find it.*) Her name is Jenn—, Jenn—

ANNA: Jenn . . . Jenn-fer.

SPEECH THERAPIST: Wonderful! Let's go on. Where do you live? (*Anna can't find it.*) Where do you live? (*Anna can't find it.*) Do you live in New York?

ANNA: Yes!

SPEECH THERAPIST: Good. Again. Where do you live?

ANNA: New . . . newapple.

SPEECH THERAPIST: You mean the Big Apple?

ANNA: Yes, yes, bignewYorple.

SPEECH THERAPIST: Right. The Big Apple, New York. Can you tell me what country that's in? (*Anna strains for word, can't find it; laughs.*) Where is New York?

ANNA: . . . Sss . . . sssss. . . . tttt. . . . .

SPEECH THERAPIST: States?

ANNA: . . . Sssstar.

SPEECH THERAPIST: We live among the stars. Can't deny that. Very good, Anna. We'll do more work tomorrow. (*Rises to leave. Anna restrains her.*)

ANNA: Wait. Want—want—

SPEECH THERAPIST: What is it? What do you want?

ANNA: Want—Want—elbow! oboe! oh!

SPEECH THERAPIST: Be patient. You've only been in the hospital six weeks. Just try to find the word. What do you want?

ANNA: (*Goes to window.*) Want—Want—Want—toe. Lo— sco. No. Want yellow! no! no!—(*She continues trying to complete the sentence using the words "telpho", "elphote", "soap", etc. while the Speech Therapist moves into an anteroom and speaks to Jennifer and Daniel.*)

SPEECH THERAPIST: She knows what she wants to say but she can't get it out. Maybe she wants a sandwich, or needs to go to the bathroom, or maybe she wants to hear a piece of music—but she's lost the words, they're scattered over the terrain of her mind, and without cues, she can't retrieve the ones she needs. Imagine a violent wind tearing all your clothing from your closets and sending them flying to the four corners of the world; you need your blue socks: where would you begin to look for them? Everything's whirling around, tangled up, in chaos. She struggles; she finds one word here, another there, but then she can't string them together to express herself. What's happened to her is earth shattering. It's more than a problem with communication. Her entire inner world has come apart . . .

ANNA: Want . . . sco! sco! tesco!

JENNIFER: (*Turns to Therapist.*) She wants her telescope!

ANNA: Jenn-fer.

BLACKOUT

SCENE THREE

Lights up on Bill addressing his class, holding a glass of milk in one hand and an empty glass in the other.

BILL: Is she going to be "all there?" I don't know. But during a solar eclipse, the sun is still there, isn't it? And when a star collapses in on itself, isn't that star still there? We have to make the connections; it's all hooked up, the macrocosm and the micro-cosm, the inter-stellar dust and the dust that our bodies will become, the dark matter of the universe and the dark matter of the brain, the black hole in the cosmos and the black hole into which we will be thrown at the end. And leading our minds backward and forward from earth to heaven and from heaven to earth, we have been given a river, a bridge, the via lactea—billions of stars in a luminous galaxy—(*He pours milk back and forth from glass to glass*)—galaxy from 'galactos,' meaning—(*He pours it into his mouth*)—milk.

As lights go down there, two candles are lit in Anna's home. Daniel has almost finished setting the table, and is placing a bottle of champagne in an ice bucket. Anna is watching admiringly. Throughout, Anna searches for words but is better able to communicate. She is still not well coordinated—but both try very hard to keep the atmosphere 'normal'.

ANNA: You everything?

DANIEL: I alone.

ANNA: Cook, too?

DANIEL: You could say that.

ANNA: Never cook after . . . no no no no. . . . before!

DANIEL: Never had to.

ANNA: Very nice. Very very nice.

DANIEL: Wait till you taste it.

ANNA: Exper.

DANIEL: No, I'm not an expert.

ANNA: You cook. Exper. Exper-man.

DANIEL: Expert man.

ANNA: (*Laughs; tries again.*) Exper. Sci.

DANIEL: Sigh . . . You're relieved I'm so competent. . . . ? No, wait. I get it, I get it! A scientific experiment! Right?

ANNA: Confabulations!

DANIEL: Confabulations to you too. We'll be fine, hon. I know it. Nothing's changed.

ANNA: Big change. Like earthcake! Allfalldown. Very disaster. Break. Ending you me.

DANIEL: You think we're going to break up?

ANNA: No bedding ring. Easy talkout—walk out. Maybe soon.

DANIEL: Why? There's no law that says I have to stay with you.

ANNA: Yes law, yes. Law pretty—pity.

DANIEL: No. Love.

ANNA: . . . True?

DANIEL: True glue. (*She grabs for him, starts kissing wildly, wanting to express herself physically, without the burden of words. But she's forgotten exactly what to do. She's all over him, like a child, polymorphous perverse. He responds at first, then gets confused by what's happening, then somewhat frightened. Gently he extricates himself.*)

DANIEL: Wait, darling. Wait. Wait.

ANNA: Wait?

DANIEL: We have champagne. (*Picks up bottle.*)

ANNA: No pain. You bottle, me bottle . . .

DANIEL: Our bottle, right. Here . . . (*Opens it with a pop.*)

ANNA: No! No pink. Better now fex.(*The champagne fizzes over. She holds up her glass to catch it; points to the flowing liquid.*) Look. You. (*Shakes her glass.*) Me. (*He looks blank.*) Youme! Splash fizzlove. Botty. Fex.

DANIEL: Ohhhh. Fex!

ANNA: (*She nods; a big smile.*) Now!

DANIEL: I may have forgotten how.

ANNA: I perfect memory that!

DANIEL: (*Raising his glass in a toast.*) Here's to memory then! And to the future! And to us—now. (*They clink glasses: she is too forceful, and the glass breaks.*)

ANNA: (*Upset.*) Stupid. Cum . . . cum . . . cumsy.

DANIEL: (*Wiping the spill.*) Don't worry. It's nothing.

ANNA: Me. Me nothing.

DANIEL: Don't be silly.

ANNA: (*More upset.*) Meglass. Break! Bittypieces. You big strong pickup pickup. No good.

DANIEL: (*Sharply.*) Forget it, will you, Anna?

ANNA: Forget. Yes. Forget everystar. Forget . . . words . . . shames—names and shine in sty—spy—sky! Skyyyy!

DANIEL: The Doctor said it takes time.

ANNA: Take shovel! Fill holesin head. Stu-pid. Dummy. Brain brain brain eclipse!

DANIEL: Please, please Anna! You're killing yourself.

ANNA: Good. Die.

DANIEL: Well that *is* stupid! A glass breaks and you want to die! Where's your will power?

ANNA: Will!? Youpower. You! You talk meaning clear. I am aphasia! Anna aphasia!

DANIEL: But it was my fault! I screamed you into that car! It's all because of me!

ANNA: No! Me anger, locked in self, go run! Me!

DANIEL: What can I do? What? I've been reading everything I can, trying to get inside your head—

ANNA: Head—dead!

DANIEL: No. No! Your head is not dead! It's just the words! Understand? The words are lost inside! You have to find them again . . .

ANNA: When?? WHEN???!! (*She breaks down.*)

DANIEL: I'll do anything. Tell me. What do you want?

ANNA: Want—want working.

DANIEL: You want to go back to teaching?

ANNA: No possible now teaching ass—(*Laughs through her tears.*)—teach class. Now want papeh-con. Con—Con—

DANIEL: You want to be at my next concert?

ANNA: Yes. No. Con—con . . . Want con-fiss—

DANIEL: You want confidence?

ANNA: Paper. . . . Tow-el.

DANIEL: Paper towel?

ANNA: (*Agitated, trying to explain.*) Paper. Eye towel, fly, fly confiss. (*Stops; starts again.*) Working con. Fly eye—fly con—

DANIEL: Take it easy, sweetheart.

ANNA: (*Sinks back in chair; tries again.*) Jenn-fer. 87. 87. Test.

DANIEL: French test.

ANNA: Yes!

DANIEL: (*Working it out.*) French test . . . Paris! That's it! The big conference in Paris!

ANNA: Yes!

DANIEL: Your paper! Paper towel! Eiffel Tower! You want to give your paper. Why not? You've got two months . . . You might be able to make it.

ANNA: Work! Will!

DANIEL: I'm with you darling. We'll fly together.

ANNA: Fly you . . . flyme, high—fex! Fly! Fly now! (*She blows out the candles. The stage goes dark as they move into each other's arms. In the blackness, Bill's voice is heard:*)

BILL: Lights out. Total darkness. Can you see me? No—but I'm here—I exist—like a black hole, a mass of matter so dense, so compressed, that no light can escape from it. But inside the hole, where your eyes, where even the most powerful telescope cannot penetrate, the light is shining, we believe, the light is simply trapped inside, unable to reveal itself . . .

SCENE FOUR

Spotlight on Anna. For this scene, she remains in the center while the other characters move in and out from the periphery. She often doesn't even have time to form a word before she's barraged by someone else. Underscoring the live assault of words is a running tape of recorded voices and sounds, which might include: A news report, rap or rock music, a paid political announcement, a football sports-cast, a commercial, etc. The scene should move very quickly and build to an hallucinatory intensity. Lines may be repeated and voices over-lapped to create the desired effect.

WAITER: Our specials today are butternut squash soup, penne with porcini and sun dried tomatoes, salmon smothered in leeks, and wild hen glazed with honey.

ANNA: . . . . Okay.

WAITER: Okay what? (*Anna stammers. He speaks louder and slower as if Anna were hard of hearing.*) Butternut squash soup? Yes?

ANNA: Butter . . . ?

WAITER: Soup! (*Demonstrates eating soup; goes on.*) Penne—pasta—with porcini—mushrooms. Salmon—fish, fish! river! (*Demonstrates fish swimming.*) Wild hen—like chicken! (*Demonstrates chicken, squawking. Anna tries to respond but a recorded voice on an answering machine cuts her off.*)

ANSWERING MACHINE: I'm sorry. I'm not at home to take your call but if you leave a message at the sound of the beep tone, we'll get back to you as soon as possible. Have a good day! BEEP.

ANNA:—name Anna. Call you—call me—house. Home—(*A woman friend interrupts.*)

FRIEND: (*As if to a child.*) I will come to your house, all right? We will go to the museum, all right? We will see the Cezanne show. Many many paintings. Beautiful paintings. That will be fun, won't it? We can see the paintings together. Then we can have tea in the garden. Won't that be nice? (*Jennifer calls to her.*)

JENNIFER: Yo, mom! Teacher conferences! You gotta sign up! (*The ticket seller claims her attention.*)

TICKET SELLER: Tickets available orchestra, mezzanine balcony January 26, 27, 30 evening or February 2 matinee and evening. Which date, please? Which section? What price? (*The telephone rings.*)

BILL: (*On the telephone.*) Just wanted to let you know that Herbert and Holden are forming a study group with the Missing Matter Astronomy Society to work on Neutrinos and WIMPs and they asked me to ask you if there's any chance you can—

ANNA: Can yes Wimp—(*The party guest interrupts.*)

GUEST AT PARTY: Hello. My name is Albert. Awful party, isn't it? Oh, don't say a word! I can see you agree with me. Bean sprouts! Tofu! I hate these California style eats, don't you?

ANNA: California, yes! Visit redwoods. Eu-nuch.

GUEST AT PARTY: I beg your pardon . . . !

ANNA: U—nique! U-nique! (*Daniel's voice comes at her.*)

DANIEL: I can't read this message! When is that callback?! (*Her Acquaintance interrupts.*)

ACQUAINTANCE: I know just what you're going through, really I do. I had strep throat and bronchitis last year—yes, a double dose!—and I couldn't get out a word, not a single word, it was hell, really, and it lasted for two full weeks! I thought I'd go crazy! So I know just how it feels, and if you ever want to talk to somebody about it . . . (*The Person Giving Directions cuts in.*)

PERSON GIVING DIRECTIONS: You go out, you walk three blocks north to the subway station and take the number 9 or 1 to 86th street, then walk uptown four blocks and turn left, walk two more blocks, and you'll be at number 301 W. 90th Street, right near Riverside Drive, right where you want to be, and take the elevator to the 3rd floor, make an immediate right, I mean a left, and that's the apartment. Now if you prefer the bus, you can get the number 11 uptown and change for the cross-town—(*Anna screams. She stands there, utterly overwhelmed and in despair. Elsewhere: lights up on the Speech Therapist.*)

SPEECH THERAPIST: She's like Sisyphus, rolling language up a hill. She has to search for every word and once she finds it she has to struggle to hold it in her mind so it won't run away from her and then she has to move it very carefully from her mind into her mouth, and from her mouth into sounds that can be understood. Can you imagine doing that every time you speak? Can you imagine what a strain every conversation is? Someone asks me what kind of work I do. "I'm a speech therapist," I'd want to say. What could be easier? But if I have to pronounce every word backwards—(*Painfully slowly.*)—Mi a hceeps tispareht. (*Directly to audience.*) You try it. Where were you born? City and state. Backwards. Go on. Try. (*Waits for the responses to come.*) It's not automatic any more. You have to work at every syllable. Try something even simpler: your name. Backwards. (*The audience will respond but in this instance Anna is there before them: her name is a palindrome.*)

ANNA: Anna! Anna! (*The Speech Therapist looks at her with pride.*)

BLACKOUT

INTERMISSION

SCENE FIVE

Lights up on Anna at home, fussing with the room and herself in preparation for Bill's first visit, setting out a teapot and cups, a cake, etc. Elsewhere: The Speech Therapist sits with a patient, helping him to read a children's story.

APHASIC PATIENT: (*Very slowly, with eccentric rhythm and accent.*) One day, when HennyPennywas scra-scra-scrap—

SPEECH THERAPIST:—scratching.

APHASIC PATIENT:—scratching among the leavesinthebarnyard, an ache—an ache!—acorn dropped from a tree and hit! hit! heron the head. (*Stops.*)

SPEECH THERAPIST: "Oh goodness gracious me!" . . . Go on.

APHASIC PATIENT: "Oh goodnessgracious me!"

SPEECH THERAPIST: Good. (*The doorbell rings. Anna freezes, then composes herself to open the door.*)

ANNA: Bill!

BILL: Hello, Anna. (*Uncomfortable.*) You look terrific.

ANNA: You thinktank—No. You thank—

BILL: Thank Heaven, that's what I say. Really, you look great. I don't know what I expected but I'm dumbfounded; you look just like yourself. I mean, not that you're not yourself but what happened was so awful, unspeakable, really—

ANNA: Teacup cake?

BILL: Teacup—? (*Stares; gets it.*) Sure, I'll have some tea. No cake. I'm watching my middle now, intensely watching, especially since I started this new study at the observatory. You know about it, don't you?

ANNA: Know nothing from—about you.

BILL: (*Oblivious; settling in.*) Well, I'll tell you then.

ANNA: Tell—tell—(*Blurting.*) Why no visit?

BILL: Why . . . no . . . visit? (*Shocked; stumbling over himself.*) Oh . . . Well. You know how it is, work work work, double duty in the classroom, seeing students, trying to write a paper, time disappearing and—

ANNA: Shit!

BILL: What?

ANNA: Shit bull—Bill.

BILL: I guess . . . that's . . . my name. (*She pours tea, while elsewhere:*)

APHASIC PATIENT: HennyPennycr—cried out: "The sky is failing."

SPEECH THERAPIST: Falling.

APHASIC PATIENT: Falling.

ANNA: Working.

BILL: Like a dog. That's what I was saying—

ANNA: I. I working.

My paper.

From before accident.

Read paper you, okay?

Daniel no understand theory.

You Bill fatpig.

BILL: Fat—?

ANNA: *Guinea* pig. (*Gets her manuscript. Elsewhere:*)

APHASIC PATIENT: "I must go and tell the King." So she buriedalong and buriedalong and buriedalong—

SPEECH THERAPIST: Hurried. Hurried along. That's what you're doing. Take your time.

ANNA: My paper tired—Title. (*Reading painfully, stumbling, with odd inflections and errors.*) "Comic—Cosmic Hide-And-Seek, Pen— Pin-The-Tail-OnTheDar-Dark ness, and Bind—Blind Man's Buff . . ."

BILL: I remember. You were working on this—before. The search for missing matter as a game. Go on.

ANNA: "—children's games, child's pray—play. But that is exactly our situation viz-a-visa the costume—cosmos. Confronted by the miseries—mysteries of infinite space, the blackness in which most of the universe is hiking—hiving—hiding, we—(*Gives up in despair.*) Awful! Too hard.

BILL: I didn't realize . . . God, Anna!

ANNA: (*Bitterly.*) No God.

Stars.

BILL: I could read the paper for you . . .

ANNA: No!

My paper.

BILL: But you can't stand in front of a thousand people and read like that . . .

ANNA: *You* want light.

My light.

BILL: No, I don't. I want you to find your own.

ANNA: (*Erupting.*) Own! Alone!

I missing!

You no find me.

Why? Why?

BILL: I'm sorry, Anna! I'm sorry! I don't know what else to say.

ANNA: *You* hiding! Terror—terrible no talking, nightmirror! And I . . . I sicktrouble, wanting work, conversion—conversation from friend astromy.

BILL: All right, I admit it, I wasn't there for you!

ANNA: Lost in stars!

BILL: I could kick myself now; I do kick myself. I just kept putting it off. But I thought of you every day. Believe me. And I missed you; we all missed you. The students are sick to death of me. Everyone wants you back. Gregory's not hiring anyone else till you make your plans and . . . what's his name? . . . wants to use your research in his paper on dwarf stars . . .

ANNA: Who?

BILL: What's his name . . . in our department . . . short . . . glasses . . . it's on the tip of my tongue . . . you know, had a hair transplant. . . .

ANNA: Nathan.

BILL: Right! Nathan. (*They regard each other. Elsewhere:*)

APHASIC PATIENT: So she hurried along and soon she met Co-ck-y Lo-ck-y. Cocky Locky?

SPEECH THERAPIST: Cocky Locky, that's what it says.

APHASIC PATIENT: Cock-yLock-y. (*Flings the book to the floor.*) "Warand Peace!" "King Leeeeear!" No Cocky Locky! No! No! (*Lights out on them.*)

ANNA: Now tell jerk—work youBill.

Observtry. Why?

BILL: I've been studying the cycle. Watching the stars go through it, birth to death. And wouldn't you know it? They don't age any more gracefully than we do! I'm writing my paper on middle-aged stars.

ANNA: You middleage crying—crisis.

BILL: That's it! The title of my paper: "Mid-star Crisis!" You're still fabulous.

ANNA: Still Billshit.

BILL: I love you, too. Can I stay a while? (*She nods. He relaxes, settling in.*) I've been discovering that middle-aged stars have problems exactly like middle-aged people. It's a fact. They experience more inner turbulence—indigestion, ulcers! Their energy slackens; they turn more slowly; they lose their youthful glow, get washed out, dull! Even their waist lines thicken. I'm the living analogy. Look. (*He starts to pull his sweater off, but his head gets stuck in an armhole just as Jennifer jives into the room, her Walkman playing music through her headphones, humming to it, oblivious. Extricating himself, Bill's hand lands on her chest. She screams, pushes him away.*)

JENNIFER: Hands off, dude! Don't play pig with me!

BILL: (*Getting his head through the neck.*) Sorry, Jen. I couldn't see. I didn't mean to—

JENNIFER: Sure, sure! That's what they all say! Accident on purpose!

BLACKOUT

SCENE SIX

Lights up on Jennifer and Anna, later that evening.

JENNIFER: Like, I'm standing on the subway and all of a sudden a hand just sort of drifts over my chest. Or a bunch of boys are messing around behind me and next thing I know my bra's being snapped. How do they even know I wear a bra? It's really gross. (*Anna nods.*) So what do I do? It makes me so mad but like, I don't want everybody to think I'm a nerd . . .

ANNA: Bill. Accident.

JENNIFER: I'm not talking about Bill. (*Anna nods.*) I'm afraid to go to the dance, even. I mean, what if some boy presses into me, you know, or puts his hand where he shouldn't? (*Anna picks up Jennifer's hand, slaps it; nods emphatically.*) Slap his hand? You don't do that in modern times, mom!

ANNA: "Body my body."

JENNIFER: I'm talking about *my* body, mom.

ANNA: Me, too.

JENNIFER: Well, I don't want to talk about you. I don't want to talk about your body. Or your brain. I mean, aphasia's not the only problem in the world, you know?

ANNA: Grow up. Hard.

JENNIFER: Like, did you have to go through all this yucky stuff, boys hitting on you and—

ANNA: No hit. Never hit!

JENNIFER: Chill out, mom! I mean hit like coming on, you know, flirting! God, I don't know what's worse, if they try to make out or they don't. Like, what if nobody asks me to dance? What if all my friends get asked and I'm left standing there all by myself, like a dummy?

ANNA: No dummy.

JENNIFER: Maybe I shouldn't even go. I don't have anything to wear anyway! No offense, mom, but my clothes look like they died last year; I gotta have a killer dress for that dance, something way rad.

ANNA: Cool dress.

JENNIFER: Hot, mom. I want to look hot!

ANNA: Hot. Boys touch hot.

JENNIFER: (*In despair.*) Oh god, mom, you don't understand anything!

ANNA: Understand yes.

Mixed up. Teen-age.

(*Picks up a hairbrush and starts to brush Jennifer's hair.*) Hair, straw.

JENNIFER: Right, beat me up a little more, I need it.

Elsewhere: Lights up on Bill, against the night sky, brightly colored stars surrounding him.

BILL: . . . and just like human beings, stars don't burn indefinitely. They travel through the life cycle the way we do. Their evolution is even color coded! Just look. These blue stars are the young ones, hot, throbbing with energy; the yellow ones are less intense, growing sedate, with a hint of flab around the middle; the reds are elderly already, sending out their tired rays of light; and these white dwarf stars are literally burned out, cooling into black dwarfs, like dying embers . . .

JENNIFER: (*As her hair gets pulled.*) Ow! You're killing me!

ANNA: No kill. Trans-form.

Get make-out—

No, no, make-up!

Put on cosmics!

I mean—cos-metics.

JENNIFER: Isn't your speech ever going to get better, mom?

ANNA: Maybe no. Forget talk now.

Big night come. Dancing fuck—

JENNIFER: Mother!

ANNA: Dancing fun! Fun!

Cool Jennfer!

JENNIFER: Hot, mom, hot!

Blackout there and lights up again on Bill, as before:

BILL: We used to think those stars were all that existed, and that our earth was at the center of everything. Now we know that we're just one infinitesimal planet drifting through an eternity flecked with a hundred billion galaxies and a billion trillion stars. And perhaps, as we gaze at the night sky, near one of those faint glimmers of light, someone quite different from us, in one of those other universes, is contemplating a star we call the Sun, and wondering, wondering . . . (*Blackout there and lights up on Anna with a Saleswoman:*)

SALESWOMAN: You're looking for a dress for your daughter? (*Anna nods.*) What size is she?

ANNA: —small—

SALESWOMAN: (*Perplexed; uncomfortable.*) Oh. Yes. But I need to know her size. (*Anna doesn't know it.*) An eight? A six?

ANNA: Eight.

SALESWOMAN: Fine. An eight. Now, what kind of dress are you looking for?

ANNA: Dance. Hot.

SALESWOMAN: A . . . hot . . . dance? (*Anna nods. The saleswoman stares, thinks Anna is deranged, but tries to be polite.*) You mean something for the summer? . . . a light material? perhaps a chiffon, a bit décolleté?

ANNA: Pretty.

SALESWOMAN: All our dresses are pretty.

ANNA: Hot pretty! Cool! Hot!

SALESWOMAN: (*Pause.*) Really, dear. Don't you think it would be better if you brought your daughter in with you? (*Turns to leave; Anna pulls her back.*)

ANNA: No! Surprise! Now!

SALESWOMAN: (*Frightened.*) Don't touch me. I'll call the police. You're obviously on drugs—

ANNA: No no no! I—

SALESWOMAN: Well then what? If it's not drugs, you should be in a hospital! Or some sort of . . . home.

ANNA: No! I—I—hell! Hell! (*Gets inspired.*)—Holland!

SALESWOMAN: . . . You're Dutch?

ANNA: Dutchyes.

SALESWOMAN: Well . . . ! Why didn't you say so? All right. Let's start over. I'll show you what we have . . . (*Anna breathes a sigh of relief.*) I adore tulips!

Lights dim there and come up on the Aphasic Patient, trying to match word and emotion.

APHASIC PATIENT: I a door. A door? I adore. You. I fate-hate you.

I sorrow.

I pappy—peppy—heppy—happy. Happy!

I scarr—scarred—scared.

I furrrrr—furious.

I long—lonnnng—lonnging. . . .

I bitter—better.

I gory. Glory. I glory!

BLACKOUT

SCENE SEVEN

A Reporter is interviewing Anna while Daniel hovers around.

REPORTER: . . . So you're making a marvelous recovery.

ANNA: Very struggle.

REPORTER: How long has it been since the accident?

ANNA: Three—five years.

DANIEL: Five months.

REPORTER: You still have therapy?

ANNA: Yes yes. Many therapy. Everyday. But now also walking own hands—feet.

REPORTER: It's wonderful that you're still going to give your paper at the international conference.

ANNA: Im-imp-impotent.

DANIEL: Important. It's important to her.

ANNA: *Paper* important.

REPORTER: You're able to continue your research in the observatory?

ANNA: No observtry. Problem. Air thin. Bad go high.

DANIEL: She can't risk the oxygen deprivation at that height.

REPORTER: Then how can you keep up with the newest discoveries?

ANNA: Con—confuser.

DANIEL: The computer. She uses the computer.

REPORTER: And you'll continue to teach?

ANNA: Yes! Next week.

REPORTER: Really!

DANIEL: Year. Next year. Possibly.

REPORTER: Can you give me some general idea about the subject of your paper? Nothing very complicated. This is going to be a human interest story, not a scientific article.

ANNA: Matter about cold and dark.

DANIEL: She's studying the dark matter question.

ANNA: Dark matter cosmos, yes.

Universe hiding.

Wheelchair man . . . great science—

DANIEL: Stephen Hawking.

REPORTER: Oh yes.

ANNA: He say two mysteries only.

One cosmos, one brain.

Many missing between and between.

No supper—No separate human and stardust.

Same matter.

Life part from all universe,

connect ocean, water of body—

REPORTER: What is she trying to say?

DANIEL: She's saying that all human life is created from the same matter as—

ANNA: (*Furious; to Daniel.*) No you put words in mouth!
(*To reporter.*) Listen me. Me!
I astromer. *I* know.

REPORTER: I'm sorry, I didn't mean to imply—

DANIEL: Look Anna, I was just trying to ex—

ANNA: Trying to big man.
No speak my thinking!
Go make aria.
I talk newspaper.

DANIEL: (*Furious too.*) Fine! Talk for yourself! You think I don't have better things to do? (*Storms out.*)

REPORTER: (*After a silence.*) Well. You certainly are a tough cookie.

ANNA: Good. Now.
Coffee with cookie? Tea?

BLACKOUT

Lights up on Daniel in his space, singing at the top of his lungs, in a mounting rage. Anna enters.

ANNA: Voice, Daniel! Very lion!

DANIEL: Oh, a big bad lion scared your reporter away?

ANNA: Newspaper go.

DANIEL: (*Singing vehemently.*) Addio, Addio, Addio, Addio . . .

ANNA: Stop now! Wake dead!

DANIEL: I guess so. Got you in here, didn't I?

ANNA:. . . . What??!

DANIEL: Don't want me to talk, don't want me to sing. Yes, madam. At your service. Just whistle for me. That's something you can still do, isn't it?

ANNA: I little words, yes.
But you, you little heart.
Hurting feel good. (*Jennifer, hearing the loud voices, steals out of her room to listen.*)

DANIEL: I'm a saint. Everyone knows that.

ANNA: Everyone know you nothing.

Zero. Creeping from failure.

Anna weak, now you big pants,

walk cockcockcock.

DANIEL: Oh yeah, it's terrific for me. What power I have! I get to put you in a taxi, tell the driver where to go; I get to work with Jenny on her homework, talk to her teachers; I get to write the checks, talk to the doctors, write down your appointments: oh, am I lucky! Mozart can wait; it's an honor to be your nursemaid, your caretaker, your longtime companion—

ANNA: Stop!!!!!

Years, years I *everything!*

Stoop, you stoop—stupid!

From auditions I call,

I with love, I do infinity!

DANIEL: All right! I wouldn't have a career if you hadn't pushed me, made me audition, shamed me into rehearsing. Okay! So now we're even, right? . . . But what about the next ten years? The next twenty, forty, FIFTY YEARS?!!!

ANNA: Free man.

DANIEL: Free? Oh no, honey, I'm locked up with you. We're a team. The prisoner and the guard. The puppet and the puppeteer. Can't have one without the other. What would you do if I walked out?

ANNA: . . . Make new life.

DANIEL: Really? All alone? On your own hands—feet!?

ANNA: Go! Go! Take freedom!

DANIEL: You don't have to ask me twice. I'm out of here! (*He leaves the room. Lights dim on Anna remaining there, stunned and confused.*)

Lights up again on Daniel, with Jennifer.

JENNIFER: You're not gonna split, Daniel; you can't!

DANIEL: She takes up all the air. There's no space for anyone else.

JENNIFER: But she can't help it. You know that. She hates being so dependent on everyone, so she fixes on herself. So she can be somebody. It's part of her sickness.

DANIEL: *I'm* sick! Sick of being her memory, her eyes, her ears, her mouth, her super supernumerary! I can't go on like this! (*Anna positions herself so she can overhear them.*)

JENNIFER: But what about her? She can't go on without *you!* She needs you!

DANIEL: Me? Oh no. She needs hands to pick her up when she falls down. She needs a crutch to lean on. She doesn't give a damn if it's me or the man in the moon.

JENNIFER: *You're* the man in the moon to her! . . . And to me. . . . God, Daniel, you'll be walking out on me, too.

DANIEL: Oh, Jen, don't you get upset now.

JENNIFER: But if you go, I'll be stuck with everything! I'll have to be the daughter and the mother and the boyfriend and the nurse and you know how I'll end up, don't you? I'll be one of those little old ladies who spend their whole lives taking care of their little old moms, and I'll never have a life of my own!

DANIEL: Don't, hon, don't. I love you; I'm not going to desert you!

JENNIFER: Don't you love her anymore?

DANIEL: Oh love! Love isn't everything!

JENNIFER: Oh, right! So how come all the movies are about it? And novels? And your operas? I know. Every opera I've seen is a tragedy about love. And they always have the same plot, too. The guy falls in love with a woman and then runs out on her. They're all wimps, or studs, or slimes—

DANIEL: Not *all* the guys—

JENNIFER:—And what happens to the women? They commit suicide. Or go crazy. Or cough themselves to death.

DANIEL: Believe me, Jen, your mother is more like The Queen of the Night than Violetta.

JENNIFER: She loves you.

DANIEL: What makes you think that?

JENNIFER: My daughterly instinct. . . . Besides, she told me.

DANIEL: Really? When?

JENNIFER: During our private times.

DANIEL: She did? In words? (*Anna enters.*)

ANNA: More, more than words.

JENNIFER: (*After a silence; gives an exaggerated yawn.*) . . . Man, I'm tired. See you later. (*Exits.*)

DANIEL: You have something to say? (*She touches his arm.*) You sure were able to talk to that reporter. What's the matter now? Cat got your tongue? (*She flings her arms around him; he flings them off.*) The power of speech, language: that's what separates us from the animals, honey! What do you want?

ANNA: Want . . . . . . Very need you. (*He doesn't respond.*) Very love.

So miss—so misery!

Words dis—dispate—disappear! Despair.

Heart in jail. No can move love to mouth.

DANIEL: (*More gently.*) Try.

ANNA: You . . . Daniel . . . Wish on stars belove man Daniel. Waking up nightmare, face smiling bright. Breathing life. Big luck from me.

DANIEL: Big luck *for* you.

ANNA: Yes. (*Puts arms around him again.*) Giant luck. Thank you.

BLACKOUT

SCENE EIGHT

In the blackness, an enormous elongated balloon, a dazzling glowing color, like the sun, the stars, is slowly being inflated; there is the sound of breath filling it. Then Bill is seen behind it, addressing his class.

BILL: . . . and after all these stars pass through middle age, class, after they burn out and die, we are faced with the ultimate question, the final mystery: how will our world end? (*Inflating the balloon further, to its limit.*) It could go something like this—the entire universe pressing outward, expanding indefinitely in all directions, every atom stretched to the limit until, inevitably— (*Releases the end so the balloon makes a deflated sound and sputters off.*)—it fizzles off into space, whimpering . . . (*He picks up the balloon.*) Or maybe it will end like this . . . (*He stretches the rubber taut until, as he lets go of the ends, it snaps together with a loud pop.*)—on a day when the expansion suddenly reaches an end, and the universe rushes together with incredible force, smashing itself into nothingness again with a reverse big bang . . . (*Lights dim on him and come up on the Aphasic Patient reading from a book, struggling through the lesson on prepositions, and trying to match words and actions.*)

APHASIC PATIENT: I walkaround the room . . . around . . . I hop in frontofthe chair . . . in front . . . I stand on tip—on top of the table . . . on top . . .

(*At home, Anna is in her robe, sitting at a vanity table, putting on make-up. Jennifer is also getting dressed for the dance. Daniel is off-stage, rehearsing phrases from the Papageno/Papagena Duet in "THE MAGIC FLUTE."*

ANNA: Newspaper read. New tesco from orbit today, superno.

JENNIFER: You mean a new telescope is being sent into orbit today and will study supernovas?

APHASIC PATIENT: I look down at the floor . . . down . . .

ANNA: New tesco being sent for—

JENNIFER:—into—

ANNA:—into orbit—

JENNIFER: You got it!

APHASIC PATIENT: I place my hand undermy chin . . . under . . .

ANNA: Learn supernova. See if they runaway.

JENNIFER: Runaway stars? Like kids? That is fresh!

APHASIC PATIENT: I lay my fingernext to mynose . . . next to . . .

ANNA: Many mystery. Look find why universe big lumpy all over.

JENNIFER: Lumpy?

ANNA: Like porridge. Cosmos is opposites, smooth *and* lump same time.

JENNIFER: I never heard that before.

ANNA: You about teen-age. Not science.

APHASIC PATIENT: I press my fish—fist against my chest . . . against . . . (*Jennifer takes a look at her mother; her make-up is a mess.*)

JENNIFER: Oh, gross! And you were the one who taught *me* how to color inside the lines! (*She helps her mother correct the make-up as the Aphasic Patient tries his last sentence:*)

APHASIC PATIENT: Sometimes God has to hit us over the head . . . over . . . (*Looks up, down, around for God; then exits.*)

DANIEL: (*Still singing Papageno's role, leaving a space for Papagena's part.*) Pa. Pa pa pa pa. Etc.

JENNIFER: He's really got the role?

ANNA: Yes.

JENNIFER: That is fly, mom, that is really fly! God, he could be a star. I mean, you'll be studying the stars and he'll be one. We'll be a family of stars! Far out!

ANNA: Very far. Voice like music from spheres.

JENNIFER: You really like the way he sings, don't you?

ANNA: Love. (*They both listen. At the silence left for Papagena's part, Anna inserts herself, singing tentatively and then with increasing conviction.*) Pa. Pa pa pa pa. ETC. (*The duet continues, with Daniel offstage and Anna facing in his direction, until he enters and together they sing the final phrases:*)

DANIEL: Papapapapapapapapageno!

ANNA: Papapapapapapapapagena! (*Lights dim there and come up on Bill as music from "THE MAGIC FLUTE" continues.*)

BILL: Press your ear to the cosmos and you hear it: the music of the spheres. Centuries ago, Pythagoras, listening in the night to the movement of the seven planets, made out the seven notes of the musical scale and exulted to know that harmony exists between heaven and earth, and that the universe sings, yes, it pulsates with rhythm; out of nothingness, out of its own motions, it makes a divine music, if you listen for it, and the celestial bodies dance . . . (*He dances. Jennifer enters the gym in her 'hot' dress. Anna, as chaperone, stands on the sidelines and watches. A young man taps Jennifer on the shoulder.*)

YOUNG MAN: Killer dress. (*Jennifer smiles shyly.*) Blows me away. (*She smiles again, at a loss for words.*) Dance?

JENNIFER: Okay. (*They dance awkwardly.*)

BLACKOUT

SCENE NINE

Sound: On a tape recorder, the conclusion to Jennifer's language tape is being played.

TAPE: French is a romance language, capable of expressing many subtle shades of meaning. For this reason, it has always been considered the language of love and of diplomacy. It is spoken all over the world, in parts of the Caribbean, Polynesia, Antarctica, Africa, the United States and naturally in France. This language tape has helped prepare you for your future travels. Voila. Un de ces jours nous recontrerons á l'Arc de Triomphe au Place d'Etoile! Bon Voyage! (*A spotlight picks up Anna, dressed elegantly, with her restrung beads around her neck, at the International Conference in Paris. She reads from the paper in her hands, speaking slowly into a microphone, while one Interpreter translates her words into French, and Another into sign language.*)

ANNA: (*Struggling with the scientific language, making many errors of pronunciation.*) . . . past mystical—miscal—mis—cal—cu—lations of light abyss—ab-sorp-tion by dust has caused cigar—sig—nif—i—cant underwear—underes—ti—mates of gallant—galactic masses. The dark matter problem may be partially solved by corking—correcting this missing—mystic—mistake—(*Pained, she stops.*) Mistakes. Too much. (*Hesitates; decides.*)

Ladies and genmen, forgive.

Big words, astromy.

Elephants on tongue.
No science paper. (*Puts down paper and speaks spontaneously; the interpreters try to follow her.*) Look at cosmos, and you see.
Great spaces between stars.
Now for me, spaces between words,
holes in listening,
holes in talking.
I searching many truth
I feel but cannot express.
Ideas in head but pure—poor words.
I in black hole aphasia,
climbing out.
You know story Alice in Wonderland
fall down hole,
not dying
but explore new world.
Now better my open heart.
Surprise in living, everyday.
I working.
To find shining light.
Night sky beautiful.
And missing, and mystery.
Wonder—
Wonder full. I. You.
All world.
Speechless.

BLACKOUT

END OF PLAY

Kathleen Tolan

APPROXIMATING
MOTHER

Author's Introduction

Lyn Austin of the Music Theatre Group asked me to write a play about the adoptive triangle. I said I'd mull it over, do some reading, see if anything occurred to me.

I knew it would have to ask the question, what is a mother? This is a question, being a mother, I consider constantly: what is the impulse to mother, to have (own?) a child? Where is the impulse generous, where is it selfish, narcissistic, a wish to control, to live vicariously through one's child, thereby changing the past, getting a second chance? Where is it letting go of the wish to remain a child and accepting a natural, important step?

I thought that I'd want to include some of the moments shared daily between a mother and her child: those tedious, loving, exasperating, desperate, hilarious, incredibly intense moments.

I found certain reading incredibly helpful as I considered that act of adopting, giving up a baby, of the society that supports such an act, of the possible impulses and circumstances behind such an act, of our society's attitude toward procreation and toward female sexuality. *Recreating Motherhood* by Barbara Katz Rothman; *The Baby Brokers* by Lynne McTaggart; "The Missing Discourse on Desire" an essay that appeared in the Harvard Educational Review by Michelle Fine. In a less direct way, I was helped in reading Faith D. Ginsburg's *Contested Lives* and Eileen Simpson's *Orphans*. And I found a conference organized by the American Adoption Congress very helpful in illuminating the complicated, often painful experience of giving up one's child, adopting a child, and being an adopted child.

In the end, I didn't know how to write a music theatre piece (or, anyway, this play didn't seem to want to be one). Lyn was gracious, wished me well. After a couple more drafts, Julia Miles offered to produce it. The last draft was written after very helpful notes from Julia and from the production's wonderful director, Gloria Muzio, who never ceased expressing enthusiasm for the play, at the same time giving me honest reactions (never in the form of judgments or conclusions; usually expressed as questions) to various moments, which subtly guided me to greater clarity.

Approximating Mother was produced by the Women's Project & Productions under the directorship of Julia Miles at the Judith Anderson Theatre, New York City from October 29 to November 24, 1991. It was directed by Gloria Muzio.

Set design by David Jenkins
Costume design by Elsa Ward
Lighting design by Jackie Manassee
Casting by Judy Dennis

Production stage manager   Robert L. Young
Sound designer   Mark Bennett

Approximating Mother is made possible in part with public funds from the National Endowment for the Arts, the New York State Council on the Arts, and the New York City Department of Cultural Affairs.

The action takes place in New York City, now, and, in the scenes with Jen, somewhere in Indiana.

CHARACTERS

MOLLY
FRAN, Molly's best friend
JACK, Molly's husband
ELLIE, the midwife
MAC SULLIVAN, a lawyer
JEN
SYLVIA, a social worker
EUGENE, Jen's father
BRENA, Jen's friend
GRACE, a nanny

Seven actors could do this, with an actor playing Eugene and Jack, and an actor playing Ellie, Sylvia, and Grace.

SCENE ONE

*A Japanese restaurant. Molly sits at a table, thinking. She is very
pregnant. Fran's coat is draped over the opposite chair. Now Fran
comes in and joins Molly.*

FRAN: No message. He's not interested. I have to face it. The
first relatively interesting male I've encountered in I'd say about a
year and a half—if I get to count Peter—

MOLLY: He really can't be counted. He was *not* available for
the long—

FRAN: Yes but—

MOLLY: And he wouldn't let you *say* anything during sex.

FRAN: Did I tell you that?

MOLLY: Yes.

FRAN: But he *was* interesting. Face it.

MOLLY: Yes but he still doesn't count.

FRAN: Then it's been like five years.

MOLLY: Evan was the last.

FRAN: Dear Evan. Why did I . . . ?

MOLLY: That's what you say now. You were miserable. He
only cared about you when you'd decided to leave him.

FRAN: True. Then why do we get to count him?

MOLLY: Well. You were with him six years.

FRAN: True.

MOLLY: But why have we written off this guy Ted? Just
because he hasn't called—

FRAN: Molly. He said he'd call me the next day. It's been
two weeks.

MOLLY: Maybe he's gone out of town. Isn't he a journalist or
something? Maybe he had a hot tip.

FRAN: Right. Head for the hills and don't look back. I checked
with his service. He's in town.

MOLLY: Oh.

FRAN: I knew it anyway. These fucking cowards. I knew it at
the time. It's just that he'd actually brought me *flowers* and a box of
candy. I mean, he was really, you know, paying *attention*.

MOLLY: Uh huh.

FRAN: It was so . . . *heterosexual,* so old *fashioned.*

MOLLY: Yeah.

FRAN: And he didn't spend all of dinner talking about his mother like that guy Francis did.

MOLLY: Right.

FRAN: Nor did he do an hour on his body building technique.

MOLLY: Uh huh.

FRAN: Though he didn't ask me a single question about myself. Talked non-stop about himself, his work, his perceptions of various things, but it was interesting and I thought maybe he was nervous, as I was. All I did was nod and smile, really. He must have thought I'd recently had a lobotomy or something.

MOLLY: Oh, Fran.

FRAN: He did tell me this story about how his best friend who's this very eccentric, unconventional, brilliant Parisian woman writer-journalist—

MOLLY: How nice.

FRAN: They were in a restaurant and she was served an omelette and called the waitress back and said it was rubbery and the waitress said it was the best they could do and she picked it up and slapped it against the wall and said "I didn't order a fly swatter." And I guess he's telling me this story so I know who his model is and isn't it fantastic to be so witty and irreverent and I just nod and smile dully and feel incredibly old and tired.

MOLLY: Yes.

FRAN: Anyway, we went back to my apartment, had some more wine and I decided I needed to make more of an effort. This is really embarrassing. I pulled out my violin.

MOLLY: Why is this embarrassing? What did you do with it?

FRAN: Molly. I played it. I hadn't played it since *highschool* when I decided the best and most effective revenge on my mother was to quit playing the violin. It was awful. There I was, the performing seal, playing Paganini *terribly.*

MOLLY: You really like him.

FRAN: Then I showed him my scrapbooks.

MOLLY: Really?

FRAN: Then when he said good night—I know this is shocking, but I had known him, you know, peripherally, for *years*—

MOLLY: You slept with him.

FRAN: I just took him and gave him this long kiss and we ended up in bed and it was nice but I thought as he responded to my initial embrace, "He obliges."

MOLLY: Oh, god.

FRAN: He was *obliging* me.

MOLLY: Right.

FRAN: Very polite.

MOLLY: Uh huh.

FRAN: But it had nothing to do with whatever his own impulse might've been.

MOLLY: Right.

FRAN: The whole thing was, let's face it, humiliating.

MOLLY: Right. (*Pause.*)

FRAN: Anyway, the next day I took him up to Esther and Phil's and we all hung around with the baby.

MOLLY: Are you serious?

FRAN: And, yes, it's true, I thought it was a good test. I really don't want to waste time on these guys who don't want families.

MOLLY: But—they really are, so often, cowards, you know, you can't just—

FRAN: I know, I know, but I'm really sick of it. I just plopped the baby into his lap and I saw this like veil drop over his cool blue eyes as he smiled this slightly frozen smile and then made all the appropriate coos and continued to be quite charming but I knew that was it. I'd done it. (*Pause. Molly watches Fran eat her sushi.*)

MOLLY: God, that looks good.

FRAN: Help yourself.

MOLLY: I can't. It has little bugs in it or something that could make Bob sick.

FRAN: Bob?

MOLLY: Oh. Jane said, "When the baby pops out of your tummy and the doctor catches it, I will call her Bob."

FRAN: Great.

MOLLY: First thing I'm going to have, sushi and Jack Daniels.

FRAN: Mmm. I'll buy.

MOLLY: You're on. (*Beat.*) Janey asked me last week how I got pregnant.

FRAN: And . . . ?

MOLLY: I say the stuff about having an egg . . .

FRAN: Uh huh.

MOLLY: She wants to know if I eat an egg.

FRAN: Oh.

MOLLY: I say no, inside my body, and Daddy planted the seed.

FRAN: Right.

MOLLY: She wants to know if the seed was from the garden, I say no, then I'd've had a carrot! We laugh. So she asks where he planted it, I say in my vagina. She says, Oh. Two days later. We're walking home from school, and she says, did Daddy plant the seed with his hand?

FRAN: Oh oh.

MOLLY: And I say, no, it came from his body, out of his penis. She says, oh. Two days later, she says, but, that seed of Daddy's— did it just fly across the air into your vagina?

FRAN: How sweet.

MOLLY: So I have to break it to her, and she says, absolutely horrified, "He put his *penis inside* your *vagina?* Are you *serious?* And then she asks if it tickled a little bit. I say yes, a little bit. And she laughs and says that's really strange and that's it.

FRAN: God. (*Pause.*)

FRAN: (*cont.*) You don't want me there, let's face it.

MOLLY: Where? Face what? Yes I do. What are you talking about?

FRAN: Bob's birth.

MOLLY: You're chickening out.

FRAN: You have a husband! He doesn't want me 1

MOLLY: He loves you.

FRAN: But it's your special thing.

MOLLY: He was delighted you were going to be there. It'll let him off the hook. He was terrible when Janey was born, completely frantic, hit an intern, threw up on the floor, they had to take him out. Don't you remember?

FRAN: Yes.

MOLLY: He told me the other night I never loved him.

FRAN: What?!

MOLLY: I was telling him how Jimmy had told me *he* feels like *Doreen* doesn't really love *him,* they never, like, spontaneously hop into bed, it always has to be planned, and he doesn't feel she's reacting to *him, exactly,* and Jack says, well, that's how I feel about you. I've never felt you really love me. And I say, what are you talking about? How could you feel this? You've always felt this and never told me? You've just been living this lie, sleeping beside me every night? And I just lose it. And he calls me a lunatic, says only *I* am so convoluted that I would consider *me* not loving *him his* betrayal. Which in a way makes sense I guess but at the time I felt, christ, I couldn't sleep beside him for one night much less six years thinking he didn't really love me and didn't he care?

FRAN: Jesus. Why do I want to get married? That's the real mystery

MOLLY: So I'm completely hysterical. And he says, see, someone else would've said something reassuring like of course I love you, but *you*—it's all about *you,* isn't it. Methinks thou doth protest too much. And I really think he's driving me crazy. I thought he hadn't been making love to me because he's a fattist which is kind of despicable if you focus on it but most people are that way and really if you focus on every little thing you really will just stop.

FRAN: (*Thinking about herself.*) Right.

MOLLY: Just stop.

FRAN: Yeah.

MOLLY: So I thought, don't get upset about it, it'll pass, this is just a temporary condition, of course wishing he was one of those guys who was completely into the whole thing, you know? Who get completely turned on by their wive's ripening, marvel at the miracle—

FRAN: Good luck.

MOLLY: Right. Anyway, I just couldn't get up the next morning. Jack got up with Jane who had a fit, came sobbing into the bedroom begging me to get up but I just couldn't and she refused to go to school and Jack got the babysitter to come and I just lay in bed crying all day. Finally, Irene had to leave so I got up and went in and lay on the couch and Jane gave me this really strange look and I said, "I was sick. But now I'm better." And she smiled this kind of fake smile and said, "Oh." And I said, "Were you worried about me?" And she said, "Yes. I thought you were going to die of sadness."

END SCENE

SCENE TWO

Molly, Jack, Fran and Ellie the midwife are in the birthing room. Molly is in the last stages of labor. She huffs and groans, pacing back and forth, stopping to lean against a chair from time to time. Jack sits in a rocking chair, next to the birthing bed, reading aloud from War And Peace. *Ellie sits in a chair on the other side of the bed. She is reading a dog magazine. Fran stands, leaning against the wall for support or clutching a chair.*

JACK: " 'Impossible!' said Prince Andrey. 'That would be too base.' 'Time will show,' said Bilibin, letting the creases run off his forehead again in token of being done with the subject."

MOLLY: Oh, Jesus. Fuck.

FRAN: (*Herself about to faint.*) Molly?

JACK: "When Prince Andrey went to the room that had been prepared for him, and lay down in the clean linen on the feather-bed and warmed and fragrant pillows, he felt as though the battle of which he brought tidings was far, far away from him."

Molly is moaning, groaning. Ellie gets up, goes to Molly, holds her, does the rhythmic breathing, blowing out in three short breaths and then one long, until Molly joins her.

ELLIE: Want some ice chips? (*Molly nods. Ellie goes out.*)

JACK: "The Prussian Alliance, the treachery of Austria, the new triumph of Bonaparte, the levee and parade and the audience of Emperor Francis next day, engrossed his attention.'

MOLLY: Jack.

JACK: Yeah?

MOLLY: Stop.

JACK: The reading? It's enough?

MOLLY: Yeah.

JACK: Okay. (*Ellie comes in with a cup of ice chips.*)

ELLIE: Here we go.

Ellie gives Molly the ice, goes back to her chair, picks up the magazine.

FRAN: (*Weakly.*) Molly, is there anything I can do?

MOLLY: No, Fran, it's okay.

ELLIE: (*To Jack:*) Do you guys have a dog?

JACK: No. We did have. Actually, Nickel was killed in traffic.

ELLIE: Really?

JACK: It was very sad.

ELLIE: You've got to keep them on a leash.

JACK: Yeah. (*Molly moans, grunts.*)

MOLLY: Fuck.

JACK: Then we got Lucy. But it turned out she hated kids. So when Molly got pregnant with Jane we gave her away.

ELLIE: Uh huh. We have the most wonderful airedale. They are absolutely fabulous dogs. Very smart, very friendly, don't shed— great for allergies—(*Ellie jumps up, goes to Molly.*)

MOLLY: Oh, god.

ELLIE: Let's see how you're doing (*Ellie guides her over to the bed, Molly's bent over, resists getting in. Jack gets up to help.*)

FRAN: (*Weak.*) You're doing great, Moll. Jesus.

ELLIE: Atta girl. Let's get you up—up on to the bed. (*Molly continues to groan, shriek, pant. She leans against the bed.*)

ELLIE: (*Firm.*) Upsie daisy. Come on. I need to see what's happening. Come on, Molly.

JACK: Come on, honey. (*Molly manages to get up and onto her back. Ellie listens to Molly's abdomen with a stethoscope. Jack holds her hand.*)

ELLIE: Okay. Let's get her out.

MOLLY: Can I push?

ELLIE: Go. (*Molly pushes.*)

FRAN: Oh, Moll. Oh, honey. Oh my god. God.

ELLIE: Good. Hold on. Hold on. Okay. Push. (*Molly pushes.*)

JACK: Here she comes. Oh, my god.

FRAN: I can't believe it.

ELLIE: Good. Good girl. (*Ellie catches the baby, puts it on Molly's stomach.*)

MOLLY: Oh, my god.

JACK: Oh. Look at her.

FRAN: It's a girl. It's a miracle. I feel sick. (*Fran goes to a chair, sits.*)

MOLLY: Hello. Hello, sweetheart.

JACK: She's so sweet.

MOLLY: She's a little fish.

JACK: She is a little fish.

MOLLY: Oh, god, what a relief.

END SCENE

SCENE THREE

Jack and Fran in the hospital cafeteria, at a table, sipping tea.

JACK: You know, it isn't so simple, to stand on the outside and watch something so, so primitive, so profound. All these months, watching her get bigger, and myself not feeling . . . comfortable about it. That sounds absurd. It's just, you know, if you want some supper, you can just order it. You don't need to go wring the chicken's neck, pluck it, drain it, singe it, whatever one does to chickens, cook it. And so on—nature—and the time things naturally take—it's all so divorced from one's life these days. I mean, it really did seem incredible to me that, once we decided to have a baby—this happened with Janey and again now with whatever her name will be—got any ideas?

FRAN: Um . . .

JACK: She had an amnio, we could've known it was going to be a girl, we'd've had all this time to think of a name. The doctor knew. There it was, in her file, maybe it was the fear of getting too attached, if it didn't work out. And Molly felt it took the mystery out of it, although I must say I think there's plenty of mystery left.

FRAN: Right.

JACK: But—it did seem incredible to me that we couldn't just order it. That it really would take nine months and that Molly would have to go through the whole, you know, physical experience.

FRAN: Yes.

JACK: That we are, still, in the hands of nature. It really is quite—incredible.

FRAN: Yes.

JACK: And . . . to see her in such pain and not be able to do anything. Not being a woman, feeling on the outside, maybe threatened in some way. Feeling very . . . male.

FRAN: Yes. (*Fran, her head on her hand, begins to fall asleep.*)

JACK: And, of course, we men . . . There are all those classic fears, if you subscribe to that . . . of disappearing into her, of all her secretions, of blood, of milk, how foreign her body is. And the fear that she doesn't really love me, is just using me. The ease and intimacy she has with other women, and with our daughter. When I speak to Janey I always see the quotation marks.

END SCENE

SCENE FOUR

Hospital room. Molly in bed. Fran holding the baby.

FRAN: (*Moved, tender.*) Oh, Moll.

MOLLY: Sweet, huh?

FRAN: God. And she's all here?

MOLLY: Um.

FRAN: All the fingers and toes?

MOLLY: Oh. I guess so.

FRAN: (*Incredulous.*) You haven't checked?

MOLLY: No.

FRAN: Incredible. You're so . . . stable. It's the first thing I'd do. I'd be terrified I'd had a frog.

MOLLY: Huh. Well . . . I guess I'd've noticed. (*Beat.*) Why don't you check? (*Fran unwraps infant, counts fingers and toes.*)

FRAN: All here. (*Beat, then she blurts out.*) I'm sorry.

MOLLY: What?

FRAN: I failed you.

MOLLY: What are you talking about?

FRAN: What's the point of having a friend if she's going to feel threatened, thrown, overwhelmed, frozen at the sight of her best friend's pain, panicked at the—the—physicality, the biology of it all.

MOLLY: (*Laughs.*) You were fine. I was glad you were there.

FRAN: (*She focusses on the baby.*) God. You realize she's no heavier than a five pound bag of sugar? You go to the grocery store and get a five pound bag of sugar and this is what it weighs. This whole human.

MOLLY: Yeah.

FRAN: (*To baby.*) Can you say, "Fran?" Say, "Hi, Fran, you're looking gorgeous, I wish I could go home with *you*—my mommy already has a kid—she'll be too distracted, exhausted, I won't get enough attention—

MOLLY: How was your date last night?

FRAN: You don't want to know.

MOLLY: Yes I do.

FRAN: We ate, went back to his apartment, kissed, he fell asleep, right there in the chair, I'm sitting there wondering what to do next, and he wakes up and tells me he's just dreamed that he and I were lying side by side and suddenly he realized a scorpion was crawling up his leg.

MOLLY: Good god.

FRAN: I left.

MOLLY: Jesus.

FRAN: (*After a beat.*) Molly, I'm not waiting to get the guy. I'm going to have a kid.

MOLLY: What do you mean?

FRAN: I'm too desperate. I'll just get married to get to be a mother and it won't be fair to the guy or the kid or me and anyway it's just too difficult, I really do feel too desperate.

MOLLY: But—how will you do it?

FRAN: You think it's a terrible idea.

MOLLY: No.

FRAN: Just because you have this ideal life doesn't mean that the rest of us can't—aspire to something.

MOLLY: I don't have an ideal life. We're always fighting. We're completely broke. We can't pay our taxes. They just put a lien on our bank account.

FRAN: (*Devastated.*) Molly, why didn't you tell me?

MOLLY: It happened last week. I've been busy. It's just that, you know, lives can seem quite ideal, from the outside.

FRAN: But I thought I was on the inside.

MOLLY: You are. (*Beat.*)

FRAN: What are you going to do?

MOLLY: I got a call from Babs Silverman—remember her?

FRAN: Sort of.

MOLLY: She said there was an opening in the art department where she is in South Carolina.

FRAN: What a terrible idea.

MOLLY: Jack says he'll die if he has to leave New York. There are no newsstands outside of New York. I said, subscribe. But he feels he has to be able to walk into a newsstand and be surrounded by three hundred publications from all over the world, it gives him this necessary energy or something. That and the Mets.

FRAN: The Mets are in terrible shape.

MOLLY: That's what I said.

FRAN: I don't want you to go. Who will I have to pick on?

MOLLY: True. (*Beat.*) So. How're you going to do it?

FRAN: Oh. I thought about just getting laid or artificially inseminated or adopt. I'll probably adopt. I mean, no offense but if you can avoid the extreme conditions—

MOLLY: They do get pretty extreme.

FRAN: So I'll get a kid and then I won't feel so desperate anymore and the right guy will come along and I won't scare him away because I'll already have my kid and I'll just be like most thirty-eight year old women who are divorced with a kid and we'll fall in love and it'll be fabulous.

MOLLY: I answered the phone this morning and this little voice said "Hi, Mommy." I didn't recognize her. I'd never talked to her on the phone, never heard her voice isolated from the rest of her. She sounded like any little kid. Tears started streaming down my face. She said she missed me, I said I missed her, she told me what had happened since she'd gotten up. They'd spilled the box of Cheerios on the rug. Daddy'd called our downstairs neighbor and he brought his dog up to clean up the Cheerios. She has a cold so they won't let her visit. I hung up and felt so far away.

END SCENE

SCENE FIVE

Mac Sullivan's office. Mac sits behind his desk listening to Fran who sits across from him.

FRAN: I haven't wanted, in my life, to compromise.
MAC: Right.
FRAN: I mean, when it really mattered to me.
MAC: Uh huh.
FRAN: I don't claim to be, you know, Joan of Arc—
MAC: Right.
FRAN:—but, you know, a lot of my friends, because they wanted to go somewhere, get somewhere, you know, have a certain amount of success, um, are doing things, representing things or, um, philosophies, ideas, they never would have . . .
MAC: Right.
FRAN: And there's been, often, the question of how to support the children—
MAC: Ah ha! Idealism fades in the grim light of economic reality. The excruciating journey to maturity.
FRAN: Yes. Yes. And the question, too, "Am I really willing, at age forty, to live in quite the austerity I embraced in my twenties."
MAC: We're not Gandhi.
FRAN: Yes. And as a woman, you know, you hold out for as long as you can for the man who will really—I mean, *really* think of you as a, like, actual person, autonomous, with *really* as much of a right to a whole life.
MAC: Huh.

FRAN: I mean, I think there are men who are now able to think of a woman as separate but equal as a colleague but not as a wife.

MAC: Huh.

FRAN: Obviously there are exceptions and I haven't read a study or anything but it is my feeling.

MAC: Uh huh.

FRAN: Anyway—sorry—I am getting to the—this is leading somewhere. I just never felt I *really* would be able to, you know, not be "the wife," however "modern" he might seem. With every—not that there were so many—serious relationship, I felt, however unconsciously, that I should be serving him. Or that— that I couldn't—couldn't *really* have my own thoughts. My own private thoughts. Anyway, not pretending to be, you know, a moral arbiter, just trying to retain my integrity. Certainly I'm sophisti-cated enough to know one's own neuroses are always tied up in—in fact, often *inform*, if not *determine*, one's philosophy, one's actions. Um. (*Pause.*)

FRAN: (*Continued.*) Anyway, with all of this, finally feeling very, sort of, lonely and, you know, "Is this it?"

MAC: Right.

FRAN: And then beginning to think about a baby. Wanting that, the feeling, the sensuality—

MAC: Uh huh.

FRAN:—the basicness of, you know, the tasks.

MAC: Uh huh.

FRAN: And the clarity of one's priorities, one's own reason for, you know, carrying on.

MAC: Right.

FRAN: And of course, they're so sweet.

MAC: There's nothing sweeter.

FRAN: And I imagine I would feel more . . . connected to, you know, life, to the cycle, to the world, to humanity.

MAC: Right.

FRAN: And, I guess, it seems *manageable*. I mean, so much in the world seems so overwhelming, so impossible. This would be a life I might actually have some effect on. Not that I would—I mean, I'd try to honor her or him, to help and guide but not to impose my own . . .

MAC: Uh huh.

FRAN: And, I guess, to feel connected to the—the awe—to the mystery—I don't mean the mystery of birth and life, though, of course, but, I see it with my friends, that the most basic, most boring—to the outsider—achievements of their young children are absolutely thrilling. It's as if they themselves are children again, are experiencing the miracle of—of how the world works and what it is to be alive. And, of course the problems that arise can be quite daunting, but, again, the scale seems . . . manageable.

MAC: Uh huh. (*She's finished. She waits for his response. He studies her.*)

MAC: (*Continued.*) Well. It isn't easy.

FRAN: Yes.

MAC: Hardest thing I've ever done, raise kids. And my wife gets the credit. I last about two hours before I'm ready to chuck 'em all—or myself—out the window. I have no patience for that day to day nagging, fighting, entertaining, ga ga go go shit. Sorry.

FRAN: Yes.

MAC: Then there's the mothers with the careers who stick the kids with the nannies twelve hours a day. I'm not talking working class who maybe have no choice. I'm talking very simple motivation: selfishness, greed. You follow? Why do they have kids? For their own occasional comfort, they feel more complete, they're more socially acceptable in the community.

FRAN: I'm lucky to have work that I can do at home.

MAC: Uh huh. Well, I don't know, manageable. Compromise. Holding out for a guy who's going to think of you as a whole person.

FRAN: Yes.

MAC: You think men don't wish for the same thing? You think we're not diminished, reduced to what she wants from me, expects of me, blames me for?

FRAN: Oh.

MAC: So the freedom is lost. The more idiocencratic quirks are pushed underground. What you don't share is lost. You follow?

FRAN: Yes.

MAC: I don't know. (*Beat. Then he looks through his papers.*) Whatta we got here? Let's see. Depends on what you can afford. Let's see. Due date March 22. Prepregnancy weight, one twenty five, Baptist—(*Checks another paper.*) What'd you say you?— Catholic.

FRAN: Yes.

MAC: Practicing?

FRAN: No. But I could.

MAC: Uh huh. (*Back to papers.*) Never used drugs, cheerleader in high school, has two years of college, a time buyer for an ad agency.

FRAN: Why isn't she keeping the child?

MAC: Why isn't she keeping the child. Good question. Here you are, desperate for a baby, right? It's a mystery. I mean, why do women have abortions? The man split, you can't afford it, it isn't convenient, it pulls you out of the competition with the guys at the firm, you want to stay a kid. There are a thousand reasons.

FRAN: Uh huh.

MAC: This one's very desirable. Let's see. It would be, roughly, twenty thou.

FRAN: Oh . . .

MAC: All inclusive. We cover the birth, hospital expenses, support her for the last three months, legal fees, Indiana court fees.

FRAN: (*Thrown.*) I . . . I don't think I have that.

MAC: You don't think you have that.

FRAN: (*Trying to get her bearings.*) I'm sorry.

MAC: What do you think you have?

FRAN: I don't know.

MAC: You don't know. (*Considers her. Beat.*) I don't know. Who knows? (*Beat.*) It's a big decision. You think I don't wonder, what would it be like if carrying my family on my back like Sisyphus weren't the *center*, the main event of my life. I remember how it was, in law school, the freedom, the possibility. The law, argument. Concepts of justice.

FRAN: Yes.

MAC: I'll be honest. I look at these gays, I think, lucky bastard, he doesn't have to work like a slave, come home every day to the constant demands.

FRAN: Yes. (*Beat.*)

MAC: What about a father?

FRAN: Yes.

MAC: You know, babies are in great demand. People are desperate for babies. White—if you'll let me speak frankly—

FRAN: Yes.

MAC: —healthy babies. I could get one for you. I could pick up the phone right now and arrange it. (*Looks through papers.*) Here's something. One night stand. Not sure she's going to give it up. If she does, expenses'll be less. Could maybe get it for twelve thou. Want to try for that?

FRAN: I don't know. I think so. Yes.

MAC: Now that's decisive. Just kidding. It's not simple. (*Beat.*) Why do I have kids? Convention. Obligation. Love. A wish for ownership. Control. To have made something in my own image. To continue the race, follow God's wish.

FRAN: Yes.

MAC: Would you like to have a drink with me later?

FRAN: No. Thank you.

MAC: No harm in trying.

FRAN: Of course.

MAC: You're very beautiful.

FRAN: Thank you.

MAC: Very proud.

FRAN: Yes.

MAC: And honest.

FRAN: Yes.

MAC: I like that.

FRAN: Good.

MAC: We'll find you something, okay?
FRAN: Okay.

END SCENE

SCENE SIX

Jen and Sylvia sit in Sylvia's office. Jen is about six months pregnant.

JEN: I didn't use anything.
SYLVIA: Uh huh.
JEN: Didn't think we'd do it.
SYLVIA: Right.
JEN: And I thought about it a lot while we were doing it, thought I should say something but I guess I felt shy so I kept putting it off. And then I thought, well, he won't go all the way without asking if I'm on the pill or getting some rubbers or something. And then he was inside me and I kept putting it off and didn't want to interrupt and then he came inside me and I thought, "shit." But then I thought, well, I'm not so regular anyway, so who knows when I'm going to be ovulating. Think of all the times I *haven't* done it this month. The odds are really good I was ovulating one of those times.
SYLVIA: Hmm.
JEN: So when my period was late, I thought, "Shit—"
SYLVIA: Hm.
JEN: —but then, well, it's been late before and I just tried not to think about it. And I started feeling really bloated and my breasts started getting really tender and big but I really just tried not to think about it. Finally I couldn't zip my jeans and I faced the fact I had to do something so I called my girlfriend Brena and she helped me find a clinic and we went to the doctor and he said I was pregnant and I said I wanted an abortion and he said I had to have permission from my parents and I said I didn't want to tell them and he told me I should go to this social worker woman—

SYLVIA: Who was that?

JEN: Um. Her name was Mrs. Nelson.

SYLVIA: What agency?

JEN: Um. I don't know. He just gave me her number.

SYLVIA: Uh huh.

JEN: And said she'd help me and wouldn't tell my parents so I went to her and she told me I would regret it if I had an abortion and I said I regretted this whole thing but that's what I wanted to do and I didn't want to have a baby, I wanted to finish high school and stuff and she said if I wasn't ready to be a mother there were many wonderful couples who would love a baby and I said, well that's fine but I don't want to do that so she said I needed to have permission from my parents and then I should come back to her and she'd help me but I should think about how I'd feel if my parents had decided not to have me and I said, "huh?" And she said she knew this must be a very scary and confusing time for me and I should know she was my friend and I said I didn't think so and then she got really nasty because she knew I could see right through her and she started screaching, "Go ahead, kill the baby. Kill the baby. See how it makes you feel." And some day I'd wish I had a baby, wouldn't I and I said I don't know what you're talking about, let me out of here and went home and went up to my room and was just shaking and crying and I told my mom I had the flu and just stayed up there for a couple of days and finally I told my mom I was pregnant. And then everybody completely freaked out and here I am.

SYLVIA: Good. Good. You glad you can get this out?

JEN: (*Hesitant.*) Yeah.

SYLVIA: Good. I'm glad you're here. (*Pause. Jen shifts in her chair.*)

SYLVIA: (*Continued.*) And now you say you want to keep the baby.

JEN: Yeah.

SYLVIA: What made you decide that?

JEN: Um. Well, they wouldn't give me permission to have an abortion and here I am stuck with it. I mean, I know I could give it up but I don't want to do that. That's be really . . . I don't know. I don't want to do that.

SYLVIA: Mm hm.

JEN: And anyway, here I am and I can't go back home—

SYLVIA: They want you to come back. As soon as the baby is born. They just can't handle the baby.

JEN: Yeah, well, that's just . . . I don't want to.

SYLVIA: Uh huh. It's a tough decision.

JEN: Uh huh.

SYLVIA: So let's ask the tough questions, okay?

JEN: Okay.

SYLVIA: Whose gonna pay the medical bills?

JEN: I don't know.

SYLVIA: You're parents gonna pay them?

JEN: No.

SYLVIA: No insurance, right?

JEN: I don't know.

SYLVIA: The father's not going to pay. You got a friend maybe with some money?

JEN: No.

SYLVIA: Okay. Let's just skip that one for now. Let's say you get out of the hospital. How you gonna support yourself and the baby?

JEN: I'll get a job.

SYLVIA: Okay. And who's gonna take care of the baby?

JEN: I don't know. I'll get a babysitter.

SYLVIA: Okay. (*Beat.*) I've seen a lot of girls go through this place. Some of them choose to give their babies up for adoption, go back home, finish high school, get training, or even go on to college, eventually get married and have a family. The ones who keep the children. (*Beat.*) It's a hard road. Most cases, the father's long gone, they end up on welfare or doing some lousy job while their kids are in some kind of nightmare childcare situation and there's no way out. (*Beat.*) You know how it feels to work all day at a job you hate, come home, to a screaming baby? Never go out, never get a break. (*Beat.*)

SYLVIA: (*Continued.*) You know that most abusive mothers started to have kids when they were teenagers? They beat their kids. Because teenagers are bad? No way. It's hard. They're frustrated. They lash out. But they're ruining more than their own lives, understand?

JEN: I heard the heart beat. I hadn't been thinking of it being, you know, alive. And the doctor let me listen and I heard this thump, thump, thump . . . I couldn't believe it. And it's starting to move around . . .

SYLVIA: Uh huh. Well. Just think about it. I know you'll make the right decision, okay?

END SCENE

SCENE SEVEN

Molly and Fran sit on a bench in Washington Square playground. Molly's baby is asleep in her Snugli.

MOLLY: The other night, I'm nursing Baby Girl—

FRAN: I thought you'd decided on Priscilla.

MOLLY: Jack remembered he had an aunt named Priscilla he didn't like. We just can't agree on one. The birth certificate people finally just put Baby Girl. Janey's calling her Bob. Maybe if I could have just one night of uninterrupted sleep my brain would come back.

FRAN: Poor Molly.

MOLLY: So I'm nursing the baby while getting a bath ready for Janey—

FRAN: Jesus.

MOLLY: And I'm weak with hunger and exhausted and tense and just thinking, one more hour, they'll be in bed, I'll put my feet up, relax, eat, if I can just make it through one hour—where is she? (*They rise, look for Janey.*)

FRAN: On the slide.

MOLLY: Right. (*They both wave to Janey, then sit.*)

MOLLY: So I'm helping Janey out of her dress and she throws it on the floor and I say, very civil, very restrained, "Honey, would you please take your dress into your room?" and she says, "No." And I think, oh, oh, this could be the straw. But I cling to my calm veneer and say, "Please, dear, don't just throw your dress on the floor. Put it on your bed and I'll hang it up later." And she says, "No. I don't have to." And I lose it. "Okay, that's *it*," I say, "You're driving me *fucking crazy.*"

FRAN: Oh, dear.

MOLLY: And she bursts into tears and says, "But I'm a kid. Kids shouldn't have to do these things." And I say, "I've got to get out of here"—

FRAN: Incredible.

MOLLY: And Janey's sobbing, clinging to my skirt and I say, "Janey, I just need five minutes. I need to sit quietly for five minutes, *alone.*" And I go into my room and sit down and Janey follows, weeping. And we sit there and then she says, bitterly, "I wish that I were an older kid." And my rage instantly evaporates—

FRAN: Uh huh.

MOLLY: And curiosity takes over—

FRAN: Right.

MOLLY: And I say, "Why do you wish you were an older kid?" and she says, "So that I could kill you."

FRAN: Oh, god.

MOLLY: And I say, "Right. You're so angry with me you wish that you could kill me." And then she says, "But—what, oh what will I do, for then I would miss you so much." And I say, "Right. *That's* the dilemma.

FRAN: God. (*Pause.*)

FRAN: (*Continued.*) Molly. I think I'm going to have a baby.

MOLLY: What?!

FRAN: It looks good. She's due in a month. Seventeen years old. Knocked up by some guy she met in a restaurant where she works. Doesn't want to have the kid; wants to finish high school, have a life. Her parents are very supportive. I wrote her a letter about myself, about being a mother, and sent her snapshots of the apartment. It's so strange.

MOLLY: Fran. This is so exciting.

FRAN: Sould I be doing this?

MOLLY: I don't know.

FRAN: I'm so scared. I lie awake thinking, what if she changes her mind, what if she doesn't change her mind, what if it's a frog, what if it's a boy? I don't know anything about boys. What if it's a girl? Will I feel competitive? What will it look like? Will it be okay that it doesn't look like me? What if it's stupid? How conditional is my love? What if I don't know what I'm doing? And I hear you talk about what you're going through and I think, I'm not up to this. I don't know if I'm up to it.

MOLLY: Oh, Fran. You know, you're going through the same stuff I did when I was pregnant with Janey.

FRAN: (*Angry, controlled.*) No I'm not.

MOLLY: (*Surprised.*) What?!

FRAN: You always do that.

MOLLY: Do what?

FRAN: You don't want to deal with my feelings.

MOLLY: (*Completely thrown.*) What are you talking about?

FRAN: You want to neutralize them, turn them into what everybody else feels.

MOLLY: No I don't.

FRAN: You do to. You do it all the time.

MOLLY: Name one instance.

FRAN: Easy. (*Beat. Suddenly very hard.*) When I told you my mother was dying. You said no she wasn't. (*Beat.*)

MOLLY: (*Trying to reconstruct it.*) I couldn't bear it.

FRAN: It was *my* mother. (*Beat.*)

MOLLY: I didn't want it to be true. I didn't want you to be sad.

FRAN: I wasn't sad. I was relieved.

MOLLY: You were a wreck.

FRAN: So don't I get to be?

MOLLY: (*Beat, trying to sort her way through.*) I'm sorry. (*Beat.*) I felt you wanted me to take the rap for your mother's death.

FRAN: (*Beat.*) I just wanted you there.

MOLLY: You shut me out.

FRAN: I had to. (*Confused silence.*)

MOLLY: I'm sorry. (*Pause.*)

FRAN: I've just been . . . flooded with all these memories from my childhood, and this incredible longing for my parents . . . Such a sadness that they're not here. Even though it was so awful, actually, they were so unhappy, were terrible parents, got married too young, he wasn't her class, always resented her.

MOLLY: Uh huh.

FRAN: And she was so bitter at the loss of her career, that she gave it up for him. She hadn't meant to. She still played in a local string quartet when we were young. I always felt her impatience with our interruptions, our tedious needs. And her desperation.

MOLLY: She once told me you had great talent as a violinist. But that she'd wrecked it, had had too much wind in her sails.

FRAN: (*Shocked.*) She *said* that?

MOLLY: Uh huh.

FRAN: I can't believe it.

MOLLY: Why?

FRAN: She might have said that to me.

MOLLY: She probably figured you already knew it. You were there.

FRAN: But . . . it's so like her. She never spoke of it to me. (*Pause.*)

FRAN: (*Continued.*) I'm sorry.

MOLLY: No, I'm sorry.

FRAN: I have to go.

MOLLY: Aren't you coming over for soup?

FRAN: I can't.

MOLLY: Fran, please.

FRAN: I'm not good company.

MOLLY: That's okay.

FRAN: I'm sorry.

MOLLY: Okay. Come say bye to Janey.

FRAN: I can't.

MOLLY: Franny.

FRAN: I'll call you.

MOLLY: Okay. (*Fran leaves, Molly watches her go.*)

END SCENE

SCENE EIGHT

A room in a home for pregnant women. Jen is sitting there. She's seven months pregnant. Brena has just come in, is unloading her stuff, opening a tin of cookies.

BRENA: Oh oh. I hope I didn't give that house lady one of the hash cookies. I was going to put some regular ones in . . .

JEN: (*Taking a cookie.*) Right.

BRENA: I thought you needed a little fun in here. That lady was so uptight. I had to really lay it on thick, talk about Jesus and shit.

JEN: God. She's gonna get really stoned.

BRENA: She'll just think it's the flu.

JEN: I can't believe they still let you out of the house.

BRENA: Look who's talking. God. Melissa and I made a batch of these on the weekend, we were sitting around and she asked me something and, like, I started to answer but as soon as I get three words out, I'm, like, stranded, I can't remember the beginning of what I said or where I'm going. Like I was just sunk in the black hole, you know?

JEN: They'll kill me if they ever find out. They're so uptight. Even if they see me with a candy bar or a can of soda—and forget coffee or booze. It's like a prison. It's like I feel like Hansel or Gretel or whoever it was the witch was fattening up for the roast except in the old days the witch just gave them food, she wasn't like into what's bad for you. I mean, they could care less what's bad for *me*—I mean they're like really nice to us in this really fake way but you know it's just because the bun is in the oven still, soon as they get their hands on it, we'll see if they remember us. (*Brena produces a bottle of soda from her bag.*) (*Continued.*) All right! Brena, you're my savior. I can't believe it.

BRENA: No problem. (*They pass the bottle back and forth.*)

JEN: We better hide this stuff before Marina comes back.

BRENA: Who's she?

JEN: She's eight months. She's only gained twenty pounds so she freaks out if she sees anything with calories because her boyfriend'll kill her if she comes back fat. She's got the adopting parents to give her an extra thou for relocation or psychological adjustment or something—her uncle's a lawyer so he made this great deal—so her and her boyfriend're going to Cancun.

BRENA: Where's that?

JEN: Some island in Tahiti or something. Anyway, she's kind of a pain in the ass because she cries a lot in the night and I can't sleep.

BRENA: Can't you change rooms?

JEN: (*Distracted, troubled.*) I don't know. (*Pause.*)

BRENA: So. You coming back?

JEN: I don't know.

BRENA: I saw your mother the other day.

JEN: Oh, yeah? How is the bitch?

BRENA: Who knows.

JEN: She's going through this whole fucking god trip on me. She writes me this letter full of all this flowery bull shit, "I won't abandon you in your distress, hate the sin but love the sinner, you are my child and will always be my child" but underneath clear as day is "You slut, you disgusting pig, how could you do something so dirty and disgusting, didn't I tell you not to let those pricks into your pants?!"

BRENA: Yeah . . .

JEN: But she'd never let me come back with the baby, god, that would be too terrible to have this daily reminder of what a whore her daughter is and for all of her friends and neighbors to know—

it's just too, too disgusting. (*They're high, each thinking her own private thoughts.*)

BRENA: Yeah.

JEN: I always feel like two people, you know?

BRENA: Uh-uh.

JEN: The person who had these feelings, these secret feelings and it's about feeling good, you know, from when you're little and you get that people don't like to see you rubbing yourself up against stuff to feel good, know what I mean?

BRENA: You're bad. (*They laugh.*)

JEN: So you like go underground . . .

BRENA: You better!

JEN: And then when a guy kisses you or feels your tit or says something in your ear and you feel really hot and silky . . . and on top of it, really intense, riding a wave. And . . . it's so far from your life, the rest of your regular life. And it's fabulous. And it has nothing to do with, like, sex education—

BRENA: Huh?

JEN: Like everybody says, you asshole, why didn't you use anything—

BRENA: Who said that?

JEN: Anyway, everybody's thinking it. And they talk about how it makes *guys* feel . . .

BRENA: Uh huh.

JEN: Like *they* have this, like, urge, these strong feelings but nobody wants to like admit—like they're scared or something that girls have these really hot feelings—

BRENA: (*Sarcastic.*) They don't.

JEN: So all they talk about is it's up to the girls to not let the guys into their pants—

BRENA: That's right.

JEN: And don't get pregnant and watch out for diseases and getting raped and, shit, I know there are a lot of assholes out there and I don't want to get diseased or raped but—shit.

BRENA: Yeah. (*Pause.*)

JEN: (*Putting her hand on her stomach.*) Hey, hey, hey!

BRENA: What?

JEN: She's kicking me. (*To stomach.*) Don't you listen to this, baby. God. She sure is lively.

BRENA: How come you call it a she?

JEN: 'Cause they did an amnio.

BRENA: What's that?

JEN: It's when the adopters want to know if it's going to be a boy or a girl. It's a girl.

BRENA: Wow. Cool. (*Pause.*)

JEN: I got a letter from the lady that wants to adopt her.

BRENA: Wow.

JEN: She lives in New York City. She isn't married. I thought that'd be good 'cause I'm not married. And the kid wouldn't grow up with a lot of arguing and stuff.

BRENA: Right.

JEN: She has some kind of job that she does in an office but she can do it at home if she wants.

BRENA: Wow.

JEN: Editing.

BRENA: Huh.

JEN: She lives in an apartment and she also has a house in the countryside in Massachusetts that she goes to sometimes on weekends and summer vacation. She has a garden.

BRENA: Wow.

JEN: I wonder what you have to do to get to be an editor.

BRENA: Yeah. (*Jen pulls out a letter, reads.*)

JEN: She says she's thirty-eight years old.

BRENA: Wow.

JEN: And she thinks that's good because she had a lot of time to get to know what she wanted to do in her life and have fun.

BRENA: Huh.

JEN: She says, "There's nothing I can think of that would be as gratifying as to bring up a child. To nurture and guide and teach and love."

BRENA: Huh.

JEN: Sounds good.

BRENA: Yeah. (*Pause.*)

JEN: I had this thought. That I could write her and say, okay, you can have the baby if you take me too.

BRENA: She's not going to want you.

JEN: I know, but maybe.

BRENA: No way.

JEN: She sounds so nice.

BRENA: She wants your baby.

JEN: Yeah. Or I was thinking I could just go to New York and find them.

BRENA: How're you going to find them? You got her address?

JEN: No. They don't let you know that stuff But, like, I could just look in all the playgrounds.

BRENA: They don't have playgrounds in New York.

JEN: They don't?

BRENA: No way.

JEN: Why would I want my kid to grow up in New York then?

BRENA: (*Excited.*) Oh—god—Jason went to New York. He just split.

JEN: (*Excited.*) I read about it in the digest. What happened?

BRENA: He found out Marcie's baby was really from Tom.

JEN: She should've told him.

BRENA: She was too scared.

JEN: Did he start drinking again?

BRENA: Not yet. And Chester stole Benny back.

JEN: Oh my god.

BRENA: And he doesn't have his medicine.

JEN: God. What happened to Babs?

BRENA: She's left Howie. She found out he was sleeping with Bernice. But he doesn't know she knows. And she and Rick are back together.

JEN: Wow. (*Pause.*) I really dig Rick.

BRENA: Yeah. (*Pause.*)

JEN: It's weird. Like, sometimes I think about Frankie, like, what if he knew about it, what would he do, and what if he comes through the restaurant again and I'm there. I mean, maybe she's gonna look like him or something.

BRENA: Yeah.

JEN: Then I think, what if I could get a hold of him and maybe he'd lend me some money, just to get me started, just 'cause maybe he wouldn't want to give away his kid or something.

BRENA: Yeah.

JEN: It would just be so cool to have a baby and, like, you'd never feel alone anymore and if you ever needed a reason to, like, work hard or if you just felt, what's the point, just look over at her and that's it.

BRENA: I don't know.

JEN: But I don't even know his last name. I'm such a fool. (*Pause.*)

JEN: (*Continued.*) You never saw him again after that night, did you?

BRENA: Uh uh.

JEN: (*To stomach.*) Hey, hey, easy does it. We're talking about your daddy, the fuck. (*They laugh.*)

JEN: (*Continued.*) No—not really. I'll always say he was a cool guy, like, you don't want to grow up thinking your daddy was a shit.

BRENA: Right.

JEN: I'll just say he lost my number or something.

BRENA: Yeah.

END SCENE

SCENE NINE

Night. Molly and Fran standing arm in arm at a bus stop.

FRAN: His father had a furniture shop. They fixed antique furniture. And he'd have the truck and we'd go there at night and sit in the dark with all the furniture. We'd smoke Camels and he'd tell me about Plato and Aristotle and then we'd drink Grand Marnier and neck.

MOLLY: (*Laughs.*) Oh, god.

FRAN: I remember one night he touched my breasts and I stopped him and he said, why, and I wasn't sure. I had to think about it. It wasn't—natural—for me. Being raised a Catholic this was all a sin so I was pretty tense, pretty cut off. But I liked the idea, you know, of romance and intimacy and disobedience.

MOLLY: Right.

FRAN: I remember sitting in the dark in this big room full of beds and up-ended chairs, making out their outlines in the dim light, trying to work out what I thought about him feeling my breasts, whether it was okay, whether I really thought it was a sin. I decided I didn't think it was a sin so we did it. It was very strange—I felt very outside it at first, but after a while I began to enjoy it. One night I remember getting really, you know, aroused—

MOLLY: Uh huh.

FRAN: And getting on top of him and pressing myself against him. Later, he told me that was the one time he didn't like. It seemed too forward or gross or something. So I stopped seeing him, just avoided him, never told him why. Until a couple of years later and we'd both had others, we each lost that precious virginity—

MOLLY: Uh huh.

FRAN: We met at a party and ended up at the shop and made it on one of the beds. I guess we were each proving something to the other. I guess he was showing me he now knew what to do and wasn't scared of it, which I now realize was the problem but at the time, of course, I just felt so completely humiliated and—and that I shouldn't trust, you know, these feelings—

MOLLY: Uh huh.

FRAN: And I guess I was just—this sounds absurd—just being polite. I pretended I was, you know, into it—

MOLLY: Uh huh.

FRAN: But I kept remembering that one night and how it had turned him off. That was it. We never saw each other after that night. But that's how I got pregnant. I was eighteen. And . . . Daddy knew a doctor. And it was taken care of.

MOLLY: Huh.

END SCENE

SCENE TEN

Hospital room. Jen in bed wearing hospital gown. Sylvia sitting in a chair next to the bed.

JEN: I want to see the baby. I just want to see the baby.

SYLVIA: I know, dear. I know.

JEN: Where are my clothes?

SYLVIA: Your parents have them. They'll be here soon.

JEN: You stole my clothes.

SYLVIA: You'll get them back.

JEN: I want to see the baby.

SYLVIA: I know. (*Jen's father, Eugene, comes in. He has flowers.*)

EUGENE: Hi, Jen.

JEN: Hi, Daddy.

EUGENE: Okay?

JEN: Yeah. (*Sylvia begins to leave.*)

SYLVIA: I'll find a vase.

EUGENE: We'll take them home.

SYLVIA: (*Flustered.*) Okay. I'll just . . . (*Sylvia leaves.*)

EUGENE: I brought you something. (*He gives her a toy stuffed animal.*)

JEN: Thanks.

EUGENE: For your collection. And here's some clothes your mother packed. (*Hands bag to Jen who takes it behind a curtain and dresses.*) She's feeling sick. Says she'll see you when you get home.

(*Beat.*) We cleaned up your room, got it all ready for you. But I wouldn't let her take down the posters, said that was up to you. Your Uncle Harold and Aunt Grace are coming over for dinner. They want to see you. (*Sylvia comes in, goes behind curtain to check on Jen.*)

SYLVIA: Mr. Sullivan is here. (*Mac comes in.*)

MAC: Don't let me interrupt the family reunion. (*Jen comes out, Sylvia leaves.*)

MAC: (*Continued.*) Hello, dear. They tell me you were a real trooper.

JEN: They put me to sleep.

MAC: Uh huh.

JEN: I wanted to be awake. I wanted to see the baby.

MAC: (*Smiles at Eugene.*) She wanted to be awake. (*To Jen.*) Believe me, there's nothing romantic about this event. Ask my wife. (*To both.*) The first kid she tried natural—after that, with the other two, they knocked her out. She said, please, we don't go through enough, we have to go through that hell as well? She said she got to hating men so bad during that first birth she thought the whole thing—procreation!—was a plot against women! She went crazy—almost turned her into a lesbian. Luckily, by the time I saw her she'd pretty much recovered. So you're glad the doctor took pity on you (*To Eugene.*)—right?

EUGENE: That's right. (*Mac pulls out some papers, takes them to Jen.*)

MAC: (*To Jen.*) Anyway, you'll have many more opportunities if you really want to go through it. You'll finish school, meet the right guy, settle down—you've got another chance for that ideal life—a lot of girls don't get that. Now, honey, just sign here. Just a formality. (*Jen looks at the papers, blurred by tears. Can't move.*)

MAC: Come on, honey. It'll all seem like ancient history tomorrow.

JEN: (*To Eugene.*) Do I have to?

EUGENE: That's right. (*Jen signs the papers.*)

MAC: (*Relieved.*) Good girl. (*Mac brings the papers to the Eugene. He signs.*)

MAC: Good. Now. Fine. All set. Okay, Jenny, you come along with me. Just a legality. We need to bring the package together into the lobby. (*To Eugene.*) Why don't you come along? (*They all go out.*)

END SCENE

SCENE ELEVEN

Hospital lobby. Fran and Sylvia stand, waiting, across the lobby from a band of elevators.

SYLVIA: I'll take the money.

FRAN: Oh. Right. I'm sorry. Um. (*Fran fishes in her bag, pulls out an envelope, surreptitiously hands it to Sylvia who opens it and without pulling the money out, counts it, and puts it in her purse.*)

FRAN: I feel sick.

SYLVIA: It's all right. It'll be okay.

FRAN: Why is it taking so long?

SYLVIA: It isn't taking so long.

FRAN: Our flight leaves in an hour.

SYLVIA: It's twenty minutes to the airport. You'll have plenty of time. Mr. Sullivan knows what he's doing.

FRAN: What if she's changed her mind?

SYLVIA: There's always another baby.

FRAN: Fuck. She's changed her mind, hasn't she?

SYLVIA: No. Believe me, she has no alternative.

FRAN: (*Thrown.*) What do you mean?

SYLVIA: She's a kid. What's she going to do? How's she going to take care of a baby? Her parents aren't going to help.

FRAN: Oh, god.

SYLVIA: Believe me, justice will prevail, thank god.

FRAN: What?

SYLVIA: You get a baby, the baby gets a mother, and the mother gets her future served up on a silver plate. Understand? (*Pause.*)

FRAN: Why can't I have a receipt?

SYLVIA: For what?

FRAN: The money I just gave you.

SYLVIA: Don't panic.

FRAN: I'm not. I'm just asking.

SYLVIA: (*Working to maintain control.*) I know Mr. Sullivan made it real clear that if you got a receipt for every expense in the operation, it's gonna jeapordize the operation, understand? There is absolutely nothing illegal in this exchange, okay? I'm a professional. I did my job. But when you go to court for the finalization, how's it gonna look if you got all these receipts and fees you paid all along the way? It's gonna look a lot more organized than it really was and that's gonna make the judge real uncomfortable. If you want to do that, then fine.

FRAN: (*Trying to drop it.*) Okay.

SYLVIA: I'll say one thing: if my daughter'd been such a fool I'd'a knocked her upside the head.

FRAN: I'm sorry?

SYLVIA: I'm talking hanging on to what you got or you're just handing over your life for them to trash and burn.

FRAN: Yes.

SYLVIA: You gotta give these children the tools to survive, understand? I'd be on my daughter every day, year after year and she's at a great university now, you hear me? I'd kill for that child. (*The elevator door opens, out come Eugene arm in arm with Jen, and Mac holding the baby. Mac turns to Jen and Eugene, says good bye, sees Fran and Sylvia and walks quickly over to them. Jen and Eugene stand there watching.*)

MAC: (*Angry, under his breath.*) I told you to wait in the car. (*Fran is completely flustered, aware of the baby and of Jen across the lobby.*)

FRAN: Oh . . . I thought . . .

MAC: Let's go. Don't stop. (*Mac starts out the door with the baby. Fran and Jen are frozen, looking at each other. Mac comes back, takes Fran's arm, escorts her out.*)

MAC: (*Hisses.*) Goddamnit, you want to wreck the whole thing, for christsake let's get the fuck out of here. (*Fran glances back at Jen as Mac escorts her out. They're gone. Then Jen looks blankly at Sylvia who waves, embarrassed, and leaves. Jen weeps in Eugene's arms.*)

END SCENE

SCENE TWELVE

Washington Square playground. Fran sits on the bench with Grace. There are two strollers, each with a sleeping child.

GRACE: My father, he had a bakery. My mother had a shop. In the morning, my sisters, they would comb my hair. We would have breakfast, an egg and bread and Ovaltine. Or some days, oat porridge. My sister, she always had a cup of coffee, from the time she was two years old, she always liked it and my father, he let her have it. (*Pause. They watch the children.*) My mother, she had a car so sometime she drop us to school. On the way home we would be by my grandmother. She was the first house on the road home, so that's where we would go. (*Pause.*) For supper we would have rice with beans and vegetables, sometimes meat. Goat meat sometimes. Junji, a kind of corn meal. Eggplant. We like it spicy. Some days, you would hear the horn blowing and you would go down and get your fish. On Saturdays you would go down and get your meat. My father, his favorite thing was Campbells vegetable soup. He would put that on everything. (*Pause.*) My sisters, they came here first. They say there are more opportunities here and they can make out better. (*Pause.*)

GRACE: (*Continued.*) When I come here, the most surprising thing is that in the winter the sun is shining. I thought it would snow all the time. But that it could be cold and the sun shining I never thought could be. And the tall buildings, I never saw this. And the subway. And the way you have to be locked in, you know, locking the windows and locking the doors. And . . . all the planning. You always have to be planning here. Back there you could just pass and drop in. You don't have to call. (*Pause.*) My baby, Carl, he is five. Daslele is eight. Junior is nine. They stay with my mother. And my sister, too, is there. When I first came I'd be thinking it's three o'clock, four o'clock, five o'clock, oh, they're home now, maybe now they're doing their homework, maybe now they're having their supper, now they should be in bed. I call twice a month. They complain to me. They tell me what they want. I send Daslele a cabbage patch doll with corn silk hair. And some Jordash jeans. Junior I send a little computer game and a camera. Carl, he only want money. (*Pause.*) I never wanted nobody to take care of me. Because then you can't say what's on your mind. Or if they don't like it then they stop taking care of you. So if they say jump, you jump. Now, if you say jump, I sit. (*Molly comes in, flops down between the women on the bench.*)

MOLLY: Hi!

FRAN: Molly! You made it!

MOLLY: I have exactly forty-two minutes before I have to be back. She's asleep! I can't believe it. (*Grabbing stroller, pretending anger.*) Carly! I'm here. I've got forty-two minutes of quality time and you're copping z's?!

FRAN: We tried to keep her up, gave her coffee, dexidrine, nothing seemed to work.

MOLLY: (*Resigned, pulling sandwich and drink out of paper bag.*) Oh, well. It's a fabulous day. It's great just to get out of there. How you doing, Grace? Everything went okay today?

GRACE: She wanted to stay with Janey at school.

MOLLY: Oh, dear.

GRACE: But after that she was fine.

MOLLY: How was the birthday party?

FRAN: Great. Except your daughter kept on grabbing all of Tara's presents. I finally had to promise her that you'd bring home lots of presents for her tonight.

MOLLY: Fran!

FRAN: It was my last recourse. (*Beginning to gather her things.*)

GRACE: Maybe I'll do those errands now, while you're here.

MOLLY: Great.

FRAN: You look quite smashing.

MOLLY: Do I? The proper tension between funky and chic? Makes you want to hand over all your loot to the Children's Art Fund?

FRAN: Absolutely.

MOLLY: Thanks, pal.

GRACE: Maybe I'll do those errands now.

GRACE: I'll be back.

MOLLY: Okay.

FRAN: See you soon.

GRACE: All right. (*Grace leaves.*)

MOLLY: Look at them. They're such grown ups.

FRAN: Aren't they?

MOLLY: I can't stand it. How do people stand it?

FRAN: I don't know.

MOLLY: I mean, you work. You've always worked.

FRAN: It is easier, to work at home. To take breaks, have lunch with Tara. Knock off early. Work at night. That flexibility. And Mrs. Schmidman is great. And I do, often, actually enjoy my work. Of course, it is exhausting. I'm exhausted all the time.

MOLLY: If I could just get back the afternoons, going with Carly to pick up Janey from school, walking through the park, actually having a sense, over the months, of the seasons changing.

FRAN: Yes.

MOLLY: Stopping to examine a stone, a leaf, a piece of glass, an old condom . . . (*They laugh.*)

FRAN: Ah, exotic nature!

MOLLY: Going to the market, visiting with Myung and Sun Jung, examining vegetables, imagining what I might cook. They'd give the girls Gummy Bears . . .

FRAN: Mmm.

MOLLY: Stopping at Frankie's practicing our Spanish, fighting over whether they can have more candy, dragging them, screaming, out of the store.

FRAN: Sounds delightful.

MOLLY: Going home, they'd play, or watch Sesame Street, or help me. Sometimes some little personal thought or question or event of the day would pop out . . .

FRAN: Uh huh.

MOLLY: And I'd scrub the potatoes, scrape the carrots, chop the broccoli. Mundane tasks I never really thought about. But there's something nice about having that . . . the smell and texture and color and shape of this stuff from the earth . . .

FRAN: Huh.

MOLLY: Now, I come home, they've had supper, the day's over. They seem fine. But . . . I feel so distant. I pretend to connect. The other night, I was giving them a bath, they were arguing, complaining about something, I just lost it, screamed at them to shut up, stormed out, leaving them crying, hysterical. It was awful.

FRAN: You were always bad around bath time.

MOLLY: I was?

FRAN: Yes.

MOLLY: (*Thoughtful.*) I guess that's true. Maybe, if I had a snack before . . . I get them tucked in, and if we have enough cash Jack and I order Chinese. Otherwise we have beer and granola for supper.

FRAN: That's really pathetic.

MOLLY: Isn't it?

FRAN: I have a confession to make.

MOLLY: Oh-oh.

FRAN: Tara and I mainly eat in coffee shops. When I cook it's fish sticks or chicken pot pies.

MOLLY: I did know that about you.

FRAN: Oh. I suppose you did. We like it like that. (*Pause.*)

MOLLY: If we can just catch up on our taxes, I could go back to part time. If I could start selling my paintings. If I could ever get back into the studio. If I ever paint again. (*Pause.*)

FRAN: I've been thinking about the mother all day.

MOLLY: You mean . . . ?

FRAN: Wondering if she remembers it's Tara's birthday, whether she thinks about her, what her life is like. I don't correspond with her. I gather she has the pictures I sent to her through the lawyer. Sometimes I want to talk with her, be with her. Other times I feel so threatened . . . just that she's out there. (*Pause.*)

FRAN: (*Continued.*) I wonder whether she'll be in Tara's life when she's older . . . Of course I won't keep the information from Tara, I'll dutifully follow the current thinking on letting the child know her history. (*Beat.*) I dreamed we were all together—she and Tara and I—on some rocks, a coast somewhere, very windy, wet. That's all I remember. (*Pause.*)

MOLLY: She's your daughter, you know.

FRAN: I know. Mine. The toddler's possessive.

MOLLY: Sorry?

FRAN: A clue on a recent crossword puzzle.

MOLLY: Oh. (*Pause.*)

FRAN: I've started to play the violin again.

MOLLY: That's wonderful.

FRAN: Yes, like returning to an old friend. And to be inside these pieces of music I'd banished myself from for so many years . . . I tried to bring myself to play for my mother before she died. She'd be lying in bed, wasting away, becoming less, less of what she'd been, vaguer, sweeter. Or . . . it was easier to project onto her. Or . . . I had less need to project onto her. I remember, when we were driving her especially crazy, she'd tell us we were killing her and she'd lock herself up in the bathroom and we'd be hysterical, weeping, banging on the door, begging her to come out, not to die, we'd be good. I'd run and get my fiddle, play everything I knew, she'd eventually come out.

MOLLY: Oh, Fran. (*Beat.*)

FRAN: Once she told me how when Mozart was seventeen his father scolded him, told him he could be a great violinist if only he'd practice. He wrote six concerti between the ages of seventeen and nineteen. So the concerti were his way of malingering. He was avoiding practicing. (*Beat. Fran watches Tara.*)

FRAN: (*Continued.*) God, I adore her. (*Beat.*) I've composed a couple of songs for her. I can't get them out of my head.

MOLLY: Fran! How wonderful! What are they?

FRAN: The first is so she's inspired to drink her milk.

MOLLY: (*Delighted.*) Oh.

FRAN: (*Sings.*) "Milk, milk, milk, it comes from the cow or the goat. It goes right down your throat to your tummy! And we love a dove a dove a dove it! Oh, the farmer goes to the cow and he says 'Thank you, cow, 'cause you know how to make milk, and we love a dove a dove a dove a dove it.' And the farmer pulls the teats of the cow and milk spurts into the bucket. And he takes the bucket of milk and pours it into some cartons. And he puts the cartons of milk on his truck and drives into the city and he sells the milk to the people in the store—you know what for—what for? For milk, milk, milk, it comes from the cow or the goat. It goes right down your throat to your tummy. And we love a dove a dove a dove a dove it."

MOLLY: (*Watching the sleeping girls, happy.*) God, look at them. They're such angels. (*Checks her watch.*) I don't want to go back.

FRAN: And the other is so Tara will sit on the potty and poop.

MOLLY: Oh. How handy.

FRAN: (*Sings.*) "Oh, poop-a-doop-a-doop, oh, poop-a doop-a-doop, how I have to poop. Oh, poop-a-doop-a-doop, oh, poop-a-doop-a-doop, how I have to poop. Well, there was a boy, he was sitting on the bus, and he had to poop. And he said to the bus driver, sir, what should I do . . ."

END PLAY

Pearl Cleage

CHAIN

Author's Introduction

Chain and *Late Bus to Mecca* are the first two plays in a series of what I am calling morality plays. My intention is to accurately reflect contemporary African American female reality and in the process begin a collective redefinition of our sisterhood with an eye toward our survival.

Both plays explore the vulnerability and isolation of young black women who find themselves abandoned by the culture, preyed upon by those who should protect them, and forced by circumstance to question the traditional values that sustained their mothers and grandmothers, but have no relevance to their own lives.

Chain was coproduced by the Women's Project & Productions and The New Federal Theatre under the directorship of Julia Miles and Woodie King Jr., respectively, at the Judith Anderson Theatre, New York City from February 28 to March 22, 1992 with the following cast:

ROSA   Karen Malina White

Stage Manager   Melody A. Beal
Stage directions   Betty Vaughn and Erika Vaughn
House Manager   Cory Washburn and Sheri Wilner
Casting   Susan Haskins

Chain was commissioned and developed by the Women's Project & Productions and the Southeast Playwrights Project of Atlanta through a grant from the Multi Arts Production Fund of the Rockefeller Foundation.

TIME

1991

SETTING

A one bedroom apartment in a battered Harlem, New York apartment building.

CHARACTERS

ROSA JENKINS, a sixteen-year-old black girl, addicted to crack.

DAY ONE

The stage and the house are completely dark. A slide comes up on a screen at the rear of the stage: DAY ONE. *The slide holds for ten seconds and then disappears, leaving us again in complete darkness. The sounds that we can hear should come from this darkness suddenly, starting with a loud scream. These are sounds of scuffling, struggling, trying to escape and being caught. Only one voice is heard, the voice of Rosa Jackson, a sixteen-year-old crack addict. It should be clear that there is a struggle going on, but the cause of the struggle should be completely unknown, adding to the frightening nature of the sounds.*

ROSA: (*Screaming, crying, pleading in the darkness.*) *What are you doing?* No! Stop it! Don't, Daddy! Please don't! Stop it! Stop it! Daddy, don't do that! Please don't do that! Daddy! Daddy! Wait, Daddy! Wait! Don't do it! Please, don't do it! Please, don't do it! Daddy, please! Please!

The sounds of struggle suddenly stop, but the loud sobbing continues. There is the sound of footsteps and then the sound of a door slamming and a deadbolt lock clicking loudly into place. Silence, suddenly broken by Rosa's shriek.

ROSA: Da-a-a-a-a-deeeeee!

Lights up full. Rosa is crumpled in a heap in the middle of the floor. She is sobbing loudly. The apartment around her is small and crowded with well worn furniture, a television set, plastic fruit or flowers, a cheaply framed picture of John Kennedy, Martin Luther King and Bobby Kennedy. Another framed dime store painting of a white Jesus.
Rosa cries bitterly for a few minutes, then she sits up suddenly.

ROSA: Mama? (*She listens intently and then speaks tentatively.*) Mama? Is that you? (*Listens again and then speaks angrily.*) I hear you out there listening. *What kind of mother are you?* How can you let him do this to me? You don't love me! You never loved me! You hate me! You all hate me! (*Crumples again, sobbing. Stops suddenly*

and sits up. This time her look is more crafty. She is still listening.)
Mama? Mama are you still there? I didn't mean it, Mama. You
know I didn't mean it. I know you love me. It's me. I know it's me.
I love you, Mama. (*Listens.*) Mama? Can you hear me? I know you
can hear me. I can hear you breathing! Talk to me, Mama. Say
something. Say *anything!* (*Angry again.*) Well, don't then! I don't
care what you do! You can't keep me in here if I don't want to stay!
I'll get away just like I always do. You know I can do it, Mama!
And you know I will! So you might as well go on to work and stop
waiting to see what I'm gonna do. I'm gonna do what I damn well
please and there's nothing you can do about it. *Not a goddam thing!*
Now! How do you like that? (*Listens again. Suddenly frightened.*)
Mama? Please let me out, Mama? Please let me out! I'm scared
to be in here like this! Please let me out, Mama! I won't tell Daddy,
I promise. He'll never know the difference. I won't go nowhere,
I swear. I was just kiddin'. You can trust me, Mama. Honest!
(*No sound at all from outside. She is suddenly enraged.*) Open this
door and look at me! You scared to see me like this? (*Laughs
crazily.*) Well, that's just too damn bad because you gotta deal with
it. Look at me!

> *Rosa lunges for the door and for the first time we see that she is
> chained to the radiator with a long, thick chain. The chain is about
> six feet long and strong enough to hold her. She is shackled by her left
> foot. The chain is long enough for her to have some range of motion,
> but not long enough for her to get to the door. As she lunges toward
> it, the chain jerks her back, twisting her ankle painfully. She yelps in
> pain and falls down again. She grabs the chain and tries to pull it off
> of her leg, but she can't. She goes to the radiator and tries to pull the
> chain off of the radiator, but she can't. She becomes more and more
> frantic as she pulls on it futilely. She is like a caged animal and she
> growls in her throat in a way that expresses wordless rage and
> frustration. She paces around the apartment as the reality of what
> has happened settles on her. She is wild. Almost out of control. She
> pulls on the chain, shakes it, rattles it, etc. She stands breathlessly
> looking around at the apartment. Suddenly, she grabs a portrait of*

her mother and father and herself at a younger age and throws it to the ground. The glass in the frame shatters against the floor and the noise seems to dissipate her rage. She collapses near the glass fragments, weeping loudly. After a minute, she sits up and looks at the glass. She picks up a large shard and, still weeping, holds it over her wrist. She slowly tries to bring it down across her arm, but she doesn't have the nerve. She holds it trembling there for a long moment and then throws it away and collapses in a silent heap on the floor.

BLACK

DAY TWO

Lights up. Rosa is searching through the house as far as her chain will allow her movement. She is moving awkwardly. She tangles the chain in things, stumbles over it, etc.

ROSA: (*Jerking the chain angrily.*) Damn! (*She flops down on the sofa, frustrated and angry. She is facing the audience and seems to see them for the first time. Her face is startled, but almost immediately takes on the craftiness of the dope fiend.*)

ROSA: Got a match? (*She holds up a wrinkled cigarette.*) *Hey!* I'm talking to you! Y'all got a match? (*Disgusted at the lack of response.*) It ain't no reefer, okay? It's a *Winston* or some shit. (*A beat.*) Oh, I see. I'm invisible, right? You looking right at me and nobody see me, right? Okay. No problem. (*A beat.*) Y'all probably don't smoke no way. Right? Lookin out for your health and shit. You probably wouldn't give me a damn match if you had it. (*A beat.*) My dad told you not to talk to me, right? Not to listen to anything I said cuz I'm a dope fiend and I might trick you into doin something bad.

Fuck it. (*She tosses cigarette aside. Throughout her talking she moves restlessly around. She touches the chain a lot because the awkwardness and horror make it impossible for her to keep her hands off of it. She is also a dope fiend and she is already feeling the effects of being deprived of the drug.*)

These country ass niggas think they can keep me chained up in here like some kind of freak. But that's where they wrong. I ain't no dumb ass dog! I can figure this shit out. Be back on the street before they country asses get home from work tonight.

I wasted a lot of time yesterday cause I was in a state of shock or some shit. I couldn't believe this shit was really happening to me. *Of all people!* Now I know I have been kind of crazy lately, but this shit . . . this is like some movie of the week shit, here. Geraldo and shit. I mean, when I got home, they was actin so glad to see me and shit and now *this?*

My Dad just gave the guy the money without talking a whole lot of bullshit about what he was gonna do if they didn't leave me alone and shit. Now even I was surprised at that.

He used to go off! Hollerin and shit. Talkin about callin the cops and turnin everybody in. Next time I'd get loose and come around, nobody wanted to let me in cause they were scared my pops was gonna come back and turn out.

He would, too. Every damn time. Them niggas used to crack up behind that shit, too. My Dad would start tellin them how they ought to be ashamed to be sellin that shit to kids and wadn't nobody in there more than seventeen. Buyin or sellin! He didn't do it this time though. I guess he was just tired of the shit.

Or he was tryin to throw me off. Make me think he wadn't gonna do nothin and then *wham!* Here come this shit! I slept all day Saturday. I been up for three days. Maybe four. Next morning before they went to work, I came out to tell 'em good-by and they sittin at the table talkin real quiet and they stop real fast when I come in. Then they look at each other and my dad pulls out a chair for me. They was lookin so serious, I thought they was gettin' ready to send me back to rehab and then my dad goes to the closet and pulls out this big ass bag and comes over and sits down beside me and hugs me and shit and starts talking about how happy they were when I was first born and shit and how I'll always be their daughter and they love me so much and I'm thinkin', yeah, okay for this *Father Knows Best* crap, but what's in the damn bag? Then I looked at Mama and she's *cryin'* and shit.

Mama ain't cried when I went to rehab since I was thirteen, so I know this is some serious shit. I know this sounds crazy, but I thought they was gonna kill me. I could tell it was something heavy in the bag and I thought maybe Daddy had, like a sledge hammer, or something and they was gonna beat me to death and then put me in a bag and drop me in the river. (*Laughs.*) Crazy shit, right? But you know your mind give you all kinda shit when you get scared.

Then Daddy takes out this big ass chain and shit and I freaked. I started running around the room and I tried to hold onto Mama and she was holding me and we was both crying. Look like *The Color Purple* and shit. "Save me, Mama! Save me!" But that shit didn't work on Daddy no better than it did that nigga in the movie. He pulled my hands offa her and made her go on to work. She didn't want to go and I was screaming and crying and begging her not do this to me and she was crying, too, but Daddy was holding me so tight I could hardly breath and he kept talking to Mama in this very calm voice and reminding her that they had talked about this and telling her that this was the only way and it was for my own good. Shit like that. So she looked at me and then she grabbed her purse and ran out the room. Then it was just me and Daddy. (*She picks up the cigarette again.*)

I know one of y'all got a damn match. I swear this is a *Winston*. If it was some reefer I'd eat it, okay? (*A beat.*) Fuck it. I hate cigarettes anyway. My junior high school teacher used to catch us smokin in the bathroom and make us flush them down the toilet. I didn't care. I was just doin' it cause Paula was doin it and she my girl. *A nasty habit,* that's what Miss Young would say. *Smoking is a nasty habit!*

Paula say smokin ain't nothin. She can tell the bitch about a couple of sho nuff nasty habits if she really interested. (*Laughing.*) Paula would do that shit, too. She crazy. She say anything to people and just walk away. Most of the time they too surprised to say anything back or they just start laughing. I can't do that shit. If I say some smart ass shit to people they wanna fight. That's cause she cute. They don't care what she say cause they like lookin at her while she standin there sayin it. (*She touches the chain and jumps, having forgotten it for a minute.*)

I told Paula she better stop smoking cause she pregnant now and that shit make your baby come out real little and be sick all the time. She say she gave up smokin reefer 'til the nigga born. She ain't givin up nothing else. Then she roll her eyes and wink like she know somethin I don't know. I ask her do she mean her and Darryl still fuckin, big as her stomach done got and she say that is a personal question, which mean yes! Paula a freak anyway, though, so you never can tell. I told her she don't ever need to start smoking no rock cause she would be a coke hoe in about ten seconds. (*Laughs.*)

Me and her used to smoke a lot of reefer together when we was in seventh grade. Miss Young's class. She used to read to us at the end of the day right before we went home and I'd be so high, Paula had to keep wakin me up about every two seconds.

A lotta people like they reefer, but I'm not down wit it. I figure, what's the point? If I'm gonna go to all the trouble to get some money and go buy some shit, I wanna get as high as I can. I don't want to be somewhere sleep with my mouth all open and shit. I want to be awake so I can *feel* something! (*Looking around, disgusted.*)

They didn't even leave the t.v. in here. One of those tight ass blond bitches at my last drug rehab told my mom that she thought maybe watching t.v. was "overstimulating" me and making me wanna do drugs. And my moms went for it! Made me stop watchin t.v., except for *The Cosby Show* cause she think the Cosby kids are role models and shit. Yeah, right. Put my ass in a great big house with a whole lotta money and I'll be a role model, too.

I tried to tell her that t.v. ain't shit stimulation compared to what's up on the street! It's always somethin happenin out there.

They just don't see it. Or they see it and they scared of it. I ain't scared of nothin. I seen more shit in sixteen years than they seen in forty and I know how to handle it. Jesus (*NOTE: His name is pronounced in Spanish – "Hey-suess"*) say you either got to get into *it* or *it's* gonna get into you. (*A beat.*) No. What he says is if it's gonna get into you, you gotta get into . . . no. Wait. (*A beat.*) If it gets . . . (*A beat.*) Fuck it. It sounds like it makes sense when he say it, but I can't get that shit straight. (*A beat.*) I feel like shit. (*A beat, then louder.*) *I feel like shit!* (*A beat.*) And don't nobody give a fuck. They say they do, but they really don't. Otherwise, (*this rises to a shriek by the end of the sentence,*) they would leave me the fuck alone and bring me some damn rock up in here so I can get high! (*A beat.*) Always tellin me how hard life is. Didn't nobody tell them to be workin at Harlem Hospital every damn day of the week. (*A beat.*)

They never would have found me if Jesus hadn't a told, with his ignorant *"I'll be right back"* ass. Nobody else knew where I was to be sendin somebody bustin up in the place. No reason to. Daddy hadn't offered no reward. *"Have you seen this girl? Twenty-five-dollar reward."* Goddam crack addicts will turn your ass in for a quarter so muthafuckas got signs all over the neighborhood. People be turnin in they friends and shit. Ain't no crack addict gonna keep no secret if there's dope money comin from tellin' it. If my Daddy had offered a reward, I'd a turned *myself in!* Shit! I figure ain't nobody got more of a right to collect a reward on somebody than that same somebody, right? (*Forgetting the chain, she rises and heads for the kitchen. The chain jerks her back.*)

Damn! (*Rising anger.*) Damn! (*She sits again, drawing up her knees and rocking back and forth with some agitation. She really wants some crack. She suddenly sees some matches under the couch. She drags the chain awkwardly over and finally reaches them with great effort. She sits on the floor exhausted and lights the Winston. She inhales deeply and then explodes into a terrible cough. She cannot get her breath for several seconds. When she regains her composure, she takes a deep breath and looks around. She snubs out the Winston and begins to crumble. She hugs her knees to her chest, bows her head and begins to rock silently back and fourth.)*

BLACK

DAY THREE

> *Rosa is trying to sleep on the couch under a child's worn bedspread with colorful cartoon figures on it. She tosses fitfully, but can't figure out a way to sleep comfortably with the chain on her leg. She sits up in frustration.*

ROSA: Help! (*She waits. Listens. Then louder.*) Help!! (*Listening.*) *Help, they're killin me!* (*Listens.*) Yeah, right. Niggas run the other way when they hear that shit. (*Thinks for a minute.*) *Fire!* (*Listens. Still nothing.*) Shit! I could burn up and nobody would even know I was in this muthafucka. I ought to have them arrested for doing this to me. (*A beat.*) I wonder if I really could . . . Daddy would kill me! (*A beat.*) He couldn't kill me! *His ass would be in jail.* That would kill Mama. Shit!

Maybe Jesus will rescue me. That'd be some shit he would do. Come busting up in here with the Fire Department and shit. I'd be out before Mama and Daddy even got home!

Jesus ain't gonna do no shit like that. He probably figurin I'll get out this time just like I been gettin out before. He don't know nothin about no chain. He probably figure they sent me down south again. Naw, he know that ain't happenin. (*Laughs.*) They ain't looking to see Rosa Jackson no time soon in Alabama. Country ass niggas. Tellin me how worried my Mama was about me and what a good girl they knew I still was *underneath*. Yeah, right. I hate when people are so stupid they just *make* you take their shit. You know, like before you got there, they was on the honor system and shit cause they in Alabama. I know they act like I killed somebody when I tried to cash one of grandmamma's social security checks. It ain't like the government won't replace that shit! If you tell em somebody stole your check, they send you another one. People up here do it all the time. I didn't think that shit was no big deal, but the man at the store knew my grandmother and he called her and told her I'd been there with her check and he had cashed it this time, but could she please send a note the next time. My grandmother just thanked him and said she would, but when I got home she had called my uncle for back-up and they *both* went off on me. Both of them! I had never heard my grandmother talk so much shit. I thought they were goin to have me arrested and shit, but they didn't. They just sent me back up here.

My grandmother hates to hear me cuss. She heard me on the phone once talking long distance to one of my friends. It might have been Jesus, I don't remember, but I was talking . . . like I talk. My grandmother took that phone and said: "I apologize for my grandaughter's language. She did not learn how to talk like that in this house." And she hung up the phone and took me in the bathroom and washed my mouth out with Ivory soap. I was almost fifteen years old, but grandmothers don't care about your *real* age. They got a age they want you to be and that is the age you gonna be when they around you. My *grandmother age* ain't but ten. That's how old I was the summer we moved up here, and she can't get past it. I was ten *then*, and to her, I'm gonna *be* ten. She heard all those *muthafuckas* coming out of my mouth and she just couldn't handle it.

Nobody talks like this in Tuskegee. They cuss and shit, but not like in New York. *Everybody* in New York cuss *all* the time. When they happy, when they mad. They just be cussin. The first day we moved on this block, I was sittin on the stoop out front while Daddy moved our stuff inside and I was lookin at this guy staggerin down the street, bumpin into people and shit. I had never seen anybody that drunk before, so I was starin at him, with my country ass, and he saw me doin it. *Cussed me out! (Laughs.) What the fuck you lookin at?* He hollered right in my face. I like to died!

New York is so different from Alabama it might as well be on another planet or some shit. When we got here, I was freaked out. I had never even been to Montgomery, except once on a church bus when I was three. My parents call themselves movin to New York so I could go to good schools and have better opportunitites and shit. Yeah, right. *Opportuntities to do what?*

I ain't complainin though. It was exciting as hell. I had never seen kids my age do the shit these New York niggas were doing. They did *everything*. I mean eleven-, twelve-year-old kids drinkin and smokin and fuckin like they was grown already. It was like nobody had control of them or somethin.

I didn't do none of that shit for a long time. I was real *goody goody*. The kids at my school used to call me 'Bama and shit and make fun of me because I wadn't down wit the shit they knew from birth or some shit. It was kind of a drag at first, but then I met Jesus and he hipped me to a lot of shit about living in New York. Stuff I really needed to know, right? And plus, he was real fine and real cool and a Puerto Rican. Wadn't one Puerto Rican in Tuskegee, Alabama. *Period*. He thought I was Puerto Rican before he met me because my name was *Rosa* and some nigga told him I had a *accent*. He thought they meant a *Spanish* accent, but they was talkin about a *Alabama* accent. He thought that shit was real funny, too. Pissed me off til' I saw he didn't mean nothin by it.

See, it wadn't about *me*. Jesus thought *everything* was funny. Not the regular stuff you'd think somebody'd laugh at. A lot of weird shit. Like he thought it was funny that my parents had come here so we would have a better life. *And look at 'em now*, he says. *They got shitty ass jobs and a crack head kid*. He thought that was real funny. Jesus parents came all the way from Puerto Rico. Well, his mother did. He never said nothin about his father and I never did ask him. People in Alabama ask you your life story if they sit next to you on the bus, but people in New York don't play that shit.

My parents used to do all that tourist shit when we first got here. They walked my little ass all over New York City lookin at shit that was supposed to make you go *"O-o-o-o-o, shit! New York City!*

Ain't this a bitch?" It's like that Stevie Wonder oldie where the country ass guy gets off the bus and says *"New York City! Skyscrapers and everything!"* And then the New York niggas take everything he got! (*She laughs.*)

We went to see The Statue of Liberty and shit. Everbody standing around there looking at it like it mean something and this guy with a uniform and shit tell you about how old it is and how they got it and shit and you call tell he say this shit twenty-five times a day cause he don't even look at you while he talkin. He just be talkin. If you wanna listen, fine. If you don't, that's fine, too. He's gettin' paid to say that shit, not to make you listen. Muthafucka shoulda been a teacher! (*Laughs.*)

Jesus' momma was scared to take him a lotta places cause she didn't speak English too good yet. So he been here since he was five and he still ain't never seen the Statue of Liberty. I told him we should get high and go down there one day and listen to that guy say his shit. Jesus momma look like that woman in *West Side Story*. The one with the purple dress and the fine boyfriend? Jesus like to look at the video cause it make him think about his momma. Jesus don't look like that, though. He ain't that kinda Puerto Rican. He look just like a nigga, in fact. I always thought Puerto Ricans looked like Mexicans or some shit, but a lot of them look just like niggas. Maybe there was some country ass Puerto Ricans in Tuskegee and I just didn't recognize em.

Ain't nothin country about Jesus. He hard about shit. Not that he mean or nothin, not to me, anyway, but don't nothin fuck with him. He can look at terrible shit and just walk away. He won't even blink. We saw a kid we knew get blown away one time. He owed some people money and he had been talkin around bout how he wasn't payin *shit* so they came up to the school and waited for him. When he came out the front door, they jumped out the car, shot his ass and drove the fuck away, cool as shit. Everybody freaked. Runnin and screamin and shit. Jesus didn't even jump. He just kept walkin. It was scarey unless you was wit him. Then it made you feel good. Like *whatever* happen, it ain't gonna be no *surprise* to this nigga.

I think it was because he had seen such terrible shit already, you know? That's how he started smokin rock in the first place, behind some really terrible shit. Shit like you would hear about, but not know anybody who been through it personally. Well, Jesus had some of that shit happen to him. (*A beat, then a shrug.*) He don't care if I tell it . . . and I don't owe him shit any damn way!

Jesus mama had a boyfriend, right? And the nigga was a crackhead and she hid his shit from him. Call herself tryin to help him get off it. Well, she wouldn't tell him where the shit was, so he shot her right there in their apartment, went through all her shit until he found it, and was sittin there smokin it when Jesus came home. Jesus mama layin right on the floor in the next room, dead as shit, and this nigga so high he don't even give a fuck. Jesus say the nigga didn't even tell him she was dead. He just looked up when he walked in and said, *"Your mama in the kitchen."* When he came back out, the nigga was gone. (*A beat.*) I told you it was some terrible shit.

So after they buried her and shit, Jesus said he started thinkin about that nigga just sittin there smokin while his mama layin in the next room dead and he said he just thought, well, fuck it. *If the shit that damn good, let me have it.* I told him he was just thinkin that way cause he felt bad about his mom and shit, but he said he wadn't askin me if he *should* do it. He was just tellin me.

He didn't act like no addict either. He don't act like one now, unless he can't get the shit, then he start actin weird. Talkin crazy and shit. When Jesus need to get high, he talk about killin people a lot. He ain't never killed nobody, but he talk about that shit a lot when he can't get high. I know it's because of his mama, so I try to change the subject so he won't go off on it. Paula be scared of Jesus when he talk that shit, but she ain't know him as long as I have. I been knowin Jesus since I was eleven years old. How he gonna scare me after all that?

I don't think I woulda started smoking this shit if it wadn't for Jesus. It didn't seem to be doin' nothin so bad to him and he was sellin it so he always had some. Plus, he still had the apartment from his mom's insurance, so he didn't have to go to no crack house or nothin to get high. He could just kick back at his own crib.

But then he told me it made people nervous for me to be around so much if I wadn't gonna be smokin. They was tellin him I was fuckin up their high. People thought I might be a cop or some shit. That's cause niggas watch too much t.v. Like the cops really gonna hire somebody to live in this neighborhood undercover, right? They gonna train me to spy on a bunch of poor ass niggas don't nobody care about no way. But niggas are so paranoid, they believe that shit. I actually heard two niggas talkin about whether or not I was a undercover cop and one of them said no because anybody the cops used undercover had to be fine. It made me mad as hell, and then I said, *Rosa! You goin' off on some shit you overheard a crack addict say. What is wrong with you, girl?* But I didn't like hearin that kinda shit just cause I wadn't down wit it. So, I said okay, fuck it.

And that shit is *good.* I am not lying. I mean if you like to get high, it will get you high real fast. Now some people ain't down wit it, and that's cool, but if you wanna get high, that rock is the shit. I mean, it feel so good, you don't care where you are, what you look like, what is happenin to the other niggas in the room or any of that shit. You just feel *good.* And like in a real personal way. It ain't like you need nobody else to feel good with you. You feel so good, your own high be keepin you company. (*A beat.*)

The only problem is that shit don't last long. And once you feel that good, you gotta feel that good again, right? I mean, why wouldn't you? You gotta want *something.* Rock good as anything else you gonna want. And if you careful, you can handle that shit and not let it handle you.

See, my Daddy got this old timey attitude that if he don't like it, I'm not spose to like it. And since he don't smoke no rock, I'm not spose to smoke none either. I wish my dad would get high one time. I'll bet he would be a funny muthafucka. With his country ass. My dad don't even drink nothin but *beer!* My mom don't drink *shit.* So they don't know what the fuck I'm even talkin about. They brought me all these phamplets and shit—*"Just say no!"* What the fuck does that mean?

I used to think my dad knew everything. But you can't know everything about New York City. Not even about Harlem. Not even this one block in Harlem! When I was gone a whole week, I wadn't two buildings down from here. I used to watch my mom and dad out the window. I saw em asking who had seen me and shit. Half the niggas they asked had been smokin with me half the night! They didn't give a fuck.

My dad wanted to kill Jesus when he found out I was smokin it, but I won't tell him where Jesus live. He act like it's Jesus' fault I'm smokin it. Say this shit about if Jesus was really my "friend" he wouldn't give me that shit. (*Laughs.*) I told you my dad be trippin! He never did like me to be around Jesus after what happen to Jesus mom. I told him that wadn't none of Jesus fault, but my dad didn't wanna hear that shit. Jesus had his own place so my dad thought I'd be over there all the time fuckin and shit. I don't even think he thought about me gettin high. He just didn't want me to be fuckin.

(*Laughs.*) Jesus place was usually so full of crack heads wadn't no place to be fuckin if we wanted to. Jesus didn't care nothin bout that no way. I don't know why. I think all of Jesus weird shit is because of how that shit went down with his moms. But I know he didn't care nothin about it cause I used to try get him to do it with me, and he wouldn't. Jesus like to get high. Everything else is take it or leave it. I think that's why he wanted me to start smokin rock, too. He wanted us to do it together. *Romantic* and shit, right? (*Laughs.*) He always used to tell me he just wadn't down wit no whole lot of fuckin, but that if I wanted to do it with somebody else, he wouldn't be pissed off or nothin. Well, that wadn't what I wanted, so I kept bringin it up and bringin it up and finally he said he would teach me how to do somethin that he liked to watch. And I said okay . . .

At first I thought I could do it in here to pass the time, right? I mean no t.v. No Nintendo. No telephone. *Shit!* But I can't do it if nobody ain't watching me. I don't know why. I guess I'm as big a freak as Paula, with her pregnant ass.

Sometimes when we needed money, he'd get me to do it in front of some niggas. They thought it was funny that I could get off like that and still be a virgin. It was just Jesus watchin me, I guess. He'd be lookin right in my face, too. I'd be goin off and he just be lookin' at me, thinkin about gettin high, calm as shit. He said he used to hear his mother and father fuckin when he was real little and sometimes he'd pretend his mother was doin' it with him instead of his father. I told him not to tell me none of that freak Puerto Rican shit!

I love to hear Jesus say my name like it was Spanish. *"R-r-r-r-r-rosa!"* He rolls that "r" around so long I can't stand it. Shit sound like rollin lemon heads around in your mouth. If I was doin *it* and he called my name like that, I'd get off in a second. When it was somebody I didn't want to do it in front of, he would tell me to just *listen for my name* and it would be easy. He wadn't lyin either. Worked every time. (*A beat.*)

Last night when they got home, my Mom was still cryin and shit. They had both worked double shift, too, so it was late and they was good and worried about how I was gonna be when they got here. I started to lay out like I was dead so when they opened the door they'd see me layin there with my eyes open and shit. But I knew that would really fuck with them and I didn't want my daddy to go off. So I was just sittin here when they busted in all hyper and shit. My Mom started huggin me and my Dad was lookin real relieved and shit and it seemed like they were surprised to see me still there, right? They were scared I had figured a way to get out and wouldn't nothin be here but the goddam chain. *No Rosa!* Well, they was wrong this time, but they gonna be right pretty soon.

I shoulda asked them how they figure I could get away, but I know they wouldn't tell me. They did unchain my ass while they were here, but then they followed me around like Dick Tracy. My mom even went in the bathroom with me, which was embarrassing as hell, if you know what I mean, but she didn't care. She started sayin that shit about how she used to change my dirty diapers and she didn't care nothin bout standin there until I got through. *And she did.* She sat in there while I took my shower, too, and then when we all got ready to go to bed, Daddy got this really sad look on his face, and he put this muthafucker right back on me and carried his happy ass to bed like *"this shit is hurting me more than it's hurting you."* I hate when people say that shit to their kids. That is bullshit. Muthafuckas be whipping their kids ass saying some shit like that. The kid should stop cryin and say, *just beat me, okay? Don't beat me and bullshit me, too.*

(*Laughs.*) Like I'm gonna say some shit like that to my Dad. I used to try to scream real loud when he would beat me so he'd feel bad and quit. It usually worked. He didn't wanna be whippin me in the first place. I didn't even get my first whippin til I was thirteen. I kept runnin away from rehab and hangin out and he didn't know what else to do. Me, neither, so we lookin at each other like, *well?* And I'm thinkin, *do somethin if you gonna do somethin or leave me alone so I can go get high!* So he took off his belt and hit me a couple of times, but it wadn't bad or nothin. My dad don't have the heart for that shit.

See, the shit they don't understand is that *I like to be high.* I like the way it *feels.* I was in rehab last time and they was goin around the circle like they always do so you can introduce yourself and confess how sorry you are to be a dope fiend and then everybody cry wit you and tell you some shit about yourself they just thought of since they met you ten minutes ago and you suppose to say, *"oh, shit!"* and decide not to smoke no more rock. It's bullshit, so when they got around to me, I said, *My name is Rosa Jackson and I just like to get high!* So everybody laughed and started sayin shit like *I know that's right!* and the counselor got mad at me and told me wadn't nothin funny about bein a dope fiend and I said, that's where you wrong. *Everything* is funny about being a dope fiend! And that was before my pops had even come up with this chain thing. But I already knew the shit was out. Here lately, I been laughin at the same shit Jesus find funny, and you know that *that* mean!

The real bullshit of it is when people talk to you about this shit, the part they always leave off is how good it feel when you doin it. Ain't nobody robbin their grandmother for some shit that don't feel good. That don't make no sense.

I gotta pee. I can't close the door all the way with this mutha-fucker on, so don't look! (*She crosses awkwardly toward the bathroom door.*)

BLACK

DAY FOUR

Rosa is pacing as rapidly as she can with the chain. She is smoking a cigarette. She has mastered walking with it well enough so that her turns now include a practiced flip of the chain that allows her to progress much more efficiently than she did the first few days. The chain is now less a strange imposition and more a constant irritant.

ROSA: (*Snubbing out her cigarette in an ashtray that is already overflowing. She continues pacing. Reaches into her pocket and takes out another cigarette. Lights it with a Bic lighter, still pacing. Inhales deeply, coughs, snubs this one out too.*) My dad says I should try not to start smokin cause it's bad for my health. (*Laughs.*) Still trippin. (*Lights another cigarette, inhales, makes a face.*) I hate cigarettes, but I gotta smoke something. I am jonesin' like a muthafucka. My mom keeps tellin me to just take it one day at a time and shit like they tell you in rehab. That is bullshit. This is like a minute by minute trip, right? I want to get high so bad . . . damn! My fingernails wanna get high. My damn toenails wanna get high! *"One day at a time."* I hate that bullshit.

Jesus shoulda been lookin for me by now. That muthafucka. He don't give a shit about me. He never did. He just hung around me for the . . . Shit, I don't know why he hung around me. He don't even know I'm here. I know he don't know I'm here or he woulda figured out some way to contact me. He could slide a note under the door or some shit. (*Sudden thought.*) Damn! If he could slide a letter under . . . (*She goes to check how wide the space is under the door. She becomes very agitated. She tears a few pages out of a magazine and folds them like a business size letter. She runs this under the door to see how wide a piece of something could be slipped underneath. There is plenty of room.*)

Goddam! Goddam! (*She paces excitedly.*) He could slip me some shit under there. He could slip me some shit under there every goddam day. They'd never know it. I'll smoke it in the morning and by the time they get home, they won't even be able to smell nothin. Shit! Why didn't I think of that before? I gotta get word to Jesus. I gotta let him know what he needs to do. (*She looks around for a piece of paper and a pencil and begins to write a letter quickly.*)

(*Slide fade in and hold for twenty seconds while she writes:* Dear Jesus, They got me chained in the house. Bring dope. Rosa.)

(*Rosa looks critically at the letter and makes an alternation. Slide changes to reflect rewritten letter.*)

(Dear Jesus, They got me chained in the house. Bring dope. Forever your girl, Rosa.)

(*Slide fades out.*)

(*Rosa folds the letter and then looks around quickly. It dawns on her that she doesn't have any way to get it to him.*) Shit! (*She drags the chain toward the window, but can't reach it. She tries to tug it toward the telephone. Too short. In frustration, she begins to pull and tug at the chain in a rage.*) Goddam it! I . . . want . . . this . . . shit . . . off . . . of . . . me!

(*She tears up the letter to Jesus in a rage and sits down, rocking back and forth rapidly.*)

I'm not gonna make it. I'm gonna die up in this muthafucka all by myself. I feel like shit and can't do a damn thing about it. I know where the shit at. I know who got it and how to make em give it up and I can't get a goddam thing. They're killin me. They're killin me. (*A beat, then trying to calm herself.*) But it's gonna be okay. I just gotta hang in there til I'm eighteen, then they got no power over me no more. Jesus say when I get eighteen, I should move in wit him since he got plenty of room. I'm down wit it. I know Jesus dig me and he always got enough rock for us to get high. (*A beat.*) Where is that muthafucka? He shoulda come up here and beat on the door and hollered or some shit. He could ride up the hall on a big ass white horse like they do in the movies. I would love that shit. I love when somethin weird happens. Somethin you ain't seen two hundred times a day every day. Sometimes I feel like I seen everything they got to show and ain't none of it shit. *Ain't none of it shit.* (*A beat, then Rosa yells several times in loud succession in complete frustration.*) Jesus ain't shit. I ain't shit. Ain't none of it shit. (*Begins to laugh.*) So what the fuck am I cryin about then, right? If ain't none of it shit, who gives a fuck about it? I just wanna get high, you understand? I don't give a fuck one way or the other, I just need to get high. Goddam, I need to get high!

When you start smokin this shit, they don't tell you how bad your ass gonna feel when you ain't got none. They forget to tell you bout that shit, right?

You know the funny shit is, I was almost glad to see my daddy when he came to get me. I hadn't seen Jesus in two days and them niggas was acting crazy as shit. He told them he had the hundred he owed them at the crib and he was gonna leave me there with em while he went to get it so they would know he wadn't bullshittin. He ain't said shit to me about that shit, so I said, *say, what?* He hadn't even told me about owing nobody when we busted up in there or I wouldn't a gone in the first place. Niggas be slitting people's throat for two dollars and here he come owing some niggas I ain't nevah seen before a hundred dollas. He knew I was pissed, cause he said, don't worry bout that shit, baby. I'll be right back and we'll go over to the house and I'll put the rest of the niggas out and we'll get fucked up, just me and you.

Bullshit, right? But I'm so stupid, I believe the muthafucka. *Okay, baby,* I say, or some stupid shit like that. I shoulda said, *no, muthafucka. You tell me where the shit is, I'll go get it and they can hold you hostage til I get back.* But I was tryin to hang, you know? That's where I fucked up. That muthafucka kissed me good-by and shit and walked on out the damn door and I ain't seen the nigga since. At first them niggas had a lot of shit to smoke, so we kept getting high and they didn't say too much to me about nuthin. But then when Jesus didn't show for a long time, they started askin me where he was. Like I knew anything about the shit! I said I didn't know where the nigga was and they said he better bring back a hundred dollars or they gonna fuck me up. I ain't even in the shit, right, but they gonna fuck *me* up!

So I start figuring what I'm gonna do to get out of the shit and one of em asks me how much would I charge him for some pussy and I say a hundred dollars and he say I must be think my pussy made outta gold and I tell him I can make him get off good by just *watchin* me cause I'm that good and he look at the other one and they both laugh and say, *maybe the ho do got a pussy made a gold. Show me,* say the one who started the shit in the first place and I tell him it gotta be just me and him cause I don't want them to jump me or anything. Niggas get brave when they got they boys watchin. I know I can handle one, but I ain't down wit muthafuckas tryin to run a train and shit. So we went in the bedroom and he closed the door and told me to hit it.

So I pulled my panties to the side like Jesus showed me and started rubbin myself and lookin at his face and he grinned at me and started rubbin hisself through his jeans. I always watch their faces cause that's how you know if they dig it or not. Then he unzip his pants so he can hold his dick in his hand and it was feeling alright to me too, even though Jesus wadn't there to call my name, and I'm thinkin maybe this ain't gonna be so bad after all, but then the nigga reached out and grabbed my hand and tried to make me sit down on his lap while he still got his thing out and shit! And I'm tryin to tell him I ain't down wit it cause a AIDS and shit and he tellin me he ain't no faggot and we sorta wrestlin around and I'm tryin not make no noise cause I don't want his boy to come in to see what's up, and that's when my dad started beatin on the door and hollerin and shit and all hell broke loose.

They was gettin ready to shoot through the door at first, and I said *no, that sound like my dad!* So they told him if he didn't pay the hundred dollars *I* owed them they'd blow my brains out right in front of him. My daddy just stood there for a minute lookin at that nigga holdin his 9 millimeter against my head and I'm thinking, *my daddy ain't got that kinda money! I'm dead!* And then he reached in his pocket and took out a roll a money and handed it to the nigga who had been in the bedroom with me. The nigga counted it right in front of my daddy and it was a hundred dollars *exactly*. That's how I know Jesus the one told him to come get me. How else my daddy gonna be walkin around Harlem with a pocketful of cash like he the dope man and shit.

Then that nigga told my daddy to get my little crack addict ass outta his place and pushed me so hard I fell against his chest. My daddy didn't even look at me. He took off his jacket and put it around my shoulders and we walked the three blocks home with him holdin my arm like you do a little kid when they been bad. He wadn't sayin shit. When we got home, my moms was there and she started cryin and holdin my face up so she could look at me and shit. I know I looked like shit. I hadn't eaten in two three days and my clothes were all twisted around from tusslin with that nigga in the bedroom. And I know my hair was all over my head cause she kept smoothin it down and I could feel it risin right back up again and she'd smooth it down again and it would rise on back up. My head was itchin too, but I couldn't scratch or nothin because my mom was huggin me and she had my arms pinned down at my sides and you can't push your momma off you, even if you want to, so I'm standin there tryin to get her to calm down and I catch a eyeful of my pops sittin at the table and tears just runnin down his face. He ain't cryin or hollerin or nothin. He just sittin there lookin at me and momma stumblin around the room like we drunk.

That hurt me worse than anything. I never seen my daddy cry in my life. *Never.* I seen him mad plenty of times, but not over me.

He be mad about some niggas actin a fool or some crackers fuckin over him or somethin mama said that didn't sit right, but he never cried. He didn't cry when his momma died. Took the phone call, drove down south and buried her, came back and never broke. So I felt real bad when I saw him cryin over me. I love my daddy . . .

So I got away from moma and I went over and stood in front of him and I said, *don't worry about me, daddy. I'm okay.* And he just looked at me and tears runnin all down his chin and he wadn't wipin shit. Act like he didn't even know he was doin it. I didn't have no kleenex or nothin, but I hated to see him like that, so I just wiped him off a little with my sleeve, right? He caught my hand and held it so hard I thought he was gonna crush my damn fingers and he just looked at me and started sayin my name over and over and over like he wasn't sure it was even me: *Rosa, Rosa, Rosa!* And my mom on the other side of the room runnin around hollerin and shit.

It was almost like I was somewhere else watchin it. It was too weird to be happenin to me *for real*. When I went to bed, I could still hear my mom in the other room cryin and everytime I woke up, my dad would be sittin right by my bed, just lookin at me like he in a dream or somethin. Then one time I got up to go to the bathroom and he walked right wit me and stood there outside the door and waited for me and before I got back into bed he hugged me real hard and I could feel him shakin like he was jonesin worse than me. Scared the shit outta me. I figured my shit must be even raggedier than I thought if it making my daddy shake.

It's no way for me to tell him how it feels, you know what I mean? They don't understand nothin about none of it so there's no place to start tellin them anything. They shoulda kept their country asses in Tuskegee, Alabama.

My daddy used to sing when we lived down there. He can sing, too. He sound like Luther Vandross a little bit. Him and my momma used to sing in the car. Raggedy ass car they got from somebody. We drove that muthafucka all the way up here, though. Soon as we got to Harlem, the muthafucka broke down. I used to ask my pops if the car had a broke down in Brooklyn, would he a stayed in Brooklyn and he would laugh and say he probably would. (*A beat.*)

I think that nigga was gonna rape me if my daddy hadn't busted up in there. And that wadn't gonna be the worst of it. Jesus wadn't comin back no time soon. That's why he called my pops and told him where I was. (*Laughs.*) He busted up in there, though. My daddy crazy. They coulda blown him away with his Alabama ass. (*A beat.*) I don't think he'd a brought me up here if he'd a known what these niggas up here were like. They treacherous up here in New York. You think you ready for it, but you not ready. These niggas don't care nothin bout you. Jesus spose to be my friend, and look how he act! (*A beat.*) My daddy bad, though. He was beatin on that door like he was packin a Uzi and he didn't have shit. Not even no stick or nothin. He just standin there talkin shit about: *Where my baby girl at? Where you got my Rosa?*

And I'm hollerin: *Here I am, daddy! Here I am!*

BLACK

DAY FIVE

Rosa is clicking rapidly through the channels on the small t.v. on the table. It is a tiny black and white model with a very fuzzy picture. She tries in vain to adjust it and find something she likes. Finally snaps it off, frustrated and begins to pace. The chain is still in place, but by now she handles it casually as if it has always been there.

I been tryin to find somethin to *overstimulate* me. My mom said they real proud of me cause I'm actin like my old self so they gonna let me have t.v. today. How else I'm gonna act chained to the damn radiator? *My old self.* Who the hell is that? They mean my Alabama self. My before I met Jesus self. My don't know nothin bout crack rock self. That's who they lookin for. (*A beat.*)I miss her too, but I think girlfriend is gone, gone, gone. (*She paces, but slowly. She's thinking.*)

My daddy say I been doin so good, he ain't gonna chain me but a couple more days. *Just to be sure.* I started to tell him, *it take longer than that to be sure,* but I didn't say nothin. If I say some shit like that, he'll never take this damn chain offa my leg!

He ask me was I worried about the street *takin me back* if he take the chain offa me. He sound so serious when he say shit like that, but to me, he just be trippin. Like the street some kind of weird, scary shit waitin for you in the alley instead of a bunch of niggas you know tryin to get paid and get high.

But how'm I gonna tell him that shit? So I told him no. I wasn't worried about the street *takin me back.* And he hug me and shit and tell me there is nothin out there for me. I say, *I know that's right.* (*She tries t.v. again. Turns it off.*)

The thing is, after a couple of days when you don't watch t.v. seem like when you go back to it, ain't nothin on there you wanna see. You gotta let it stay on for a little while without payin no attention, then it start lookin good to you again, otherwise that shit is *too* lame.

My pops told me I should pray instead of gettin high. No bullshit. He really did tell me that. I never been to no religious rehab, but I know some people who did. They tell you shit like that all the time. *Let God take the place of the drugs in your life. Give it all to God.* Shit like that. It works for some muthafuckas, I guess, but I don't believe all that shit. I used to go to church when I was little cause I like to listen to the choir, but I never did get into prayin a whole lot.

I used to like to sneak and look at people while they be prayin with their eyes closed. They be looking so serious, frownin up and shit. I don't know why people think they gotta look all ugly and shit to talk to God. I figure if the muthafucka—scuse me!—if *His Highness* is really *God* and a bad muthafucka, he oughta be able to let you talk just sittin down someplace lookin like you look when you just bein regular. I rather have niggas just talk me that way than be frowning up and shit, but I ain't God, right? So what the fuck am I talkin about?

I told my daddy I wish I believe in God, but I don't. It take time, my dad tell me. You have to get to know him just like any good friend. You have to put the time in to *get the goody out.* That's what he said. He talkin bout God and shit and then he come talkin bout *the goody!* He so country sometime! (*A beat.*)

I been thinkin bout if I wanna keep smokin that shit or not. No, I mean really thinkin about it for myself. It can make you do shit that is really fucked up. I done some fucked up shit myself when I was high, or tryin to get high. I told you I stole my grandmamma's check. I stole lots of people checks. Cash and carry. Old people be lookin all worried cause they check ain't come and I know I smoked that shit up two days ago. And you don't care neither! You just say, *fuck it.*

Like, I keep thinkin bout how Jesus left me with them niggas I didn't even know! He didn't care what they did to me. They coulda thrown me out the window.. *And they do that shit, too!* Old crack-head niggas threw a girl out the window right around the corner from here just a week ago. Took her clothes off first so when she hit the ground her titties and shit was all out. People standin around laughin and she dead as shit. Nobody even covered her up or nothin.

My daddy told me only God stronger than crack. I tell him this chain been doin a pretty good job. I was just kiddin, but I think it made him feel bad cause his face got all sad and shit. (*A beat.*) I told him I just meant it's hard once you can come and go when you want to not to just go anywhere you can think of goin, right? Even if you not thinkin about it by yourself, somebody gonna remind me to think about smokin that rock. They gonna be goin there, or comin from there or lookin for some money to get there or *somethin.* It's not like you gotta be lookin for the shit. (*A beat.*)

He told me he knew I was a good girl and he trusted me. I wanted to say, *hey, man! This is goddam Harlem! Trust ain't in it!* (*A beat.*) I don't trust nobody. (*A beat.*) Not about no shit like this. It ain't a goddam thing out there but a bunch of niggas gonna die and wanna take me wid em. *Ain't a thing out there. (She looks around.)*

At least in here, ain't nobody fuckin with me. I got food. I got a bathroom. I even got t.v. and shit, so how bad can it be? (*Suddenly angry.*)

And what the fuck you lookin at?

BLACK

DAY SIX

Rosa sits on the couch, smoking. She is rubbing her ankle distractedly and thinking. She snubs out the cigarette deliberately, still thinking. She gets up and walks across the room. The chain is no longer on her leg, but she is still limping slightly and whenever she is not moving, she rubs her ankle as if it were a little sore.

She crosses to the telephone, which is in evidence in the room for the first time, picks it up and dials hesitantly. She hangs up before she finishes the number. Thinks for a minute. Dials again. She waits for it to ring several times.

Who is this? . . . Let me speak to Jesus. Rosa. (*Waits for him to come to the phone, when he does, she jumps on him angrily.*) Where you been, muthafucka? Yeah, this is Rosa. Who the fuck you think it was? I know the nigga told you Rosa. You know another Rosa now beside me? Where the fuck you been? . . . No! Don't tell me shit! I don't wanna hear it! You left me, muthafucka! They could have fucked me right up and where the fuck were you? . . . I said don't tell me shit! . . . I don't wanna hear it. They had me chained up because of your triflin ass! . . . You heard me! Chained up by the foot like a goddam dog! Right in the living room. If you had brought your ass over here you would have known that shit. . . . Don't tell me that shit! You know they be workin all day just like all the other country ass niggas in Harlem. You think they boss give them the week off so they can sit home and watch out for their dope fiend daughter? You know better than that shit, muthafucka. You just didn't give a shit. Got me started smokin that shit and now you just don't give a damn, do you? Well, fuck you, Jesus! Fuck you! . . . No, I haven't finished. I got a lot more shit to say to your trifling ass . . . (*He interrupts her now until he breaks her rhythm and she begins to be listening more than she is fussing. Her demeanor changes from angrily belligerant to petulant to needy over the course of the conversation.*) No. Nobody ain't told me nothin about where you been. I ain't seen nobody, I told you! I been chained up! . . . Where you been? Why? For real? When? They came to your place? Them two you left me wit? . . . Then why you leave me wit 'em? . . . But if you don't know, you spose to take me wit you and not take a chance, you know? . . . They coulda killed me, Jesus! You know I'm not lyin! . . . No. . . . No . . . Nothing like that happened. . . . I can handle myself, I been tellin you that. . . . I ain't scared of no crackhead niggas. . . . Not even you! . . . What you mean how long since I been high? I ain't doin that shit no more, muthafucka cause I ain't no muthafuckin dope fiend, alright? I been up here without shit for five days, right? *And I handled it! I am handlin it!* So fuck you, Jesus! Fuck you! . . . No. My mom be home in a few minutes so don't bring your black ass up here. That's right. Not tomorrow either. I don't need that shit. I just called to let you know not to bring your ass around me and when you see me on the street, don't even act like you know me, *you junkie muthafucka.* . . . You . . . you . . . *You left me!*

BLACK

DAY SEVEN

Rosa is looking out the window. Smoking. She smokes it down to the end, snubs it out and lights another. She keeps her eyes fixed on the street even while she is getting another cigarette. She is waiting. She goes to the table. Sits. She goes to the couch. Sits. She stands near the door and listens. Crosses to the window. Scans the street. Nothing. She sits again in silence, then speaks slowly and fiercely to herself.

Fuck this shit, okay? Just fuck it! (She snubs out another cigarette. Turns on t.v. Off. Picks up the phone, starts to dial. Stops. Hangs up. She is very agitated. She sits and sighs deeply.)

Okay, look. This is a prayer, okay? (*A beat.*) I can't do that shit.

She is pacing again. She stops suddenly near the closet and slowly reaches for the knob. She reaches in and gets the bag her dad had the chain in. She takes it out and goes over to the couch with it. She takes it out, handling it gingerly. She feels the weight and the chill of it. It is completely familiar and absolutely mysterious. There is both resignation and comfort in her handling of the chain. She may even place the shackle around her wrist like a bracelet. She suddenly takes it off of her wrist quickly and puts it down, but not away. She realizes what she is considering and the thought horrifies her. She sits looking at the chain for a beat and then reaches toward it again.

There is a sudden furtive knock at the door. She draws her hand back guiltily. She goes quickly and quietly to the door. She listens. Another furtive knock. She speaks quietly.

Jesus? (A beat.) Jesus, is that you?

(*She begins to quickly unbolt the locks and chains on the door, fumbling in her anxiousness to get the locks open. When she does, she takes a deep breath, closes her eyes for a minute and then opens the door.*)

BLACK

Pearl Cleage

LATE BUS TO MECCA

Author's Note: "Late Bus to Mecca" is the first of a series of morality plays. My intention is to identify and highlight the values and actions that will be necessary if black women—and by extension black people—are to survive into the twenty-first century.

Late Bus to Mecca was co produced by the Women's Project & Productions and The New Federal Theatre under the directorship of Julia Miles and Woodie King Jr., respectively at the Judith Anderson Theatre, New York City from February 28 to March 22, 1992 with the following cast:

AVA   Lisa Gay Hamilton

A BLACK WOMAN (ABW)   Claire Dorsey

Stage manager   Melody A. Beal
Stage directions   Betty Vaughn and Erika Vaughn
House manager   Cory Washburn and Sheri Wilner
Casting   Susan Haskins

Late Bus to Mecca was commissioned and developed by the Women's Project & Productions and the Southeast Playwrights Project of Atlanta through a grant from the Multi Arts Production Fund of the Rockefeller Foundation.

TIME

October 24, 1970, 10 p.m.

When Muhammad Ali made his victorious return to the boxing ring after three years of exile because of his claim-to-consciencious objector status on the basis of his religious beliefs, it was cause for jubilation in the Black community. When no other state would issue him a boxing permit, State Senator Leroy Johnson was able to secure one through the state of Georgia for a match on the night of October 26, 1970.

Tickets at ringside were going for $100. Hustlers and gamblers from all over the country flocked to Atlanta to bet on the fight, enjoy the parties and show off their ladies. The event became a week long celebration of the young black champion who had faced down the American government in the midst of the Vietnam War and emerged victorious. Ali, 28, defeated Jerry Quarry by technical knockout in the third round.

PLACE

A Greyhound bus station in downtown Detroit, Michigan.

CHARACTERS

AVA JOHNSON, a twentyish black woman.
A BLACK WOMAN, also a twentyish black woman.

PLAYWRIGHT'S NOTES TO THE DIRECTOR

Ava represents the possibility of consciously extending the circle of sisterhood to include every black woman specifically, in all her complexity and terribleness. Ava has to be a prostitute because we have to see the potential for our salvation in every segment of our group. We cannot allow class distinctions, superficial moral judgements, and personal prejudices to divide and conquer us. We have to believe that there is enough resilience and residual sisterhood in any and all of us to make it possible for us to redeem ourselves and rescue each other.

It is important that Ava not be painted in broad comedic strokes. Her style and behavior are entirely appropriate to the world she lives in, as are her language and her sexual frankness. Ava must be an admirable and likeable character so that the audience's identification with her can help them confront and release their own class prejudices.

It is important that A Black Woman's silence be representative of every physically battered, spirit-bruised black woman whose words have been ignored or used against her so often they seem beside the point. While she represents all of these women, she does not pretend to know all of their pain. She is specific. She is not *the* black woman. She is *a* black woman.

She must have a strong physical presence on the stage although she never speaks a word. The audience should have concern for her overall well being and for her moment-to-moment ability to maintain balance and consciousness.

A Black Woman's face should often be averted, but it should always be alive. She must make visible on her face and in her body her increasing trust in Ava, but maintain the wariness that the harshness of her life has taught her.

BLACK OUTS AND SLIDES:

The play is arranged in thirteen scenes, separated by black outs. At each black out, a slide should immediately be projected on a large white screen at the back of the stage. The slides will contain the number of the scene coming up and a quote from the dialogue of the scene coming up. All dialogue on the slides should be framed in quotation marks. The slide should hold for ten seconds and then disappear as the lights come up. The slides are as follows:

1. *"Did they just call the bus to Atlanta?"*
2. *"That's who I'm named after."*
3. *"Are you on something?"*
4. *"Blink if you can hear me."*
5. *"Not as fine as you are."*
6. *"But animals is different."*
7. *"Maybe you should fix yourself up a little."*
8. *"I always have a plan."*
9. *"What can I say?"*
10. *"Not after I got to know you."*
11. *"I told her I wasn't pretending."*
12. *"I thought a bolt of lightening was gonna strike us dead."*
13. *"You could have just told me."*

SCENE ONE

In the darkness we hear the sound of the bus arrivals and departures being announced. The last announcement is for the midnight bus to Atlanta with appropriate intermediate stops.

Slide 1: "Did they just call the bus to Atlanta?"

As lights come up, a black woman (ABW) is huddled on a bright orange plastic bus station chair. Her age is difficult to determine because she is dirty, and disheveled. She is dressed in worn bell bottom jeans, faded tee shirt with an anti war slogan on it and runover shoes. She looks very tired. Her face is very dirty and smudged. She has a tattered back-pack tossed carelessly by the side of her chair.

There are two empty chairs next to her. She shifts uncomfortably; staring at the floor; hugging her arms around her body. She seems to be shivering although the place is warm.

Ava enters in a hurry. She is very agitated. She is carrying a large shocking pink suitcase, with a matching shocking pink make-up case. Her clothing is tight and flashy, high heeled shoes, etc., but she is not a charicature. She is attractive and has tangible physical confidence.

AVA: Did they just call the bus to Atlanta? What time did they say? Midnight, right? There's isn't one before that, is it? They told me none after 9:30 until midnight. (*A black woman makes no response.*)

AVA: Did you see a girl come in here? About my size? Leather coat? Real pretty? (*No response.*)

AVA: Red leather. You couldn't miss her. (*Ava looks around again anxiously, then back to ABW who has still made no response.*)

AVA: Hey! Look, if you do see her, tell her I'll be right back. Okay? Hey! Are you sleep or what? Hey! (*No response.*)

AVA: Shit! (*Ava dashes out. ABW remains motionless.*)

BLACK OUT

SCENE TWO

Slide 2: "That's who I'm named after."

Slide fades. Lights up. Ava re-enters, much calmer. She stacks her things in the chair between them and sits looking around with some satisfaction.

AVA: You definately have the best seat in the house. I can see everything from here. (*ABW does not respond.*)

AVA: I'm Ava. (*She sticks out her hand. ABW ignores it.*) You the strong silent type I guess. (*Shrugs.*) Suit yourself.

AVA: I'm supposed to meet my girlfriend. She's always late. I told her the bus was at ten so she'd be here on time. She probably called to check, knowing I *would* lie about that shit. Well, the bus ain't til midnight, so she's still got plenty of time to make it. I can't miss her from here! You can see the whole damn room. Plus, I got the tickets, so how far is she gonna get, right? (*ABW shifts miserably in the chair.*)

AVA: Are you okay? Hey! You okay? (*ABW wearily closes her eyes. Ava snaps open the make-up case and looks critically at herself in the mirror. She sighs and searches through the jumble in the case for her make-up. She repairs it while she talks. This routine will include lipstick, lip pencil, combing hair, putting on foundation, powder, blush, eye shadow, mascara, etc. The make-up application should run through out the scene. She looks mostly at herself in the mirror, but checks on ABW every few seconds.*)

AVA: You don't ride the bus much do you? (*Ava puts on lipstick with elaborate unconcern.*)

AVA: I didn't think so. Sitting all by yourself up in this dim ass corner. You should be glad I sat down cause you are asking for trouble. You are a sitting duck for every nigga with his dick in his hand and his eye on what you got. Know what I mean?

You see that guy over there? I saw him looking at me when I first came in. Grinning at me like I got no more class than to be picking up old half drunk niggas at the bus station! (*Ava's voice rises with indignation as she speaks in the direction of the man who offended her.*)

AVA: Somebody needs to tell these niggas when they are out of their league. *Way* out of their league.

Don't worry. He ain't coming over here. They don't mess with you unless you're all by yourself. (*Talking loudly again.*) They get real brave then. Can't tell them shit then!

See? He's leaving. I know niggas like the back of my damn hand. I know how they think! (*Ava looks at ABW with concern.*)

AVA: I told you I'm Ava, right? Most people have never met anybody with that name other than Ava Gardner and they haven't *met* her. They just know her name from the movies.

That's who I'm named after. My whole name is Ava Gardner Johnson, but I don't say all that because niggas think everything is so goddam funny when it ain't none of their business in the first place, you know? (*Ava begins combing and styling her hair energetically and efficiently.*)

AVA: Did you know she was black? She didn't tell anybody because she wanted to be in the movies, but she was. My mother saw her once and she said you could really tell it close up.

Her hair and everything. My mother used to say she was related to us, but my mother used to say so much shit you had to take it or leave it.

She said it was almost true because she was pretty sure her and Miss G. had been sisters in another life. She believed all that stuff about being alive over and over until you get it right? I don't think so though. I mean, how likely you think it is that a big Hollywood movie star like Ava Gardner is gonna have my mother for a sister in any life! (*Ava puts away hair brushes. Ties on a scarf. Looks critically in the mirror. Takes it off.*)

AVA: I usually look better than this when I'm travelling. But it's nobody but deadbeats on the bus anymore. And this late at night for sure. Present company excepted, of course! (*Ava tries on several pairs of earrings.*)

AVA: I hate the bus. I like to fly. First class all the way! First time I was on an airplane, I never wanted it to land. Except I was sitting next to this asshole friend of Tony's who kept trying to get me to do it with him in the bathroom. "Come on baby, don't you wanna join the mile high club?" (*Looks around anxiously for her friend again.*)

AVA: I'll be glad when Sherri gets here though. I know that! She's so flakey sometime. I told her she musta been a white girl in her last life!

I never knew anybody met a nice guy on the bus. Sherri met a nice guy on the train once. Well, he sounded nice when she told me about it anyway. She's taking the train down south to her mother's funeral and this guy asks can he buy her a drink, but since she's going to her mom's funeral, she doesn't feel up for a lot of chat. So she tells the guy straight up and instead of getting an attitude like niggas usually do when you try to tell them something real, he says, he's sorry to hear about her mom and how about if he buys her a drink anyway and they can just sit and *contemplate* the scenery together for awhile. That's what he said: *contemplate* the scenery.

Sounds like a movie, doesn't it? That's why she believes in so much fantasy shit in the first place. So much of it happens to her, she thinks that's real life.

Niggas always wanna talk to Sherri. She's cool though. She can handle that debonair shit niggas say and never break. If somebody offered to buy me a drink so we could *contemplate* the scenery, I'd probably think it was a con.

She said he was real suave, alright, but he kept talking suave like that all the way to D.C., which is where he was getting off. She said after awhile, she just got tired of hearing it.

Sherri's that way, though. She doesn't like a whole lot of chat. Tony's like that too. They can sit in a room with no t.v. or nothing and not say a word for an hour! They would love you!

I can't stand that quiet shit. I hafta hear some noise! (*Suddenly agitated again by Sherri's lateness.*)

AVA: I wish she would just come on!

BLACK OUT

SCENE THREE

Slide 3: "Are you on something?"

Ava is painting her toe nails carefully. She has cotton balls in between her toes. She is quiet. Concentrating on her work. ABW's eyes are closed. Ava finishes and screws the top back on the bottle, looking at her toes with satisfaction.

AVA: They talking about snow up here next week and it's still Indian summer down South. Sandal weather! (*She blows on her toes.*) You going to Atlanta, too? (*ABW looks at Ava. Panic.*)

AVA: Relax, honey. I don't care where you're going, okay? You don't have to get paranoid. Is somebody after you? (*ABW doesn't respond, but does look at Ava.*)

AVA: Well, more power to you, honey. It's every woman for herself, I say. When it's time to make a move, *make a move.* (*Ava fans her nails with her hands and blows on them.*)

AVA: I've never been any further South than D.C. Sherri hasn't either. She grew up in D.C., but she said as soon as she could, she went north. I hope it's not too country down there. I hate the country. Tony had a friend who lived way out. I thought the nigga was hiding from somebody, but Tony said he just couldn't stand no whole bunch of noise since he got back from Vietnam.

He had these big old bug eyes, too. Always trying to talk up on something and his damn eyes be getting bigger and bigger . . .

But Atlanta's spose to be a big city, so we'll see. (*Ava looks around again for Sherri.*)

AVA: She is really getting on my nerves with this shit. Sometimes I start thinking about all the stuff I don't like about my girl and I say, so what you like about her? And it's there, but it's so much harder to put into words, you know?

Don't get me started thinking about that shit! We got 22 hours between here and Atlanta. I do not want to ride that far being evil.

I hate riding the bus by myself. It's okay when you got somebody with you, but when you're by yourself, there's always a nigga with a hard on grinning up in your face, 'scuse my French. (*ABW closes her eyes again and leans back weakly.*)

AVA: (*Gently.*) You really look bad, honey. Are you on something?

BLACK OUT

SCENE FOUR

Slide 4: "Blink if you can hear me."

Ava is vigorously chomping and cracking a piece of gum. She is also examining her fingernails critically. She blows a bubble and pops it. Goes back to chomping. She is engrossed in her nails. Another loud pop. ABW is seated with eyes closed, slumped over her knees. On the third loud pop, she looks at Ava. Ava produces another huge bubble. It bursts loudly.

AVA: (*Takes gum out disgustedly.*) I hate gum when you got all the sugar out of it. Wears out your jaws trying to chew it! (*Ava wraps the gum in paper and tosses it.*)

There was a girl in my high school who was the champion gum cracker of all time. She could crack it on every chew. It didn't have to be bubble gum either. She could pop anything! Kathleen DeGracia. They were supposed to be Philippino. That's what they told everybody. Philippino my ass. They were niggas just like the rest of us. They just had that heavy hair, you know? But that don't mean shit. Look at Ava Gardner! (*Ava is sorting through her nail polish to find one that appeals to her.*)

AVA: Niggas got good hair think they can tell you anything and you gonna believe it just cause their hair is so pretty. Tony had that kinda hair. Claimed to be a Mexican, but he didn't have no accent and couldn't speak no Spanish! So who you gonna believe?

When Sherri gets mad she always says: "Niggas ain't shit!" until I remind her that Tony is a spose-to-be Mexican. It's ain't just niggas. Ain't none of them shit. (*ABW is still looking at Ava.*)

AVA: Did somebody beat you up, honey? (*ABW starts to turn away.*)

AVA: I'm sorry! Look! I'm not trying to get into your business. You just look like . . . you need some help.

Did somebody hurt you? Can you hear me? I know you can hear me. Can't you? Nod if you can hear me! Just nod, *okay?* (*No response from ABW, but she is still looking at Ava.*)

AVA: Okay. . . . it's okay. You don't have to nod. Just . . . *blink.* Blink real hard *two* times, if you can hear me. Or *once,* just do it once, but do it hard so I'll know it wasn't just a *regular* blink, you know? (*ABW closes her eyes and turns wearily away.*)

AVA: (*Choosing to interpret this as a blink.*)

Good enough. Good enough. Okay. No problem. Good enough.

BLACK OUT

SCENE FIVE

Slide 5: "Not as fine as you are!"

Ava is wiping her hands and cleaning under her fingernails delicately with a handi-wipe.

AVA: Are you hungry? I'm starving to death. I'm gonna have to break down and get a sandwich or something. Messing around trying to get out of there before Tony got back. I know how niggas will always show up when you don't need to see 'em.

First time I saw Tony, I made him feed me. I thought he was the finest thing walking. I had a gig dancing at this cheap ass place downtown and I was late again so I knew I was gonna get some shit anyway and then it started to rain.

I started running and then I said, fuck it! I quit! I'm not running in the rain to get to a gig I don't like in the first place. So I just stopped in the middle of the sidewalk to think for a minute. I needed a plan quick!

And then I heard somebody right behind me say, "Baby, you don't ever have to stand out in no rain. Not as fine as you are."

And it was Tony. With a *big* umbrella.

Niggas make me sick sometime. They always pretending it's anything but what it is. And if they halfway fine, you start pretending too and next thing you know, Fantasyland!

That shit is dangerous too. You step back and forth across that line too many times, you start believing any shit they tell you.

Me, I don't believe one word that comes out of a man's mouth. They all might as well be talking out their ass if you ask me about it.

You want a handi-wipe? No offense or anything, but you might want to, you know, wipe your face a little. They gonna pick you up for being a vagrant or something looking like that. (*ABW touches her face with some concern.*)

AVA: Here you go. (*ABW looks at her. Ava gives her a couple of handwipes. She places them in ABW's hand and she just holds them.*)

AVA: He was having dinner at the 24 hour pancake house and he told me I could get anything I wanted. I ate so much food he started laughing his ass off. Showing all those pretty white teeth. He said, "Girl, you must think this is a Chinese restaurant much stuff as you ordered!"

AVA: Go ahead, honey. Wipe your face off a little. You know . . . (*Ava demonstrates dramatically.*)

AVA: You in bad shape, honey. You know that? You in real bad shape. (*Ava, sighing, takes the handiwipes gently.*)

AVA: (*Very gently.*) I'm gonna wipe your face, okay? You want me to help you? You want me to help you do it? Huh? (*As she talks, she very slowly wipes ABW's cheek. ABW draws back almost imperceptively, but Ava is talking softly and her touch is very gentle.*)

AVA: It's okay. You just need a little help that's all. And I am the A-number-one girl for helping out, and that's the truth. Sherri will tell you. I've been through a time or two with my girl where nobody thought she was gonna make it but me. But I didn't give up on her. (*Ava finishes her wiping.*) One hundred percent improvement! Look! (*Ava turns the make up mirror toward ABW who turns quickly away.*)

BLACK OUT

SCENE SIX

Slide 6: "But animals is different."

Ava is filing her nails energetically. She looks up periodically for Sherri. ABW watches.

AVA: That girl is gonna be late for her own funeral, I swear.

She always says that's why she can't keep a regular job. Late all the time. I told her that's why she needs to work with me. I'll cut her a little slack. (*Ava gets up impatiently and paces. She looks at her watch.*)

Shit! (*Still pacing.*) Waiting around like this is gonna drive me crazy! How long you been sittin' here? (*Ava is suddenly irritated at ABW's silence.*)

AVA: Hey, look! I don't care alright. But we got another hour to sit here before this damn bus comes. Can't you say *something?* Just to pass the time? (*ABW does not respond.*)

AVA: Great! I got one on the way who can't tell time and one sittin' here who can't talk. This must be my lucky night! (*Ava sits and tries again to do her nails, but she's angry.*)

AVA: Well, I'm going this time even if she doesn't come. I told her that. She can do what she wants, but I'm not fucking no dogs!

And I don't care how much they willing to pay to watch us do it. Them niggas ain't got that much money. And I told both of them that when they first brought it up. *No way!*

She just sat there and didn't say anything, just rolling her eyes and smiling. I told him, look! I can do about anything a regular human being can think up to ask me if they paying cash money, but animals is different. (*ABW looks at Ava with specific curiousity for the first time. A flicker.*)

BLACK OUT

SCENE SEVEN

Slide 7: "Maybe you should fix yourself up a little."

Ava is carefully gluing on some long, curved fake fingernails.

AVA: Atlanta' gonna be the place to be this weekend. That's where you ought to be trying to get to, honey. People who been there tell me it's live! They said people down there call it "the Black Mecca" cause black folks got it so good. I told this Muslim friend of mine about it and he got mad. He just got to be a Muslim since high school, but the way he acts now, you'd think he'd been selling bean pies all his life! He said they all gonna burn because Mecca is about the spirit and them Atlanta niggas ain't about nothing but money.

Well, I know that's what they gonna be about this weekend. Every hustler, and every wanna be a hustler, is gonna be there for that fight. They all want a piece of "Ali! Ali! Ali!" The way these niggas are talking about it, you'd think they were gonna personally go down there an kick some ass.

Myself, I don't care one way or the other. Boxing is some man shit, even though Ali is fine! But they're gonna be spending big money to celebrate that shit and I am a celebrating something when I put my mind to it.

I told Sherri if we work this week right, we don't ever have to come back to Detroit. For what? We can retire and go to beauty school like we got some sense. I told Sherri I don't wanna be stuck in no gig where the big money comes when you start fucking dogs. We need to make plans. (*Angry again suddenly.*) If she ever get here!

Tony had tickets to the fight, til he lost them gambling. He was pissed off. His ego couldn't stand going down there and not being able to get in, so he's telling people he decided to just "cool out at the crib." I told Sherri that's why he's pressing that dog shit. Since he ain't goin to the fight, he's gotta come up with something new to impress the fellas.

Most of them stay so coked up and full of cognac they couldn't do nothing if they wanted to, which they *don't*. All they wanna do is get high and watch.

Tony was into watching, too. But Sherri wouldn't do nothing when it was just the three of us even though he used to ask her all the time . . . She said she wasn't no freak. She was just trying to make a living. *(Looking at ABW.)*

I'm not trying to talk you into anything, but there's plenty money to be made in Atlanta this weekend. Maybe you should fix yourself up a little . . . no. I guess not.

BLACK OUT

SCENE EIGHT

Slide 8: "I always have a plan."

Ava enters with sandwiches, chips, Cokes in a flimsy cardboard tray.

AVA: Okay. We got tuna and we got cheese. You can pick. *(ABW looks helplessly at Ava.)*

AVA: Tuna? No? Okay. Cheese it is. *(Ava unwraps the sandwich, puts it in ABW's hand, and sits a can of soda by her feet. Ava unwraps her sandwich and begins to eat.)*

AVA: You better eat something. It's a long ride on an empty stomach. *(ABW slowly picks up the sandwich. Ava watches her sideways approvingly.)*

AVA: Go ahead. It's bad, but it won't kill you. (*ABW slowly raises the sandwich to her mouth, sighs deeply and takes a bite. She chews slowly and swallows with difficulty. Ava smiles at her.*)

AVA: I know it ain't none of my business, but you gonna get hurt hanging around here by yourself. Do you have a ticket to Atlanta? Do you have a ticket to *anywhere*? (*ABW eats methodically.*)

AVA: Your problem is you don't have a plan. You gotta have a plan, honey. Even if you have to adjust it a little every now and then, you gotta have a basic plan that you stick by.

I always have a plan.

You're just out here, aren't you? I wish you would say something!

That's okay. I hear you. You don't have to say a damn thing. They took all of it, didn't they? Every little bit they could get their hands on. They just turned you out, didn't they? (*ABW suddenly puts down her sandwich. Her eyes fly open and she grabs her stomach and her mouth. She is clearly about to throw up.*)

AVA: What the . . . Quick! The Ladie's Room! Over there! Hurry up! (*ABW rushes out. Ava watches her to be sure she makes it to the Ladie's Room.*)

AVA: Jesus! (*Ava goes quickly over and picks up ABW's backpack. She goes through it quickly. She finds the tattered wallet, takes it out, flips through, reading the papers, looking for information. She removes several dollars and counts them. She takes out a pill bottle. Looks at the label. It's empty and topless.*

Ava looks toward the Ladie's Room, registering concern. She goes back to going through the purse, money still in her hand. She does not see ABW return from the Ladies Room until she turns to face her standing there watching.)

BLACK OUT

SCENE NINE

SLIDE 9: "What Can I say?"

Ava lights a cigarette and smokes nervously. She jiggles her foot nervously. ABW is holding her bag tightly in her lap. Both women look straight ahead.

BLACK OUT

SCENE TEN

Slide 10: "Not after I got to know you."

Look, I'm sorry, okay? It's none of my business what you do or don't do.

But I know they give you those pills and shit at the hospital for a reason. It's so you can take care of yourself out here. A girl Sherri knows was in the crazy house three times and she had these big ass pills. Horse pills. I told her they look like horse pills. She had to take them every day or she would go off. That's why she kept going back in. She'd stop taking her medicine and then go into the grocery store or something and start cussing people out. When she takes her medicine, she doesn't care how long the lines are or how long the meat's been sitting there. She's in her own world.

It ain't no picnic out here, you know. If they gave you something to take the edges off, go for it.

You throw all of them away? (*ABW looks at her.*)

AVA: Not for you, honey. If you don't want to take them, don't take them. But you can always sell prescription tranqs. It's like money in the bank. People will take anything from a hospital. It's guaranteed to cool you out.

Well, it doesn't matter. But you gonna have to start thinking about stuff like that. You sell people what they want, you gonna always make a living.

You believe me, don't you?

About the money, I mean. I wasn't gonna take your money. I was just being nosy. I probably would have taken it at first, but not after I got to know you. Well, not really *know* you since you still haven't said shit, but you know what I mean. I got no business stealing from you. All these men out here with pockets full of money. What would that make me to be stealing from you?

But that should be like a warning to you about how dangerous it is out here, honey. Just between us, I think you are way too crazy to be out here walking around on your own. They're gonna eat you alive. (*ABW looks at Ava. Ava gets up pacing again. Looks at her watch.*)

AVA: I cannot believe this girl is gonna leave me hangin'! (*Angrily turning on ABW all of a sudden.*)

You not gonna make it! You hear what I'm telling you? They ought to lock you up now and save you and them some trouble. I don't know how they let you out in the first place. I'm tired of being around crazy bitches who don't know how to make a move!

Why don't you fix yourself up!

BLACK OUT

SCENE ELEVEN

Slide 11: "I told her I wasn't pretending."

Ava is tucking in a new blouse on ABW. It is bright and flowery and very much in contrast to ABW's other clothing.)

AVA: Much better! Now what about that head? Let's just touch it up a little around the edges, okay?

Goes and gets comb and brush. Begins to brush ABW's hair back gently.

Are you tenderheaded?

Well, I'll act like you are just to be on the safeside. I always liked to do hair. Even when I was little. Your hair would probably take a press or a perm real good cause it's so thick.

My mother said Ava Gardner had to use a hot comb on her hair twice a week just to keep her edges together. (*A beat.*)

Anybody ever ask you to do something you just couldn't do? No matter what? That's how I feel about this animal stuff.

When I met Tony, I was practically living on the street. Dancing in those places where they all think they get to fuck you as part of the cover charge. He gave me some place to stay. Some protection . . . from everybody but him, I guess!

I know I owe him, but damn! I don't owe anybody everything!

You gotta have a place where you draw a line you won't cross. Period. Sherri ain't got no line. She zig zags all over the damn map, depending on who's holding the most dope.

Tony and that bug eyed nigga think because they got some money we just something for them to play with. (*Ava brushes ABW's hair too hard and she winces.*)

Sorry! Did I hurt you?

I know she ain't coming. It's almost midnight now. If she was coming, she'd a been here.

She's somewhere with Tony telling her how she is the best hoe he got and the best one he ever gonna have and how she's special in his life.

When I first met Sherri, she was so pretty. And tiny! Tony wanted to put us together right away cause I was a kid and she looked like one.

I didn't know what he was talking about at first but then Sherri started laughing and talking about how low down Tony was for trying to set us up like that when we had just met a few minutes ago.

And he said, "yeah, well, okay, that may be the maybe, but what's it gonna be? Can ya'll hang? It's big money in it for everybody if ya'll can hang."

And she looked at me and I understood what they were talking about. I said, "Hey! I'm a dancer."

So she said, "well, come on then. Let's dance."

That's the only time she ever let Tony watch us when wasn't nobody else there, but that doesn't really count, I guess, because it was sort of like an audition, you know? He wanted to see how we'd look together.

I was really nervous, too. I had never done anything like that with a woman. I hadn't done it that many time with no men. She told me to forget about Tony and just think about how beautiful we were. I knew she was beautiful. And I hoped I was . . .

When she asked me about that dog stuff tonight, I said *no* right off. And she said, "Look, little bit, this ain't nothing new. It's just like when we do each other. We don't really have to enjoy it. We have to pretend that we do.

So I told her she wasn't like no dog to me and I wasn't pretending.

BLACK OUT

SCENE TWELVE

Slide 12: "I thought a bolt of lightening was gonna strike us dead."

Ava is arranging a scarf unsuccessfully around ABW's hair, neck, shoulders.

AVA: Did you ever kiss a woman in the crazy house? When it wasn't any men around, I mean? It's really not that weird when you think about it. Niggas are who's weird! I used to be at niggas houses sometimes during the day and their wives nightgown and stuff would be hanging on the bathroom door and they would ask me to put it on, but I wouldn't do it. I knew it would make me feel bad if my old man was getting off watching somebody parading around in my nightgown while I out working.

I did it with a minister's son once. He hated his father and he had the keys. He wanted to do it right behind the pulpit. It was funny at first, but when we got up there, it was so quiet, I thought a bolt of lightening was gonna strike us dead. It was kind of exciting, I guess, but I couldn't really believe that God was all of a sudden gonna be so concerned about what I was doing that he'd start throwing lightening bolts at me.

Niggas don't care though. They'll do it anywhere. Sherri knew a coke dealer who had a girl sit in the middle of a polker game and put a snake inside herself. My mother said men will ask you to do anything, but if you fool enough to do it, that's on you! She had a lot of good advice. She just never took any of it.

It was pretty weird when Tony got me and Sherri together that first time. I thought it would feel nasty, you know, since I had never done anything like that, it didn't. Niggas always try to make you think your stuff smells funky, so you won't ask them to kiss it, but they just lying. We smell sweet.

One night me and Sherri made a bunch of money and she said, "this is what makes all that damn freak shit worth it." It just made me feel funny that she could talk about it that way when she never said that kinda stuff about the other stuff we did. I felt like at least when it was the two of us, we could be two women *together*. We could help each other out, you know?

One time, I asked her if she was ever with a woman in the crazy house, but she wouldn't talk about anything that happened to her in there. It wasn't like she was ashamed of it or anything. She just wouldn't talk about it. The most she would do is laugh sometime when I'd get on her about taking that shit and tell me she'd done a lot worse drugs than some nigga cut cocaine.

I think they scared her real bad in there. Made her think she might be crazy for real . . .

They didn't make you think that did they? (*Ava looks directly at ABW who returns her gaze and then turns away.*)

AVA: Why do you bitches believe that shit? Of *course* that's what they're gonna say. What else are they gonna tell you? "It's niggas driving you crazy. Cut them losse. Close your legs and open your eyes and make a move!" They not gonna tell you no helpful shit like that. They'd be out of a job in a minute! (*Ava catches her gently by the chin and turns her face back around.*)

I'm sorry, honey. You don't need for me to be fussing at you. You're doing real good. At least you got nerve enough to be out here trying, right? The only time it's really over is when you stop trying, right? (*Softly.*) Isn't that right? (*Ava looks at ABW, leans over and kisses her very gently on the mouth.*)

SCENE THIRTEEN

Slide 13: "You could have just told me."

Audio Announcement: Late bus for Atlanta, Georgia with intermedi-ate stops in   ,   , and   . Lights up. Ava is gathering up her stuff, looking at the final effect of a much more presentable ABW.

AVA: You can see why I'm going to beauty school, right? I told Sherri we could open a shop together and call it, "Shop Sherava." "Ah-vah" not "AA-va." I think it sounds classier if you say it that way. Sherri says there's only two sure ways for a colored woman to make any kind of independent living: slinging pussy or frying hair. I told her that the first option was working my last nerve and seemed to be driving her crazy, so what have we got to lose? She said she didn't know whether or not she'd like it. I said, fuck it! If we don't like it, we'll do something else!

I might keep that name anyway, even though, you know, it technically won't be her place. I still like the way it sounds—"Shop

Sherava." I'll do all the hair stuff and maybe some manicures and make-up. But no pedicures! I ain't messing with nobody's negro feet!

I did okay with you, though. You might make it out the bus station anyway. (*Ava puts the rest of her stuff away efficiently.*)

They're gonna start boarding for Atlanta in a minute or so . . . (*Looking at ABW.*)

So . . . You can keep that stuff if you want. The scarf and stuff, I mean. Maybe you'll make it down to Atlanta after all and this way at least you'll be ready. Well, at least you'll have a fighting chance.

Here's ten bucks, honey. (*Ava puts it in ABW's pocket.*) I wish I had more, you know, but I spent all my damn money on these tickets? I guess I'll leave Sherri's at the counter so if she comes late they can, you know, give it to her and she can just meet me down there.

You gonna be okay?

Sure you are. You got this far, didn't you? Right?

You just gotta work on your plan a little. You know, starting from now. From now on. You remember I was telling you about makin a plan.

Well, if you do get down there, look me up, okay? I'll be listed under Ava cause a lot of people that wanna call me don't know my last name is Johnson.

I gotta drop Sherri's ticket off. If you see her, tell her, you know, that I left it for her, okay? Maybe I should write her a note and you just hand it to her, okay?

Never mind. You be careful. (*Ava exits to the ticket counter.*)

(*AUDIO ANNOUNCEMENT: Final boarding call for the late bus to Atlanta.*)

(*ABW reaches up and pulls off the scarf Ava has draped on her and sits slowly, dropping the scarf to the floor. Ava reenters with the tickets still in her hand. She sees the scarf fall, but ABW is looking away and doesn't notice her return.*)

AVA: The line is too long. I'll miss the damn bus myself worrying about her *maybe* getting on it.

I could use some company, you know? (*ABW looks at her.*)

AVA: (*Reaches down to pick up the scarf where ABW has dropped it.*) If you didn't like the damn thing you could have just told me. (*Ava smiles and puts the scarf back around ABW's neck. Ava holds out the ticket in her hand to ABW, who stands slowly and looks at her.*)

AVA: At least it's warm in Atlanta. (*ABW reaches out slowly and takes the ticket. She smiles at Ava tentatively.*)

AVA: Come on then, we gonna miss the damn bus. (*Ava talking as they walk toward the bus.*) First thing we gotta do is names. I'll write down some names and you point when I get to yours. Or point to one you like. You can pick a new one! I won't know the difference. (*Ava and ABW exit.*)

The final slides come up in sequence as the actresses reenter the theater through the back doors. They will distribute fliers row by row in the theater. These fliers will list the lessons that will be shown on the final slides.

"Remember Me" by Diana Ross plays while this activity is going on.
Slide 1: The Lessons:
Slide 2: 1. Take care of your sisters.
Slide 3: 2. Be resourceful.
Slide 4: 3. Make a plan.
Slide 5: 4. Make a move.
Slide 6: 5. Don't do animals.
Final slide holds until they finish passing out fliers, mount the stage, walk to the center and take a curtain call together.

END

About the Authors

SALLIE BINGHAM (Playwright) is also the author of short stories and novels as well as a family memoir. Her work has appeared in many publications including the "Atlantic Monthly", "Ms. Magazine" and the "Transatlantic Review". Her novels include *After Such Knowledge* and the recently published *Small Victories*. Two of her plays have been produced by the Women's Project & Productions—*Milk of Paradise* in February 1980 and *Paducah* in 1985. Her latest productions include an adaptation of "The Awakening" produced at the Horse Cave Theatre in Kentucky and *In the Presence* to be produced this season at the Mill Mountain Theatre in Roanoke Virginia. Ms. Bingham is also the publisher of the "American Voice" a feminist literary magazine.

PEARL CLEAGE (Playwright) is a writer and a performance artist. Ms. Cleage's plays have been performed at theaters and colleges across the country, including The Negro Ensemble Company, Just Us Theater Company, Seven Stages, and The Billy Holiday Theater Company. She premiered six new plays in six years as Playwright-in-Residence at Atlanta's Just Us Theater Company before assuming the role of Artistic Director in 1987. Her play *Hospice*, which premiered in New York, won five AUDELCO Awards for achievement Off Broadway in 1983 and was recently anthologized in "New Plays for the Black Theater". She is author of two books—*Mad at Miles: A Black Woman's Guide to Truth* and *The Brass Bed and Other Stories*. Her two one-acts, *Chain* and *Late Bus To Mecca* were co-produced by the Women's Project & Productions and New Federal Theater in February 1992. Her latest play *Flying West* opens at the Alliance Theater in Atlanta.

DARRAH CLOUD (Playwright) adapted Willa Cather's *O Pioneers!*, commissioned by the Women's Project & Productions and given a work-in-progress in 1988. It was subsequently produced at Seattle Rep, the Boston Huntington Theatre, which can be seen on Public Broadcast System: American Playhouse, and Baltimore's Center Stage. *The Stick Wife* has been produced at the Los Angeles Theatre Center, the Hartford Stage Company, and throughout the United States. In 1990, The Manhattan Theatre Club commissioned *Braille Garden*, and *The Obscene Bird of Night* was produced at Trinity Rep that same year. The Denver Theater Center recently commissioned Ms. Cloud to write *The Sirens*, a play based on the real life accounts of battered women and victims of wife-beating.

Darrah has received grants from the Rockefeller Foundation and the National Endowment for the Arts. She was also playwright-in-residence at the Perseverance Theatre in Juneau, Alaska for two years. She received her MFA at the University of Iowa's Writers Workshop.

LAVONNE MUELLER (Playwright) had her last production, *Violent Peace* produced by the Women's Project & Productions at the Judith Anderson Theatre in February 1990 and will be given a London production later this Fall. Previously, her *Letters to a Daughter from Prison: Nehru and Indira*, was produced by the Women's Project & Productions as part of the First International Festival of the Arts and later opened in Bombay. The Women's Project has also produced *The Only Woman General, Little Victories, Colette in Love, Breaking the Prairie Wolf Code*, and *Killings on the Last Line*. Her play, *Crimes and Dreams* was produced by the Fisher Foundation at Theatre Four. Ms. Mueller has been the recipient of a Guggenheim grant, a Rockefeller grant, two National Endowment for the Arts grants, and a Kentucky Foundation for the Arts grant. She is also a Woodrow Wilson Fellow and received the NEA Artist Exchange Program to Japan. She is currently Director of the Iowa University Playwrights Workshop.

SUSAN YANKOWITZ (Playwright) is the author of *Night Sky*, produced by the Women's Project in May 1991, directed by Joseph Chaikin. The play was presented in 1992 at The Market Theatre in South Africa and is under option for a new New York production. Other major works for the stage include *Terminal, Slaughterhouse Play, A Knife in the Heart*, and *Monk's Revenge*. Her novel, *Silent Witness*, was published by Knopf and she has just completed her second book, *Taking the Fall*. Her latest play, *Real Life*, had its first workshop in July 1992 at the Powerhouse Theatre. Ms. Yankowitz is a grant recipient from the Guggenheim, Rockefeller, and McKnight Foundations, the NEA, NYEA, TCG, and others. She is a member of New Dramatists, the Dramatists Guild, W.G.A., and PEN.

KATHLEEN TOLAN (Playwright) started out acting with Andre Gregory's Manhattan Project in the early 70s. Since then she has appeared in many plays, film, and television. Her other plays include *A Weekend Near Madison*, performed first at Actors Theatre of Louisville, also at the Astor Place Theatre in New York, around the country, and in Europe. *Kates's Diary* was produced at Playwrights Horizons and at the Joseph Papp Public Theatre.